Elinor in the stage production of *Three Weeks*, 1908.

Shooting *Beyond the Rocks*, Hollywood, 1922. Elinor and Rudolph Valentino.

Le Chat Nelly by Jacques Emile Blanche, Dieppe, 1894.

Elinor Glyn

Elinor Glyn: A Biography

BY ANTHONY GLYN

Doubleday & Company, Inc., Garden City, New York, 1955

Library of Congress Catalog Card Number 55–5507

Copyright ©, 1955, by Sir Geoffrey Davson, Baronet
Copyright, 1955, by The Hearst Corporation
All Rights Reserved
Printed in the United States
At the Country Life Press, Garden City, N.Y.
First Edition

Romance is a spiritual disguise created by the imagination to envelop material happenings and desires, so that they may be in greater harmony with the soul.

From Elinor Glyn's notebook.

Elinor Glyn

We were having lunch at the Ritz.

Lunch with Grandmamma was both a treat and an ordeal, an occasion of mingled affection and apprehension. One's appearance was expected to be immaculate, one's manners flawless, one's deportment at once correct and nonchalant. In earlier days she had regularly sent her adolescent daughters out of the restaurant in the middle of a meal to fetch a wrap deliberately left behind, so that they might learn an easy and unaffected poise under public scrutiny. Such ordeals, however, were not inflicted on schoolboy grandsons. To me she was less intimidating, if not less awe-inspiring.

The sensation of walking along a knife-edge added considerably to the excitement and memorability of these occasions. But they were, even in their more alarming moments, extremely enjoyable. Grandmamma was a delightful and stimulating companion and she was always so genuinely pleased to see me. Lunch at the Ritz restaurant, an infrequent experience anyway, was made all the more exciting by being the cynosure of all eyes.

She had been lunching at the corner table of Ritz hotels all over the world for the last forty years and was quite accustomed to being covertly stared at from behind menu cards. Even at seventy her great beauty, her erect carriage, her queenly presence, her imperious glance, her green eyes, red hair, and magnolia-white skin would have attracted attention without her fame and reputation. It was pleasant to bask for an hour or two in the reflection of her limelight.

We ordered lobster thermidor. Another of the nice things about Grandmamma was that she always treated one as completely grown-up. To her children of any age were merely small-scale adults and she expected them to have the same interests and tastes as adults. She gave her granddaughter a diamond wrist watch long before she learned to tell the time; she gave me for my fourth birthday a typewriter, a scarlet portable model, on which I am typing this. She never understood about toys. Similarly, we were expected to have an adult interest in our appearance and in the opposite sex, to enjoy adult food, to like conversing about Greek philosophy or Renaissance painting or Voltaire. It was a strain, but a very agreeable one.

At the table next to ours were a father, mother, and daughter who were taking a considerable interest in us. Grandmamma told me that they were Americans, explaining the many points of manners, appearance, and speech in which Americans differed from the British. She went on to tell me about anyone in the restaurant whom she knew. Finally, as they brought our lobster, we started to play the game we always played when we lunched together.

We would discuss anyone in sight who looked interesting and whom she did not already know, indicating the person by pointing our knives lying on the table and staring in the opposite direction. After a suitable pause we would examine the person indicated and Grandmamma would describe what she imagined his character and life to be—a vivid description which would have startled the person concerned considerably if he could have heard. Her judgement about people, however, was usually sound and it seems probable that she may often have been very close to the truth. Several of her friends have since spoken of her ability to sum up with a good deal of accuracy people who were strangers to her.

The American family were clearly fascinated by our conversation and had by now given up all pretence of maintaining one of their own. Finally the father summoned the headwaiter and asked who Grandmamma was. On being told, he gazed at her more wide-eyed than ever.

We had now finished our game and I launched, with terrifying precocity, into a long exposition of the gold standard, a topic which was being widely discussed at that time. It was not a subject which appealed much to Grandmamma; money matters at any level were anathema to her. But she had much experience of lunching with politicians and it was unthinkable to show boredom while eating in a public restaurant with a young man, even a young man of eleven.

She listened politely. The American, however, could bear it no longer. He stood up and addressed Grandmamma:

"Pardon me, ma'am, but I guess these are your furs."

He picked them off the floor and gave them to her. She thanked him politely and we waited for him to sit down again. But he, hoping for a rather more elaborate conversation with Elinor Glyn, continued to hover by our table. Finally he said:

"The little boy's cute, isn't he."

Grandmamma turned the emerald stare full on him and smiled sweetly.

"He's my grandson," she said. "He's going to be Prime Minister one day."

She gave him a gracious nod of dismissal and we turned back to our lobster. The American sat down, openmouthed.

It was all a very far cry from the backwoods of Canada, where the story really begins.

BOOK ONE

The Cynical Romantic

1864–1892

1.

The Saunders family was a remarkable one. Colonel Thomas Saunders was half English, half French, his father being related to Admiral Saunders, who brought Wolfe's ships up the St. Lawrence to Quebec, and his mother a member of a French aristocratic family. Several of his mother's relatives had died under the guillotine and she herself had escaped by hiding in Abbeville all through the Terror. Thomas Saunders, who was born in 1795, was brought up in Paris, though how this was managed during the Napoleonic Wars is not known. After the battle of Waterloo he came to England and married an Irish girl, the daughter of Sir John Wilcocks of Dublin.

The young couple went first to Pondicherry in India in search of their fortunes, but the heat and the life there did not appeal to them and they returned to Paris. Soon afterwards they immigrated to Canada, together with some other young impoverished couples, trying to build a new life in a new country. Thomas Saunders bought a tract of land called Woodlands, near Guelph in Ontario, and settled down to farm the virgin soil. It was a hard task, and of all the band of immigrants who came with him he was virtually the only one to make good. He succeeded, after years of toil, in developing

Woodlands into a fine agricultural estate, and when he came to sell it and retire, it was turned into an agricultural college.

Guelph in 1830 consisted only of a few shanties and a store. It provided absolutely no amenities or luxuries. The Saunderses lived in a glorified log cabin under conditions of terrible hardship; even the elementary necessities of life such as soap and candles Mrs. Saunders had to make herself. It was difficult to get any help in the home, even during her confinements; but nothing dismayed her, neither the long cold winters nor the primitive conditions, nor the toughness of the work itself. She bore eight daughters and one son, and they all survived.

Mrs. Saunders' character must have been incredibly strong. It was not enough to survive, to make good in those conditions, to bring up nine children, to look after her domineering and much-loved husband. The children must be brought up to realise that they were by birth and breeding ladies and gentlemen, the descendants of nobility. They must be inculcated with the ideals and tenets of the aristocracy, its manners and code of behaviour, so that they would be fitted to take their place in society when the time came. Not for one moment did that indomitable woman assume that her children were going to spend all their lives farming in Ontario.

She took as her model the eighteenth-century French aristocracy, which she greatly admired and to which her mother-in-law had belonged. The classes of society, she believed, were separated by virtually impassable chasms; entry into the upper class could be effected only by birth, for it required the inherited traditions of hundreds of years of authority to produce a gentleman. But, having been born into that class, there were duties and obligations to be assumed as well as privileges. The greatest contempt she had was for gentlemen who disgraced their rank and brought opprobrium to their class. The guiding principle of her life, which she often quoted to her children, was *noblesse oblige*.

Courage and honour were the chief qualities required. Gentlemen naturally did not show fear, nor did they break their word. But there were other things, too. They must not be overbearing or ostentatious, for those were the marks of an upstart. They must shun pretence and affectation. Above all, they must have complete self-control; under no circumstances must they ever show any sort of emotion, even affection, in public.

She was fond of describing to her children the dignified bearing of the French aristocrats on the steps of the guillotine, and contrasting with them Madame Du Barry, who, for all her years in court circles, was of plebeian descent and could not help making an exhibition of herself on the scaffold. Mrs. Saunders would challenge her children: how would *they* behave on the steps of the guillotine?

She was, however, a devout Christian, and this served to modify some of the more inhuman aspects of her creed. Unlike most of the *ancien régime,* she believed in God, in marriages for love, in the sanctity of marriage vows, and in friendship and support for the middle and lower classes, which God has also created, though this did not extend to actual intermixing. One of her definitions of a gentlewoman was: "One who does not humiliate those she is paying and is not familiar with the wrong people."

Even in the Canadian wilds gentle manners were essential. Departure from these standards—"servants' behaviour" as Mrs. Saunders termed it—could not be tolerated for an instant. Every night she and her husband would dress for dinner. Afterwards they would sit in straight-backed chairs on either side of the fire, with the family grouped in a half circle between them. One of the children would read aloud from *The Lives of the Lord Chancellors of England,* or other similarly austere works, being corrected for pronunciation.

The children were taught, too, how to deal with servants—not that there were any servants at Woodlands, apart from an escaped coloured slave from Alabama who was employed later to help with the growing family. But the time would come when they would leave home and they must be fully prepared. Elinor Saunders, the youngest but one of the family, in another century and another hemisphere, would never pick up her own handkerchief or say "Please" or "Thank you" to a servant, to the despair of her grandchildren. There was nothing of highhandedness in this; no one had a kinder or gentler heart. But she had been taught by her mother eighty years before that it was not ladylike to do so, and she remembered and obeyed.

Mrs. Saunders did what she could for her children's more orthodox education. A decayed and rather drunken old scholar was engaged to teach the girls English grammar, arithmetic, history, and literature, and the boy Latin and Greek. A poverty-stricken Frenchman taught them French, music, dancing, and deportment. But this education could only continue in the long, dark winter; in the summer all hands were needed on the farm.

It was a harsh, rigid, narrow life. Once a year, however, there was great rejoicing when *le tonneau bienvenu* arrived. This was a huge barrel sent by the French relations, containing everything they imagined the exiled family in the Canadian wilds might lack—silk stockings, Paris hats, yards of material, dresses, satin slippers, books, sweets, even wigs and false teeth in case either parent might now need them.

A strange, ill-assorted existence. Yet there is a certain pathetic grandeur about their efforts in the middle of a heroic struggle for survival to maintain the standards which, far from appearing incongruous, seemed to them completely essential to life. The ideals and tenets in which they believed, and which they preached to their children, were already a hundred years out of date at that time. But the qualities they displayed—courage, fortitude, industry, refusal to compromise with what they felt wrong—are timeless.

2.

In 1715, Kenneth Sutherland, third Lord Duffus, followed the Old Pretender. He was attainted for his part in the rising, stripped of his title and estates, and was forced to flee to Sweden. Later he was given the chance to return, sue for pardon, and reclaim his estates, but by then he had fallen in love with a Swedish lady, Christina Sioblade, and was determined to pursue his suit. He succeeded and married her, at the expense of forfeiting his title and estates; but he was quite happy about this, counting both rank and riches well lost for love.

The title was, however, revived in 1826 by the House of Lords in favour of his grandson James, who became the fifth Lord Duffus. James, inheriting the family tendency to throw everything overboard for the sake of love, had earlier eloped with Lady Mary Hay, the daughter of the Earl of Erroll, Hereditary Lord High Constable of Scotland, and the wife of Major-General John Scott, to whom she had been married only a year. This ruined James's promising military career, but he was indifferent both to this and to the open scandal involved in living for fifty-six years with a lady whom he was never able to marry. They were a happy couple, but none of their ten children, all of whom were illegitimate, could inherit the title and this passed to the son of his great-aunt Elizabeth, from whom the sixth and seventh Lords Duffus were descended.

It is not clear exactly how David Sutherland, Laird of Cambusavie, was related to this family, but family tradition has it that he was the son of the third lord's younger brother Alexander, who took part in the Forty-five and is described in the Scottish Peerage as having died abroad without issue. David Sutherland's son, Andrew, fought in the American war of 1776; but he returned to meet financial disaster and he was forced to sell Cambusavie, "the Manor Place, the gardens, offices and houses thereof, also the said town and lands of Cambusavie, Cambusmore and Balvraid, with house and beggings, yards, tosts, crofts, outsets, insets, mosses, muirs, commonleys and common pasturages" to his distant kinsman, the Earl of Sutherland.

His son, Captain Edward Sutherland of the 96th Regiment, was given a staff appointment in Halifax, Nova Scotia, and when he retired, he settled in Sydney, Nova Scotia, with his wife Christina and their four children, Douglas, John, William, and Frances.

Douglas Sutherland was born in Sydney in 1838 and chose to become a civil engineer. Nothing is known about his childhood, but after he qualified, one of his first tasks took him to Guelph, and there he was entertained by the Saunders family, who were always glad to meet other people of good breeding. It was there that he fell in love with Elinor Saunders, a pretty girl with beautiful features and long mahogany-brown hair. He was then only twenty. She was sixteen.

3.

The Sutherland family viewed with some alarm their son saddling himself with a wife, a penniless girl, when he had yet hardly begun to make his career. Douglas, however, knew no such doubts; for him, as for his Duffus relations, love must always come first. But the Saunderses supported the Sutherlands in wishing the marriage delayed; Elinor, they felt, was still too young and they would prefer to see Douglas more firmly set in his career.

His youth and inexperience were, however, the only factors against him as a son-in-law. Mrs. Saunders naturally appreciated his aristocratic descent and his noble cousins. His attitude towards the gentry was very similar to her own and he spoke with deep respect of his Scottish ancestors. His ambition, when he had made his fortune, was to prove himself the rightful heir to the seventh Lord Duffus, who was an elderly bachelor, and on whose death the title would (and did) become extinct. Indeed, if Douglas were correct about his ancestry, he was already the rightful Lord Duffus. Mrs. Saunders thoroughly approved of his ambition, though obviously, as the legal costs would be considerable and the upkeep of the title in the way they considered necessary even greater, it might have to wait a long time before it was fulfilled.

Douglas Sutherland must have been a versatile young man, and it was undoubtedly from him that his two remarkable daughters inherited not only their romantic temperaments but their creative gifts. He was a brilliant engineer and held posts of considerable responsibility before he was twenty-five. He was also an artist, he played the violin and spoke several languages. On top of all this he was a dashing, masterful lover.

Elinor Saunders adored him. She was especially proud of a poem he wrote on her wedding day and which she copied into her bride's book.

Give me a *friend* within whose well-poised mind
    Experience holds her seat;
But let my *bride* be innocent as flowers that fragrance shed,
    Yet know not they are sweet.

While not showing any very great poetic gifts, the sentiment expressed has a fine masculine arrogance and Elinor fully agreed with it. For all her eighteenth-century upbringing, her submissive attitude to marriage and the status of wives was as Victorian as his.

After two years he could wait no longer and both families gave their consent. The marriage took place at Guelph in January 1861, in the heart of the northern winter.

4.

The young Sutherlands' married life was an Arcadian love idyll, punctuated by a series of personal disasters and ordeals. A few weeks after they were married, their home in Guelph caught fire. All the nearby water was frozen solid and the young bride had the experience of watching helplessly while her first married home, her trousseau, and almost all her husband's personal belongings went up in flames.

In the spring Douglas Sutherland took a post which involved their moving to New York, and here at last Elinor found the leisured aristocratic society for which she had been trained. Life in America was far more luxurious than anything she had ever known, and she was much struck by the beauty of the women's clothes and the punctilious courtesy of the men. The Sutherlands were a popular pair and were warmly received by the members of the exclusive society. Elinor noted thankfully that, for all Mr. Lincoln's speeches about democracy, New York was quite as feudal as anywhere else.

This impression was strengthened by their visits to the southern states, where they also had friends. The watering-places, in particular, with their fashionable ladies and hordes of coloured servants, delighted her, and she found the stately and ceremonious ways of the southerners even more appealing than those of the New Yorkers.

The outbreak of the Civil War that year placed them in a dilemma. They had friends on both sides; where did their sympathies lie? Feelings were running high and they began to find their position a little difficult. At this moment Douglas was offered a job supervising the building of a railway in Brazil. It was a great opportunity and railways were his specialty. He had little hesitation in accepting.

All the shipping had been commandeered and they had

great difficulty in finding passages. At last they got berths in a 250-ton schooner which was sailing direct from New York to Rio de Janeiro. The voyage was a terrible one and Elinor was to retain nightmare memories of it all her life. It was very rough and she was continually seasick. She longed for fresh water, but it was all brackish. The food was uneatable. The journey lasted no less than seven weeks and she was carried ashore on a stretcher, little more than a skeleton.

The British Minister, Mr. Christie, and his wife were kind people and took charge of her while her husband went upcountry to start work on his railway. She stayed at the Legation, regaining her strength and enjoying the diplomatic society of Rio. An unpleasant memory of the period, though, was the monthly arrival of the slave ship from West Africa. The stench was so great that all the house windows had to be kept closed for the three days while the ship was being unloaded. That and the sight of the Negroes battened down in their overcrowded holds decided once and for all her loyalties in the American Civil War.

As soon as she was strong enough, she insisted on going upcountry to join her husband. The Christies tried to dissuade her, explaining that it was no life for a woman. But Elinor was adamant; her place was at his side and they had already been parted too long.

Reunited again, the couple lived at the railhead in conditions which made Guelph seem luxurious. At least Woodlands had been clean. But here their house was an old Portuguese shack, infested with snakes, rats, and insects. The heat was terrific; there was no sanitation and almost no water. At night the rats ran up and down the posts of the ancient four-poster in which they slept, dropping off with a thud on to the pillows. On her first night Douglas grabbed the nearest garment, which happened to be his wife's white silk wedding shawl, from which she was never parted, and rigged it up as a protective canopy. The rats ate it during the night, and only a small remnant was found in a corner the next morning.

The railway, however, made steady progress, and a year later they were able to leave Brazil. They returned to New York and came on to England, which had always been Douglas' goal. Their first child was born in London in July of the following year, 1863. It was a girl and they named her Lucy.

While they lived in London, Douglas was working, in collaboration with a fellow engineer, on an invention he had made. It was an ingenious device by which railway trucks and carriages could be coupled and uncoupled without a man having to stand dangerously between the buffers, and it worked on the principle of a door latch. The invention was duly patented and the royalties from it were expected to provide, if not his fortune, at least a steady income for himself and, if anything should happen to him, for his widow.

Early in 1864 he was engaged to work on the building of the Mont Cenis Tunnel and he set off immediately for Turin. By this time Elinor was expecting another child, and he left her and Lucy in the care of a half-French aunt of hers, who was staying in Jersey. And it was in Jersey that their second daughter was born, on the seventeenth of October.

Lucy had brown hair like her mother, but the new baby was a redhead. She was called Elinor after her mother.

5.

Mrs. Sutherland was delighted by her new baby, but her joy was short-lived. Six weeks later the news arrived that her husband was seriously ill with typhoid. Immediately she hurried to Turin, leaving Lucy and the baby with their great-aunt. Douglas was clearly terribly ill. She nursed him devotedly but he seemed to get worse rather than better. One can imagine her anguish; alone in a land whose language she did not speak, desperately anxious about her husband, separated from her young children. Finally she made the decision. Somehow she must bring her husband back to England, where they had friends and where she could get help and good medical advice.

She never spoke afterwards of that journey home, but one can imagine it: the sick husband, the long cold hours in carriages and on stations, the changes, the frontiers, the channel ports. They reached London and went at once to 64 Albany Street, near Regent's Park, where they had stayed before.

It was all in vain. Douglas Sutherland died on the thirtieth of January, four years after his wedding, almost to the day. His lovely young wife was left heartbroken, penniless, and utterly alone.

She wrote in her diary:

> This morning it has pleased God to take my darling husband Douglas Sutherland to Himself. After one month of illness. May He teach me to say "Thy Will be done."
>
> Elinor Sutherland

He was buried five days later in All Souls Cemetery, Kensal Green.

6.

Douglas Sutherland's last words to his wife were a wish that his children should be brought up in England, that they should be taught to revere their noble ancestors and never demean their gentle birth. Such a wish would always have been carefully regarded; from her dying husband it became for Mrs. Sutherland a divine command.

But how was she to carry it out? She had no money and the invention was not being eagerly taken up by the railway companies. Such royalties as did come from it were appropriated by the engineer who had collaborated with her husband.

How was she, without friends or family or income, to bring up her two daughters in England?

Sadly she decided that it could not be done. For the moment she must take them back to her parents in Canada. Perhaps someday the chance would occur for her to fulfil her husband's last command.

She travelled to Jersey and brought her children to London. "The children were so good all the time I was away, though generally shy with strangers," she wrote. She was helped in London by a friend of her husband's, Bernard Beardmore, who arranged her passage home and accompanied her to Liverpool.

On the tenth of August, 1865, she

> Went on board the Steamer *Belgian* this morning with the dear children. Good-bye to dear England, where my happiest and most sorrowful days have been spent. That I may bring my dear children back there in a few years is my most earnest wish.

She was then twenty-three. Lucy was a pretty little girl of two and Elinor a sturdy child of ten months, already able to walk. Her patent-leather shoes, just two inches long, she wore down on the heel by much determined tramping up and down the steamer deck.

They reached Toronto on the twenty-fifth of August. Mrs. Sutherland wrote in her diary (the fifth and last entry she ever made):

> Arrived in Toronto at 9 A.M. Fanny and Bill Sutherland met us. Papa at the Queen's. Went up to Guelph by afternoon train. Tom and Jemima at station. Drove up to Fairview and met them all again.

Her younger daughter, a more enthusiastic diarist, would not have dealt with such a moving reunion so laconically.

7.

The Saunderses had sold Woodlands and were living in retirement at a house called Summer Hill, a gracious colonial building with a columned portico, set in a pleasant park. Life here was a good deal easier than it had been at Woodlands, but the inflexible standards of behaviour, the rigid etiquette were maintained as severely as ever. Here the Sutherlands spent the next six years and the young Elinor came under the influence of Mrs. Saunders, with results that were to be lasting.

Mrs. Saunders was now in her sixties, a frightening woman, proud, aloof, autocratic, with dramatic manners and a withering tongue. Every morning the two children were ushered into her presence and there they were made to sit without making a sound or movement for five long minutes. To Lucy, a restless, rebellious tomboy, this was sheer torture, but Elinor found it easy and indeed natural. At other times Mrs. Saunders would lecture them on *noblesse oblige,* the ideals and obligations of aristocracy, as she had done to her own children in earlier years. Lucy resisted violently but Elinor found herself once again in complete sympathy. She both emulated and adored her fearsome grandmother, whose teachings she regarded as incontestable and almost divine.

One of the earliest lessons given to the two children was, of course, the story of the French Revolution, the impeccable gayety of the French aristocracy under all conditions, and the tragic death of Marie Antoinette. This last affected the imaginative Elinor till she could hardly bear even to look at a flower with its head cut off. Her imagination was further fed by a particularly brutal murder on the next estate, and she began to be afraid of the dark, afraid to go into the woods on the boundary of Summer Hill.

Mrs. Saunders heard of this and was very angry. No grand-daughter of hers might ever show fear, no matter what the circumstances. Elinor was disgracing her class. The icy re-bukes were effective, and Elinor changed almost overnight from a rather timid child to an apparently brave one, at least as far as outward appearances went.

Elinor saw her grandmother only twice a day. For the rest of the time her chief companion was her aunt Henrietta, the only one of her mother's sisters not yet married. Henrietta was a delightful person and would read fairy stories and *The Idylls of the King* to the solemn child, both to amuse her and to comfort herself for a love affair which had come to nothing. Elinor certainly did not understand everything, especially the poetry, but one fact stood out for her. The heroes and heroines of all the stories were Kings and Queens, Princes and Prin-cesses. This was only to be expected, for they were also, on Mrs. Saunders' authority, the heroes of real life. This belief in aristocracy, by no means confined to the Saunders family, was to stay with Elinor for her whole life, though later, with an experience of the world a good deal wider than her grand-mother's, she came to realise that the gulfs between the classes were not so unbridgeable as Mrs. Saunders maintained.*

When Aunt Henrietta was not available, Elinor would amuse herself.

I wove fairy tales for myself about a blue Salvia Prince and a Fuchsia Princess, in the conservatory, which was my principal playground during the long cold winters. I lived

---

* Of the heroines of Elinor Glyn's novels, two married Dukes, one the heir to a dukedom, one a Marquis, one an earl, three Barons, five baronets, one a Scottish Laird, three commoners of ancient stock, two Russian Princes, one a Hungarian Count, and three Americans, two of these being members of the First Families of Virginia and one having risen from the Bowery on the strength of his own personality. The heroines themselves were mostly well-born English and Amer-ican girls but they included a Balkan Queen, an Emperor's grand-daughter, a peeress in her own right, a chauffeur's daughter, and a butcher's granddaughter.

in a fairy Kingdom of my own, and fancied myself as its Queen. I used to drape a tablecloth round my shoulders, and march about with measured tread, my head held high beneath an imaginary crown. I never wanted to play much with my cousins, my mother's brother's children, because they seemed so robust and noisy. My sister was their leader in every prank, but when I could not be with my mother or Aunt Henrietta, I wanted to be alone with the flowers. Even then I must have been an odd, vain, imaginative child, living in a dream world.*

Occasionally a clergyman would visit Summer Hill to teach Lucy and Elinor their catechism. He was not the most tactful of men and both children took a strong dislike to him. They rejected everything he tried to teach them, Lucy on principle, and Elinor because some of his arguments seemed illogical and against common sense; worse still, they were sometimes at variance with the sacred teachings of Grandmamma Saunders. The more Elinor tried to pick holes in his discourses, the more dogmatic and assertive the clergyman became. Since he received no great support in his proselytising from the other members of the household either, he finally discontinued his visits.

Elinor, however, was no atheist. All her life she believed in a God, and she had a deep capacity and need for worship. For the moment Mrs. Saunders' tenets were a satisfactory replacement for the Ten Commandments. But her rejection of orthodox Christian dogma left a vacuum into which a number of strange beliefs were later to find their way.

* *Romantic Adventure.*

8.

It was perhaps natural that under her mother's dominating influence Mrs. Sutherland should fade once more into the background. Her nature was always meek and docile and now she was overwhelmed with grief. She was always gentle and loving to her children but she played little part in their lives or upbringing. Any reference to her dead husband made her very unhappy and the children soon learnt not to intrude on her sorrow.

She would sit, smiling sadly, staring into the fire, thinking of her Douglas and reproaching herself for her complete failure to carry out his last commands. But she was utterly unable to devise any method of having her children brought up in England. She was still young and beautiful and several young men who had known her as a girl offered her marriage. But she rejected them all unhesitatingly because, though they might have brought consolation, and even in the end, happiness, they all meant settling permanently in Canada.

Finally, in 1871, a Mr. David Kennedy, a well-to-do bachelor, visited Summer Hill. Although he was over sixty, he was still handsome and well preserved. He had spent many years in China, but he belonged to an old Scottish family, the Kennedys of Knocknawlin. He was immediately attracted by the lovely young widow, and after a rapid courtship he proposed to her. She herself felt no more than a sort of fascinated respect for him, but he seemed fond of her and she forced herself to accept, feeling that here at last was the opportunity she had been seeking. Further, his Scottish connections might well mean that the children would be brought up in Scottish society.

They were married almost at once, and shortly afterwards

they said good-bye for ever to the Saunderses and Summer Hill. As they sailed down the St. Lawrence, Elinor, already romantically perceptive of the beauties of life, crept out of her cabin early in the morning to see the Thousand Islands in the dawn. At Montreal she watched the great cathedral of Notre Dame in the sky above them and she wondered what sort of a life lay ahead of her on the other side of the Atlantic and whether she would ever see the other and older Notre Dame on its island in the Seine.

9.

The journey to Europe was a most disagreeable one. Mountainous green waves seemed about to envelop the ship, and although Elinor had now learnt to suppress all signs of fear, for much of the voyage she was terrified. Mr. Kennedy's affection for his wife had been short-lived and his true character had already appeared—cruel, selfish, overbearing, mean. His bride, always the meekest and most submissive of wives, was cowed and terrified, grimly apprehensive of the life ahead of her and consoling herself with the thought that they were on their way to Scotland and that she was carrying out, no matter at what sacrifice to herself, both the letter and the spirit of Douglas Sutherland's last commands.

Lucy already loathed her stepfather and Elinor, withdrawn in a world of her own, consoled herself for the unpleasant present by the prospect of the castles and palaces that awaited them in Europe.

On the voyage Mrs. Kennedy used to read to her children. The first book, *Alice in Wonderland,* was not a success. Its comedy did not appeal to the solemn Elinor, its burlesque of Kings and Queens seemed distasteful and *lèse-majesté.* The next book, however, George Macdonald's *The Princess and the Goblin,* made a deep impression and later Elinor considered it to be one of the turning-points of her life. A fairy tale with a charming Princess and a dominating grandmother naturally appealed to her. So did the emphasis on courage. What was new was the mystical atmosphere of the book, the gleam of the grandmother's lamp, guiding and inspiring the hero, Curdie, as he groped his way in the black mine. The idealistic and imaginative quality of the book, in a different class from the normal fairy stories with their materialistic success endings, fell on fertile ground. Her later interest in mysticism and the occult, her idealism, her belief that it was right and proper for women to inspire men to great causes she traced back to the influence of Macdonald's fairy story at this moment of her life.

Much of the book took place in a dark mine, and this, too, struck her forcibly. All her life her greatest fear was to be of caves and tunnels. Even in her mature years it was a personal ordeal for her to travel through the Severn Tunnel and her grandchildren would watch with secret amusement her grim, set expression as she resolutely fought down the claustrophobia which she never mastered.

To the expectant Elinor the first sight of Europe was a severe disappointment. Londonderry in the wet dawn, with its muddy, unpaved streets, was not what she had imagined. The hotel was unspeakable, with strips of wallpaper peeling from the walls and bugs crawling over the floor. They did not, however, remain long, and the next day they went on to stay with Mr. Kennedy's elder brother at Balgregan Castle in Galloway.

The news of David Kennedy's marriage had come as a surprise to his family, for they had all regarded him as a set bachelor for life, and they were curious to see the presumably uncouth "colonial" girl who had captured him in such a short visit. They were even more surprised when they met her, sad, beautiful, dignified, with two impeccably mannered children. Elinor was overwhelmed with delight at Balgregan Castle.

With its great rooms, its liveried footmen, its suites of grand bedrooms, its strange staircases and turrets it was like the castle of every fairy story. It had, in fact, been a centre of Jacobite plotting, and there were several romantic legends about the place; Mrs. Kennedy told her children that it was quite probable that Lord Duffus himself had been there with the Old Pretender before the rising.

There was a large house party assembled at the castle to welcome the Kennedys home, and never before had Elinor seen such splendour and such beautiful clothes and jewels. Peter Kennedy, genial where his brother was curmudgeonly, presided in a brown evening coat with a high stock. It was all almost too good to be true. A famous London beauty of that time, a Mrs. Bovill, took a fancy to the two small children and allowed them to come and play in her huge bedroom while she dressed. Elinor was fascinated by everything—the innumerable bottles and powder boxes on the dressing-table, the pink satin peignoir, the quilted slippers. One day, she promised herself, she would be a society lady too, with hundreds of bottles on her dressing-table and pink quilted slippers.

There was, however, a darker shadow even in the golden fairy-tale atmosphere of Balgregan Castle. Mrs. Kennedy, strangely neglectful of the children for whose future she had made such sacrifices, entrusted them completely to an English nurse who bullied them severely without anyone caring or noticing. The two small girls were locked for hours each day in a dark, cold billiard room, while the nurse herself entertained a good-looking young gamekeeper in the nursery. It was at this time that both children came to realise that they must rely on themselves and not on their mother for protection against the buffets of the harsh world.

When they left Balgregan, the Kennedys went on to stay with some more relatives in Yorkshire. While there, Mr. Kennedy was taken ill with bronchitis, a complaint to which he was much addicted, and the doctor recommended that he spend the rest of the winter in the milder climate of Jersey. They set off there as soon as he had recovered sufficiently, passing through London on the way.

In Elinor's memoirs there is a vivid passage in which she described her first sight of London.

My first glimpse of London was, I believe, the greatest disillusionment of my life. I had expected to find it the Meccas of my dreams, a town of stately palaces, and filled with delightful ladies like Mrs. Bovill. I had almost believed that the streets would be paved with gold, or at least with marble.

As we drove along the twisting lanes which led from King's Cross station, through St. Giles and Seven Dials, then the worst type of slum, to Waterloo, I gazed with sinking heart upon the dingy narrow streets, the pitiful mean houses, and the rain. The pinched pathetic faces of the ragged urchins who ran barefooted beside the cab, begging for pennies with which to get some food, seemed to destroy all my most cherished hopes. There was no room for poverty within my fairy world, and least of all within the precincts of the celestial city which I had imagined London to represent. I felt cold doubts spring up as to the reality of all my dreams and I became silent and morose. The gulf which lies between the romantic and the sordid was never more clearly visible to me than on that day.

They reached St. Helier on a winter's morning at the end of 1873, a melancholy quartet: Mr. Kennedy, tyrannous and harsh like the popular conception of Edward Moulton-Barrett; Mrs. Kennedy, silent and terrified; Lucy, sullen and resentful; and Elinor, returning to the island of her birth, a sad, disillusioned little girl.

10.

Jersey in the 1870s consisted, and still does, of two separate societies, with very few points of mutual contact. One society was indigenous: the local farmers occupied with their dairy and potato farming, still speaking Norman French, shrewd, suspicious, and contemptuous of more recent arrivals, cutting down their trees so as not to shade their grass, tethering all their beautiful cattle so that the fields might be evenly cropped, polishing cabbage stalks into walking sticks for souvenirs, gathering seaweed for manure, industrious, insanitary, and tight-fisted.

The other society consisted of refugees from cold winters and high taxation: retired army and naval officers, colonial administrators, men with small private means, eking out their pensions and incomes in an easier climate. It was, of course, to this latter society that the Kennedys belonged.

The social life of the island was formal and strict, far more so than would have been found in a country town in England. A Lieutenant-Governor lived at Government House and a regiment was always stationed on the island for garrison duties. The elaborate fixed etiquette found favour with the retired stratum of Jersey society, in whom it aroused nostalgic memories of service life in India or one of the colonies. The indigenous part of the population naturally took no part in this social life beyond providing the various households with groceries. Except for the seigneurs of Rozel and St. Ouen practically none of the Jersey families were ever invited to Government House.

Mr. Kennedy liked the island so much and found the warm winter so beneficial to his chest that he decided to settle there. He rented a furnished house called Richelieu outside St.

Helier on the road to St. Clement and it was here that the Kennedys settled down to family life.

As might be expected, it was not a very happy household. Mr. Kennedy's selfish and domineering ways cast a deep cloud over everything. His ferocious temper reduced his wife to utter subjection. His meanness was extreme. Apart from some ten pounds a year of her own, his wife had nothing. She had to beg him at nicely chosen moments for money to meet the household bills and to clothe herself and her children, money which was always given only grudgingly and in part. Every night he forced his wife to play backgammon with him for three hours, an ordeal which almost drove her insane. However, such was Mrs. Kennedy's mental attitude towards marriage that although she loved her children and feared and hated her husband, she nevertheless supported him absolutely against her children.

Both Lucy and Elinor were, indeed, a serious disappointment to her. In her scheme of things children were silent, dutiful, and obedient, and she had no idea how to deal with two such turbulent personalities, both of whose characters were so much stronger than her own. As at Balgregan she left them alone for most of the time, descending on them at intervals to lecture them on being seen and not heard, on implicit obedience, on not asking questions, on the absolute superiority and wisdom of their elders and betters in all things. The house was run with the remorseless impersonality of a machine and no allowance was ever made for either girl's predilections or idiosyncrasies. Lucy became perverse, rebellious, and defiant, Elinor vain and opinionated, driven more and more into a world of her own. Both children were united in their instinctive resistance to all instruction, an unfortunate but perhaps not illogical consequence of the way they were treated. At this moment in their lives both girls badly needed firm and sympathetic guidance. What in fact they received was an uneven mixture of neglect and nagging.

A series of governesses came to Richelieu but all, faced by the implacable resistance of two difficult children, gave up the task. Elinor could not imagine that such stupid women could have anything useful to teach her and she resolutely determined not to learn the subjects upon which they concentrated —arithmetic, geography, grammar, and spelling. The music master became so impatient of her that he made the great mistake of rapping her over the knuckles. Neither threats nor punishment ever persuaded her to touch the piano again.

Despite her resistance to education and authority Elinor had a deep curiosity for life and an awareness that there was much that she needed to know over and above the official subjects of lessons. The house had a good library, which had been collected by its owner, Mrs. Combe. There were no library steps but Elinor read every book within her small reach, irrespective of subject—translations of the Greek classics, Scott, Agnes Strickland's *Queens of England, Don Quixote* in eighteenth-century French, an unexpurgated edition of Pepys's Diary, the French classics, Lady Blessington's novels, the complete works of Byron, and some rather ribald French novels. There was no one to declare that some of these books were unsuitable for a child to read and she studied them all with the care and attention which she refused to give to arithmetic.

One teacher alone earned her love and respect, Monsieur Cappe, "of the soiled linen, ridiculous moustache, and unspeakable scent of patchouli and stale tobacco." He seems to have understood how to handle difficult children and to have been able both to interest them and to get his ideas across. Under his tuition Elinor became virtually bilingual, though she successfully resisted his attempts, like all the others, to teach her spelling and grammar in either language. He encouraged a literary bent which she was beginning to develop, and she wrote for him long essays in both languages.

Her strange reading, alone in the library, had a great effect on the dream world in which she lived for most of the day. The Princes and Princesses of the fairy world gave place to the gods and heroes of Greek mythology. Her thoughts and imagination revolved round characters from Scott and *Don Quixote* and Byron, the subjects of the portraits by Lawrence, Gainsborough, and Lely which Mrs. Combe had collected and which hung in the hall, the two Pretenders, and the Kings and Queens of England, especially, after reading Pepys, Charles II.

She was always then, and later, a natural royalist, and Agnes Strickland's book had done nothing to diminish this. She believed implicitly all her life in the Divine Right of Kings. In her history book of this date she wrote under the picture of Charles II, "DEAR GOOD KING," and under Cromwell's, "NASTY OLD BEAST."

But the book which made the greatest impression on her, and which was to be still seventy years later the most dearly loved of them all, was Kingsley's *The Heroes*. As she read it, something seemed to leap into flame in her mind. She became passionately absorbed not only in the heroes, heroines, and gods of Greek mythology but in Greek history, sculpture, and architecture, literature, philosophy, and ideas. She spent long hours poring over translations of Plato and Thucydides with the same engrossed fascination which she had had two years earlier for fairy tales.

II.

Elinor's religious ideas at this time were extremely confused. Following her rejection of orthodox Christian dogma in Canada a further effort was made to indoctrinate her in Jersey, and this, too, was violently repelled. The Victorian version of the Christian ethic with which she was presented seemed full of inexplicable prohibitions and repressions. The idea of a puni-

tive and angry God ordaining "Thou shall not" was too like
Mr. Kennedy to be acceptable. Nor could she take the suggestion that so many of the good things of life which had presumably been put into the world for enjoyment (at this stage
she meant raspberry nougat rather than love) were sinful.
Her mind revolted against puritanism in any form; it seemed
to her blasphemous. She accepted the existence of a supreme
benevolent God; the rest she rejected completely.

She also believed in all the Greek gods and goddesses whom
she read about in Kingsley, and in Pan and his sprites, whose
picture, in the Italian Renaissance style, hung in the hall.
This order of gods was much more real and probable to her,
and the religion it implied more congenial than the orthodoxy
preached to her; there was no one at hand to explain to her
that it was no longer valid or acceptable. She liked to think
that Pallas Athene or Aphrodite or Psyche was with her,
watching over her like a guardian angel, and if some of the
behaviour of the gods seemed lamentably imperfect and well
below the standards which Mrs. Saunders would have permitted, that was in tune with the mood of cynical disillusion
induced by reading Cervantes and sophisticated French novels.

Later, of course, she came to see the Greek mythology in
a more normal light and relegated it with regret to her storehouse of imaginative fairy tales. But its influence stayed with
her always. In two of her novels the characters are affected
and comforted by statues of Greek goddesses, which were regarded with deep reverence.

12.

After about a year in Jersey the family returned to England
for a brief visit to the Kennedy relations in Yorkshire, and it
was on this occasion that Elinor had her first experience of

physical danger. She and her mother were watching a local meet when the horses of the carriage in which they were sitting took fright and bolted. The coachman immediately dropped the reins and jumped from the carriage, and the horses stampeded down a narrow, twisting lane.

It was a moment full of frightening sensations—the sickening lurches and jolts of the carriage, the frenzied thundering horses, the feeling of utter helplessness as they sat awaiting the inevitable crash. They were saved, in fact, by one of the huntsmen, who galloped across a field, jumped the hedge, and managed to stop and soothe the horses. Mrs. Kennedy and her daughter were duly grateful for the man's gallantry, but thinking the matter over later, Elinor was gratified to find that she had neither shown nor felt any fear.

The incident did, however, give her a lasting hatred for all horses, which was further increased by the news later of her grandfather's death stopping a runaway horse. In her later life the dictates of pride, fashion, or society occasionally forced her to mount, without in the least diminishing her hippophobia, which extended itself to cover both polo and racing. It was only with the greatest difficulty that she could be persuaded to watch either of these two sports.

A further alarming experience took place in the winter of the following year, 1875, when Mrs. Kennedy and her two children were returning from another visit to relatives in England. The ship bringing them back to Jersey was wrecked on the notorious Casquet Rocks. It hung there for many hours, gradually breaking up with the pounding of enormous waves. No one knew if the distress rockets which had been sent up had been seen. Indeed, as the long hours passed by without any sign of rescue, it seemed only too probable that no one knew of their plight.

I can still picture in my mind the gloomy scene; the dark and stormy sky, the cries of the seagulls as they circled above, and the thunder of the waves pounding mercilessly upon the slanting deck. My mother held us silently by the hand, too well-drilled by Grandmamma to show the slightest fear, although several of the other passengers were screaming. She whispered to us that we must not forget Grandmamma's teachings and that this was an occasion for us to show that we understood them.

My sister, who was always naturally brave, was not a bit afraid, and I believe she even thought it all a great adventure; but I was filled at first with a kind of superstitious terror. In my pagan imagination, storms and disasters signified the anger of the gods and I did not believe we should be saved.*

In the end they were rescued by a tug from Guernsey, just before the ship finally broke in half. Elinor, in the warmth and safety of her bed that night, recalled with some surprise that in those long hours of agony her prayers had been to the Christian God, and not to her normal, friendly guardian deity, Pallas Athene.

13.

The children's closest friend on the island was Ada Norcott, the daughter of the Lieutenant-Governor, Sir William Norcott. Several afternoons a week she would come and play at Richelieu or they would go up to Government House to be with her. They devised little plays for puppets, which they made out of paper. Elinor, who was developing a talent for pen-and-ink sketches, drew the faces, Lucy designed and painted their clothes, and Ada acted as general factotum and manipulator. The plays themselves were made up by Elinor, her first attempts in public storytelling.

* *Romantic Adventure.*

The following autumn, 1876, Mr. and Mrs. Kennedy left the two children behind when they went to England on a visit and the two girls stayed with Ada Norcott at Government House. It was at this time that Lily Langtry, the famous society beauty nicknamed the "Jersey Lily" paid a visit to her home island. Her beauty, her royal friendships, and the rather spiteful gossip that she attracted wherever she went made her the chief topic of the day. There were rumours that she was going on the stage, which would, of course, put her beyond the social pale; but this had not yet happened and she was still received at Government House.

The three children were thrilled by her arrival and hid under the dressing-table of the room where she was to leave her cloak, having cut little peepholes in the pink calico dressing-table curtains. An ill-timed giggle from Lucy, however, gave them away and they were hauled out. They could not take their eyes from the beautiful woman, splendidly dressed in white corded silk with a low, square, tight bodice and a bustle; she was the first woman they had ever seen who did not wear a chignon. She, for her part, was considerably flattered by the children's unconcealed adoration and she promised not to give them away. She even managed to send them up some supper during the course of the evening.

During the rest of their stay the children busied themselves with theatricals, which by this time had grown more elaborate, puppet shows giving way to actual performances or charades. Elinor was much mortified to find that she was never allotted the leading feminine role but made to put on a false nose and pad out her figure for comic parts. But she soon came to have no illusions about why this was. In those days red hair was a terrible disfigurement and no one so monstrously ugly could possibly be given a romantic lead.

Elinor's red hair was a sore point. Everyone condoled with her, or with her mother in her presence, on such a misfortune and openly compared her hair unfavourably with Lucy's brown or Ada Norcott's fair hair. People behaved as if Elinor were in some way almost to blame for it, and she derived a certain melancholy satisfaction from watching the same treatment meted out to another red-haired child, Ada Lloyd, the daughter of a naval captain. Mrs. Kennedy was advised by one well-meaning lady, again in Elinor's presence, to comb the child's hair with a leaden comb in the hope of darkening it. Only Sir William Norcott was kindly and expressed the view that she might not be too ugly when she grew up, as she had dark eyelashes. This conviction that she was ugly, laboriously instilled into her by all her relatives and friends at an early and impressionable age, may perhaps lie behind her later preoccupation with her appearance, her insatiable desire to be told that she was beautiful, and to preserve that beauty unlined into the furthest extremities of old age.

14.

The Kennedys returned from England in due course and the tyranny at Richelieu started again. Now it was worse than before. Mr. Kennedy's health was deteriorating and he spent much of his time in bed, a crotchety, bad-tempered invalid, with his wife a slave to his every whim. His investments, too, were not prospering and he grudged every penny he had to pay for his wife or stepchildren. All three of them were forced to make their own clothes at home, even their "tailor-made" suits. Fortunately they were all excellent needlewomen, and Lucy in particular already showed an extraordinary flair for designing clothes; they were always able to appear presentable, even at Government House garden parties.

By 1878 the position was intolerable. Lucy, almost sixteen, was on such bad terms with her stepfather that everyone agreed with relief to her suggestion that she should go and stay with her English and Scottish friends and relations. For

the next two years she was hardly in Jersey at all. The Nor-
cotts, too, left the island at this time and Elinor said a sad
farewell to her friend Ada. Finally, in a fit of temper one day,
Mr. Kennedy dismissed the governess and decided that she
should not be replaced. Mrs. Kennedy meekly acquiesced; it
never seems to have occurred to her that the education of her
fourteen-year-old daughter, now completed, lacked anything
to be desired. Nor did she notice that her daughter was now
completely alone, without sister, friend, or companion, sharing her solitude only with her collie, Roy.

The lease of Richelieu expired at this time and the Kennedys moved to a new house in St. Helier, No. 55 Colomberie,
a pleasant stone house with oak panelling. There was no library in the new house but Mr. Kennedy sent to Scotland for
his books. For Elinor their arrival was the happiest moment
of the next two years. Mr. Kennedy was too ill to arrange them
himself and they were dumped, still in their packing-cases,
in a little room on the ground floor. Elinor had plenty of
opportunity to read them in the two years that followed and
she would pore over them most of the day and far into the
night.

As at Richelieu it was a strange, rather unsuitable collection for a young girl to base her entire education upon, and
once again there was no one to advise her or guide her reading.
There were whole sets of Dickens and Thackeray, rebound
during Mr. Kennedy's stay in Pekin in old Chinese silk;
eleven volumes of the memoirs of the Duc de Saint-Simon; a
complete Gibbon; Sterne's *Sentimental Journey;* Voltaire's
Zadig; Chesterfield's *Letters to His Son;* La Rochefoucauld's
Maxims. These last four became like Bibles to Elinor. They
were always beside her bed and, having a remarkable memory, she soon knew them almost by heart.

The Saint-Simon memoirs linked themselves naturally with
what Mrs. Saunders had taught her about eighteenth-century
France and Elinor saturated herself in the history and customs

of the Bourbon court. *The Decline and Fall of the Roman Empire*, which she read from beginning to end, awoke an interest in Roman history to supplement her already considerable knowledge of Greek history, but without noticeable effect upon her later prose style.

When she had exhausted the books or wished for further information on a subject, the only course open to her was to walk to the St. Helier public library, some way away, and look it up in an encyclopaedia. She did this many times in her determined but rather pathetic efforts to provide herself with the education that she felt was necessary. One cannot but admire her doggedness, her energy, and her devotion to the cause of knowledge, but the effect of such haphazard reading was never altogether overcome in later life. The subjects which she knew and where her sympathies lay she knew in astonishing detail, which increased as the years went by; the eighteenth century in France was of course pre-eminent—by the end of her life she had an intricate knowledge of the literature, customs, clothes, furniture, art, architecture, and history (but not music) of the period. She could date a picture to within a few years from the fashions or the furniture. The seeds had been planted—if they were not already there in her Saunders blood—by reading Saint-Simon at the age of fourteen. The Italian Renaissance was another of her periods, born of an early study of John Addington Symonds. But between these overgrown islands of knowledge there were desolate gulfs of ignorance, of which she herself was always sadly aware and which she spent much care and effort in concealing.

The effect on her character was even more fundamental. The division between the two sides of her personality was already clearly discernible at this time. On one side there was the romantic Sutherland streak, nourished by fairy stories, by Balgregan Castle and the Thousand Islands in the dawn, by the Stuarts and Jacobites, by Byron and Scott, and from which she derived her conviction that the beautiful things of life were there to be enjoyed by all who had the eyes to see them. From it too came her optimism, her steadfast conviction that in the end everything would always be well.

On the other side was the French eighteenth-century background, growing out of her Saunders blood, cynical, worldly, disillusioned, melancholy, pessimistic, concerned with the outward form rather than the inner spirit; encouraged by the sight of Londonderry and Seven Dials in the rain; nurtured by Cervantes and Thucydides at an early age, and now fertilised by Saint-Simon, Sterne, La Rochefoucauld, and Chesterfield. These two warring sides of her character she was never able to reconcile and they may be held to explain the several contradictions in her views and her behaviour. It may be thought, too, that their clash provides the motive power for her almost inexhaustible creative energy.

15.

It was about this time that Elinor started to write stories, romantic subjective efforts, carefully copied into penny notebooks. The earliest one, "Valerie Charteris," delightfully foreshadows the romances to come.

"By Jove! What a pair of eyes! Who is she, Clifford?" said Guy Elmhurst as the dog-cart with the two men in it swept rapidly past a girl walking along the road.

"Don't know," answered the individual addressed, "Never saw her before, could hardly get a glimpse then," and he turned his head over his shoulder, but they were twenty yards past her by this time. "Hardly fast enough looking for one of Lady Di's friends," he laughed.

A few pages later they met again in a post office:

"Oh! I am in no hurry," he answered, "Pray serve this lady first."

Of course he was in no hurry. What idle man would be when he had the gratification of looking at anything so sweet and fresh and fair as Valerie. She blushed as he spoke. Of course it was very silly of her, a thing no "well brought-up young lady" would have done. But then Valerie was only a little country girl who had spent most of her life in a French convent and who had never before seen a handsome well-dressed man of the world.

"I want a shilling's worth of penny stamps," she said shyly, "and our paper."

All this time Guy Elmhurst—for it was he—had never taken his eyes off her face.

"By Jove!" he soliloquised, "what a sweet little wild rose. How I should like to make love to her."

The start of another one, "A Gawky Schoolgirl!" reveals, rather pathetically, the longings of her heart.

I am very pretty with straight features, big grey eyes and curly golden hair. I am seventeen and have—or will have on my eighteenth birthday five thousand a year (I dare say, dear reader, you are saying to yourself, how vain!) but I am not. I have been pretty ever since I was born and have known it ever since I could understand what the word pretty meant so I have given up all vanity on the subject. I am possessed of abundant spirits and a hot temper and my name is Kate Brandon.

Already a conscientious craftsman, she was dissatisfied with this and rewrote it in a milder version with a characteristic little bitter touch at the end.

I believe I am rather pretty with straight features, big grey eyes and curly bright golden hair. I am seventeen and have—or will have on my eighteenth birthday—five thousand a year. Perhaps that accounts for people thinking me pretty!

The time was to come when she would have far more than five thousand a year and when she would not exchange her red hair and green eyes for anything in the world.

The following year, 1879, saw the first volume of *The Diary of Miss Nellie Sutherland*—she was always called Nellie at home—which she was to keep intermittently for the rest of her life. Later it was to be written in thick uniform volumes, bound in purple velvet and fastened with Bramah locks, but at this stage it was kept, like the stories, in a penny notebook. The diary reveals only too clearly the drab, monotonous life she was leading.

> Morning sewed. Afternoon called at Government House but saw no one. Evening can't remember.

The longest entry she made at this time was devoted to the prediction of a fortune teller, which she wrote down with a touching faith and excitement. (In this one instance the spelling is left uncorrected.)

> I have been very happy but am going to have some vexation and trouble. There is a dark gentleman who loves me and will make a settlemet. At some amusement at our house I will be very vexed and troubled at somthing I here or that hapens. I will quarell with my fiance and we are to be seperated for a time but am to be eventually happy. Am to be marrade at either 19, 20 or 21. My husband is to be rich.

As a forecast it was singularly wide of the mark.

16.

That summer the world suddenly brightened for Elinor. An eighteen-year-old Eton boy came to spend his holidays on the island, and, red hair or no red hair, he was immediately attracted by Elinor. Several other young men were also apparently interested in her, as the following extract from her diary shows:

Friday 3rd September.
Morning go to Macs to clear their floor, make it up with Duncan, have great fun. Floss comes to dinner. Afternoon do my dress. Evening Duncan brings me flowers for tonight. Evening the Macs dance, have splendid fun, dance five times with Herbert and sit out four!!! In nice, nicer, nicest dance seven times with Duncan. They have a scrimmage for the end dance and I give it to Percy. Great fun altogether. Duncan jealous, Herbert triumphant.

She was already learning woman's wiles, discovering how to arouse the innate masculine hunting instinct.

However, she rapidly became very fond of the Etonian (it is never quite clear whether he was Duncan or Herbert) and recorded obliquely in her diary the diffident joys and despairing heartaches of first love. But the cynical side of her nature refused to let her believe that it was anything more than a holiday flirtation. She could not help counting the days that were left—"only three more days together"—but she had been well schooled in the control of her emotions and she saw him off on his return to Eton dry-eyed and smiling. Mrs. Saunders, had she been there, would have approved and might not have noticed the lump in her granddaughter's throat.

The episode with the Eton boy did two things for Elinor. It gave her a deathless admiration for the methods and traditions of Eton College; and, more important, it restored a good deal of her self-confidence. A good-looking young man of eighteen had found her attractive; perhaps she was not so ugly after all.

She was also reminded, before it was too late, that the spirit of romance, in spite of its sadnesses and disappointments, was far more enjoyable than a dry, aloof mood of cynicism.

Elinor's second romance took place about six months later, and this was a far more adult and dangerous affair. A French lady, Mademoiselle Duret, who was staying in Jersey, invited Elinor to return to Paris with her on a week's visit. Mrs. Kennedy, only too glad to get Elinor out of the house for a few days, agreed, and so it came about that in the spring of 1880 Elinor saw Paris for the first time.

It was a delight and an enchantment to her. She felt, she wrote later, as if she were returning to some place which she had known well long ago. All Elinor's own French relations were out of Paris and Mademoiselle Duret's family seemed rather old and uninteresting to the youthful and ardent girl. But as a treat and because Mademoiselle Duret felt that Elinor ought to see the great actress, she was taken to see Sarah Bernhardt in *Theodora,* Mademoiselle Duret believing erroneously that Elinor's French was not sufficiently fluent to allow her to understand much of the story. Thirty years later when Elinor actually met Sarah Bernhardt, she recalled in her diary her memory of that performance of *Theodora.*

It made an immense effect upon me, as she moved and undulated over her lover. Strange thrills rushed through me. Although I analysed nothing in those days I know now I had suddenly found my group—the group of the Sirens, the weird fierce passionate caressing and cruel group. I remember long sentences of her love words to Andreas. I used to say them to myself and act the scene before the dim glass in the little back room in the Rue de la Borde. I had no idea of anything sensual—it was merely a sudden flint touching steel which had ignited the tinder. I remember letting down my hair as a cloak and covering this imaginary lover with its copper waves. He had no personality—he was not Andreas. He was something for the rousing of the soul of me. The old lady who took me to the theatre believed that a child of fifteen would notice nothing, would not understand the French, would take it as a pantomime! I remember trembling in my bed the whole night through. This was a sudden awakening to the possibilities of life.

The following day, while Elinor was still in a romantic daze over the love of Andreas and Theodora, a good-looking young Frenchman who had visited the Kennedys in Jersey a month earlier came to call at Mademoiselle Duret's flat, bringing an invitation that they should visit his own family. He contrived to spend the next three days in Elinor's company, and although they were naturally never left alone together, he managed to make passionate love to her in English, which Mademoiselle Duret understood imperfectly. The three of them visited the Paris Zoo and it was there that Elinor saw her first tiger skin. As she stared, fascinated, through the bars of the cage, the young Frenchman kept whispering *"Belle tigresse!"* into her ear. Coming directly on top of *Theodora,* this made Elinor intoxicated with romance. She went about in a starry-eyed dream, murmuring *"Andreas, je t'aime . . ."* to herself.

However, the cynical side of her nature stood her in good stead and she declined the Frenchman's invitation to fly with him. She returned to Jersey a few days later with a new copy of La Rochefoucauld, a present from the Frenchman, and the firm conviction that the world was, after all, an exciting place, that she herself was both beautiful and attractive to men, and that what she had so far experienced was only a foretaste of the raptures to come.

17.

In 1880, Lucy, now a lovely girl of seventeen, returned for a while to Jersey and Elinor once more had a companion.

They both went out a good deal. Lucy, in particular, was very much in demand at parties. Many of the young officers in the regiment stationed there were in love with her and she herself was very fond of one of them, a particularly charming young man, from all accounts. Elinor felt no jealousy of her sister's success and romantic preoccupations. Her week in Paris had completely restored her self-confidence. She, too, was beautiful; her own time would come.

In the meantime, between social events, she lived in her dream world, imagining her lover to be now like the Etonian, now like the Frenchman. He would be handsome, well born, rich, utterly eligible. She would be his passionate, devoted bride and they would live happily ever after. Her cynical thoughts, it will be seen, were for the moment firmly shelved.

By the following year Lucy and her young man were completely devoted to each other and Mrs. Kennedy was beginning to congratulate herself that one of her daughters would soon be off her hands. At this point, however, the young pair had an unfortunate quarrel. It would undoubtedly have been completely forgotten in a day or so but Lucy, in a fit of pique, went straight to England before any apologies could be said.

She stayed there at an old house called Kings Walden in Hertfordshire and there she met James Wallace, a dissolute bachelor, more than twenty years older than she was. He was entranced by her youth and charm and asked her to marry him. She accepted without hesitation.

Mrs. Kennedy was appalled when she heard the news. She knew of Wallace's reputation for loose living. He had very little money; Lucy had known him only a few days; the young officer in Jersey was only too anxious to make up the quarrel. Would not Lucy reconsider her decision?

But Lucy, perverse and headstrong as always, was adamant. The more they argued with her, the more stubborn she became. It was plain to all that the marriage could end only in disaster, but Mrs. Kennedy saw that nothing would change her daughter's mind and reluctantly she withdrew her opposition.

The wedding took place soon afterwards, very quietly.

18.

After their marriage Lucy and James Wallace went to live in a little house in the grounds of Cranford Park, near Hounslow, which was owned by Lord Fitzharding, a friend of James Wallace's father. Elinor went to stay with them each year and the place became a second home to her—not a very happy home because Lucy and her husband were already beginning to quarrel, but at least it was a *pied-à-terre* in England away from that suffocating island with its unhappy associations.

Lady Fitzharding, a corpulent but kindly lady, took a fancy to Elinor and constantly invited her up to Cranford Park and, on occasion, to stay in London. It was under Lady Fitzharding's aegis that Elinor was launched in society and started her first English season.

Cranford Park was a gay place at that time. Its house parties were large and fasionable; numbers of notable people came down every Sunday from London and the house was usually thronged with young officers from the cavalry barracks in Windsor. The food at Cranford was Lucullan and the chef, François, a master of his craft. His speciality was *poulard céleste,* which Elinor was able to describe so accurately in her first novel, *The Visits of Elizabeth,* that Escoffier of the Carlton was able to imitate it exactly for the celebration lunch on publication day. François, however, was dismissed by Lord Fitzharding, soon after Elinor's first visit, as he refused to manage on less than two thousand eggs a week, and his lordship thought that excessive.

Lord Fitzharding himself was a delightful person, with a

kind heart, a neat wit, and a minute stature, causing him to be known, with relentless British humour, as "Giant." He was much entertained by Elinor's gifts as a lightning artist and especially proud of a sketch she did of him in his tall cap covered with hedgehog quills. He encouraged her to sketch the other members of his parties, and this little talent helped her to become a noticed and, unless the caricature was too mordant, a popular member of his circle.

At Cranford she received invitations to other house parties all over the country, and soon she was "visiting" like the most established members of society, an elegant girl with a haughty poise, no money, a courtly manner, and homemade clothes. On the surface she was a young lady of gentle birth, taking her rightful place in society—though some hints in her novels and the general contempt in which "colonials" were held indicate that her path was not always smooth—enjoying the pleasures of the idle rich, the companionship of good friends of both sexes, staying at great houses, relishing the unsurpassed amenities of life. But underneath her romantic heart was searching for her dream lover, for Andreas.

Her search was not altogether in vain. Several charming young men were strongly attracted to her, but they were all virtually penniless and Elinor, her cynical side for the moment uppermost, held her emotions in stern check. She knew that her mother would be deeply disappointed if she, too, married badly and her own studies in eighteenth-century thought had taught her that the success or failure of a young girl's life was measured entirely by whether she made a rich or a poor marriage. Even in Victorian times this view had not entirely been abandoned. Elinor herself had had enough of poverty under Mr. Kennedy's régime and prospects of a lifetime of love in a cottage held no attractions for her. The whole point of Cinderella was that she ended by living in the palace; if after her marriage she were to continue having to sweep out the kitchen, with or without Prince Charming to help her, the story would have lost all its appeal.

In her first two seasons at Cranford no less than three men proposed to her, all of whom were rich and influential enough to satisfy all her worldly desires. But all three were very far from being the dream lover for whom her romantic heart yearned. She had already twice tasted the heaven-sent delights of young love; she could not bear to throw away so soon all the bright dreams of her adolescence.

All her three suitors were elderly and they were all physically very unattractive. The first, a bibulous peer with a walrus moustache, disgusted her by spluttering over her as he proposed. The second was the Duke of Newcastle, and Elinor would have given a very great deal to have been a Duchess. But as she wrote later:

> He was absorbingly interested in the details of ecclesiastical apparel and this subject was so far removed from my ideas as to the things that matter most in life that I wonder that I appealed to him sufficiently for him to pay me such a compliment.

The third was a millionaire, but he was vulgar and ostentatious, with a common voice and unfastidious manners. Mrs. Saunders would not have permitted him inside the house, and all Elinor's childhood training revolted at the thought of marrying such a man. On top of everything else he had a beard. James Wallace, however, pressed her strongly to accept him and all four of them went on a yachting trip on the millionaire's yacht in August when the season was over. Elinor firmly refused the proposal when at last it came. James Wallace was furious and sent her home to Jersey in disgrace.

In 1887 she paid her first visit to Hillersdon in Devon, which was owned by Mr. W. J. Grant, himself to be one of her gayest and most steadfast friends. More than twenty years

later when she was again at Hillersdon, she tried in her diary
to describe herself as she had been on that first visit.

Twenty-three years ago since I first floated on this lake.
I remember I was unhappy even in those days. Always some
sword of Damocles hanging over me. First cantankerous
step-father. Then an unspeakable brother-in-law making
home impossible. There were long visits to French relations,
rich and prosperous, and returning laden with exquisite
clothes, flung at me as a parting gift, galling always. Then
there were those visits for the autumn balls, and the women
hated me. Why, I wonder? My old friend (Billy Grant)
said because I was so white and slim and red-haired and
could dance and speak French and had not red arms and
carried my head very highly and wore Doucet ball dresses
—and when one has no connections even in England, surely
these were causes enough in all conscience! An upstart,
half-foreign person! who dared to sail into the sacred precincts and cause havoc among the young country squires
and especially ensnare the heart of the great catch of the
neighbourhood and then not marry him!

A girl with such an appearance *must* be bad! Red hair
and black eyelashes and green eyes!! No really nice woman
creature could have colouring like that! She must be stoned!

But I had my triumphs in those days. Now that I look
back upon it all, there was something a little pitiful about
it. A poor little lonely girl hiding many troubles under a
haughtily set head, longing to be protected and loved.
Timid really and very tender hearted—and always antag-
onously treated by women for no fault except nature's
bizarre choice of red, white and green. Always the centre
of the passionate love of men—always proud—always alone.
Ah me! how I remember when I decided to marry. I thought
I would choose some good Englishman who would be kind
to me, where I could shelter from the turmoil and have

some domestic happiness and peace—and above all a home!
Ah me!

We must make allowances for the mood of disillusion in
which that was written and for the spirit of self-pity engendered so often by writing a diary. She was undoubtedly happier in those days than she remembered. She had forgotten
her youth, her romantic ardour, her delight in the society
world in which she now found herself, her thankfulness at
her release from the long years of imprisonment in Jersey.

But there was a grain of truth in it, all the same. Her
haughty bearing, her arrogance, her icy courtliness, her in-
tolerance must have often repelled many who would have
liked to have befriended the young girl. Men were drawn to
her like moths to a candle. It was her own sex that looked at
her askance.

19.

In 1888, Elinor's French cousins, the Fouquet Lemaîtres,
invited her to spend the season in France and she, hoping
perhaps to find there the dream lover whom she had so far
failed to find in England, accepted gladly.

The Fouquet Lemaîtres were an affluent aristocratic family
with a beautiful château near Bolbec in Normandy and a town
house in the Champs Elysées. Elinor found herself very much
at home in that milieu; her command of the language, her
miscroscopic knowledge of certain aspects of French life and
culture stood her in good stead, though in a young republic
they were a little surprised by the vehemence of her royalism,
about which she seems to have expressed herself with force
and frequency.

On this visit she saw for the first time the palace of
Versailles, the place which was to mean more to her than any-

where else on earth and which she ever after regarded as her spiritual home. To her earth had not anything to show fairer than the great façade of the palace seen from the steps above the *tapis vert.* She both amused and shocked her companion, the Comte de Ségur, by declining to waste her time looking for a portrait of his ancestor, a Napoleonic general, as she was not interested in *cette canaille-là.*

Although they were living in the progressive, industrious world of the Third Republic, the Fouquet Lemaîtres and their circle still conducted themselves according to the ethics and manners of the *ancien régime,* and Elinor regarded them with warm approval. The approval was mutual when they saw her own manners, her knowledge of French history and art, her undisguised admiration for France. Clearly she had been very well brought up.

They were very kind to her, loading her with presents of clothes, which she, remembering her own scanty wardrobe, accepted with mingled gratitude and humiliation. It was a gay and enjoyable summer and she did all the things that fashionable girls in Paris were expected to do. She made trips on the Seine—short ones in Mr. Gordon Bennett's fast yacht, the wash of which half drowned the washerwomen on the bank —and the longer excursion with the whole Fouquet Lemaîtres family to Rouen. This, judging from the description of it in *The Visits of Elizabeth,* must have been a farcical riot from beginning to end. She played tennis at Puteaux. She stayed at Bolbec. She took part in the cotillons. She even forced herself to ride in the Bois, where she hoped that her beautiful figure with its seventeen-inch waist would distract attention from her shocking seat on a horse.

She was overjoyed to find that the French considered her a beauty. Monsieur Marcel, the famous hairdresser, kept two distinguished clients waiting the whole afternoon so that he might have the pleasure of doing her lovely hair himself. Wearing a brand-new white tulle ball dress (a present from her cousins), she was taken to a ball at the American Embassy the same night. Feeling exactly like Cinderella, she was beyond doubt the belle of the evening. Handsome men crowded round her, she danced every dance.

Unlike Cinderella's, her beautiful new ball dress did not turn back into rags at midnight but there was no Prince Charming either. Gradually she came to realise that though she might easily find romance in France, she would never find a husband. She had no dowry.

20.

The following year, 1889, Mr. Kennedy died and his wife's long years of servitude were over at last. She sold 55 Colomberie and moved to London, where she took a little house in Davies Street, Mayfair.

A new trouble immediately appeared for the poor woman. Lucy was by now very unhappy with her husband, whose drinking habits were making life impossible at home. Her four-year-old daughter Esme was sent to live at Davies Street to be away from her father and to be cared for by her grandmother. Lucy, who for all her faults was a courageous girl, made a last effort to save her marriage.

It had, however, deteriorated past repair, and finally Lucy was forced to admit that there was no course left except to end it. Divorce in those days was a costly matter and the legal expenses absorbed the bulk of the estate which Mr. Kennedy had left. Mrs. Kennedy found herself almost back at the point where she had been twenty-four years before, with almost no money, two unmarried daughters, and now a small granddaughter to support as well.

Elinor was now twenty-five and her failure to find a husband was glaring. She wondered many times whether she had not been selfish in refusing the Duke or the bearded million-aire.

Mrs. Kennedy decided, after much serious thought, to use the rest of Mr. Kennedy's estate in starting Lucy in a small dressmaking business on the ground floor of the Davies Street house. It was registered as Lucile's, Ltd., and Mrs. Kennedy herself helped with the cutting-up and sewing in the back room. The history of that venture, romantic though it is in its growth from one room in Davies Street to the foremost cou-turier business of the time, Lucile's of Hanover Square, Paris, New York and Chicago, lies outside the scope of this book.

Elinor, meanwhile, continued the social round, now becom-ing desperate with the passing of time and the lack of money. She visited her French cousins again in the summer of that year and the following one, 1890. That winter she went once more to stay with Billy Grant at Hillersdon, and here an in-cident took place which was to alter her life entirely.

A large house party was assembled for the duck-shooting and the Exeter Ball, and at the latter event Elinor was once again in the centre of all attention, to such effect that four men of the Hillersdon party, who had been competing for her favours all the evening, threw each other into the lake on their return to Hillersdon. They then pulled off their sodden evening clothes and took baths in their host's best champagne to ward off the chills of midwinter bathing. That episode was remarkable even for the Naughty Nineties and news of it travelled fast through the social world. It reached amongst others some friends of Elinor's, the Chisenhale-Marshes of Gaynes Park, Essex, and they retailed the story to a neighbour of theirs, Clayton Glyn, a wealthy landowner who for twenty years had saddened the hearts of society mothers by firmly remaining a bachelor. He was intrigued by the story, knowing the four men concerned. Any girl who could persuade four such stolid types to jump into a lake at three o'clock on a winter's morning must be worth looking at, and he suggested to the Chisenhale-Marshes that next time they invited Elinor to stay, they should ask him, too.

The invitation materialised that autumn, Elinor having duly been told about the man who was showing such a gratifying interest in her.

"Clayton Glyn," she wrote later, "was in his ways and thoughts always instinctively and naturally the most perfect grand seigneur that I have ever met, and one of the kindest of men, generous in everything and incapable of meanness of any kind." In appearance he was striking, tall, broad-shouldered, with a dignified carriage, a good-looking face with china-blue eyes, perfect teeth and—unexpectedly—thick wavy silver hair, the consequence of a gas explosion when he was a child. He was a descendant of Sir Richard Carr Glyn, the banker and Lord Mayor of London, but Clayton Glyn had no business interests, his life being centred round his house, Durrington, and his surrounding estates. He was a fine sportsman, a magnificent shot, a connoisseur of food and wine, a great traveller, known with respect and affection by almost every head-waiter and wine waiter in Europe and the Near East. He had a dry, caustic but strong sense of humour and a merry smile.

He was obviously very far from being disappointed with Elinor when they were finally introduced. A great part of his attraction for her, she later confessed, was his mastery of the situation from the very first moment. He took it completely for granted that she would consent to marry him.

Elinor herself was excited and bewildered. The mental picture she had always had of her future husband was undergoing drastic changes in her mind. Clayton Glyn was very different, both in appearance and in manner from the young Frenchman who had captivated her eleven years before. He did not make love to her, as she expected or hoped. He did not whisper passionate words in her ear. Indeed, he had at all times an innate distrust of the sentimental, the dramatic, and the highfalutin. Elinor was a little disappointed but she managed to persuade herself quite easily that romance did not consist only in ardent phrases. And there was so much that was attractive about Clayton—his smile, his blue eyes, his grand manner, above all his hair. It was like a powdered wig. He might have been a Marquis at the Bourbon court—or Prince Charming stepped out of an illustration of "Cinderella."

21.

In February of the following year, 1892, Elinor and her mother went to Monte Carlo. Clayton Glyn, still like Prince Charming, pursued them, and there beside the blue Mediterranean he asked her to marry him. She accepted gayly and he promptly bought her a large diamond ring at Cartier's. It was decided that they should be married in London at the end of April. Then, unlike Prince Charming, he abandoned his fiancée of a few hours and returned home to see how the young pheasants were getting on. As he was a poor correspondent, Elinor neither saw him nor heard from him again till immediately before the wedding. If she could have seen it, in that moment of casual neglect on his part lay the seeds of much future disillusionment, and of more than twenty romantic novels.

Nothing, however, could shake Elinor's happiness at that time. She and her mother came slowly back, stopping in Paris to do a little shopping for Elinor's trousseau, the bulk of which, of course, was to come from Lucile's. The Fouquet Lemaîtres were astounded by the news—they had never expected their impoverished cousin to marry. Clayton Glyn, they felt, must indeed be in love with her; but in which case why was he not now by her side? Elinor laughed but did not care. In less than two months she was going to be married.

22.

Clayton Glyn and Elinor Sutherland were married on the twenty-seventh of April, 1892, at St. George's, Hanover Square, the parish church of Mrs. Kennedy's house in Davies Street. They must have been a striking couple, the tall, distinguished, silver-haired bridegroom and the slim, beautiful, red-haired bride.

It was the first fashionable wedding that Lucile's had dressed and Lucy had done her sister proud, with a beautiful full-skirted gown of white brocade and a veil of Brussels lace held in place by a diamond tiara, a present from the bridegroom, who insisted that a wreath of orange blossoms, then the usual headdress, was not fine enough for his dazzling bride. She looked, he told her, just like a fairy queen.

They spent their honeymoon at Brighton. Clayton observed that it was sad to have married the Lorelei and then give her no opportunity of displaying her charms. So he hired the public baths for two days so that she might swim up and down alone, naked, her long red hair, which when uncoiled reached her knees, trailing in the water behind her. It was a romantic, costly, and rather uncharacteristic gesture which completely won his bride's heart.

After the honeymoon they returned to Durrington in triumph. At long last the squire was bringing home a bride. They drove in their carriage through cheering crowds of villagers to the main gate, where the horses were taken out of the shafts and the farmers themselves, in Newgate-frill beards and wearing their Sunday best, drew the carriage up the drive, under the evergreen triumphal arches with floating banners and mottoes of "God Bless the Bride and Bridegroom." At the end of the drive was the fine Palladian façade of Durrington House, no mean threshold over which to be carried.

That night there was a banquet for the tenants, with un-limited punch and long laborious speeches full of hearty references to the possibility of an heir. Outside there were fire-works. It was a magnificent home-coming. Elinor was trium-phant and radiant. At long last, after all those interminable years of waiting, her dreams had come true. Cinderella had married her Prince Charming. She had everything in the world she craved. She had romance and she had riches.

The tragedy was that in fact she had neither.

BOOK TWO

The Best-Selling Novelist

1892–1907

I.

Clayton Glyn was very much the country gentleman, interested in his land and his farms, discussing the prospects of pheasants with his head gamekeeper. He was a Justice of the Peace, the squire of the neighbouring village, Sheering; the villagers pulled their forelocks or curtseyed as he passed through. For much of the time, of course, he was away from Essex, at other houses or travelling abroad, but when he was at home, his villagers and tenants regarded their lord of the manor in a suitably feudal and respectful way.

He went to church every Sunday, wearing a top hat, for it would, in his opinion, have been extremely disrespectful to God to have called on Him less formally attired. On the other hand, he was invariably six minutes late in case the vicar might get uppish and it was very many years before his children discovered exactly what happened at the beginning of Morning Prayer.

Into his country life Elinor fitted a little awkwardly. She had no experience of its special pleasures and duties and she tended to regard it all as rather provincial and dull. She had been sufficiently long in Paris to have acquired some of the urban condescension with which the Parisian *beau monde* of that date looked down upon their country cousins. In appearance, too, she was rather un-English. She had only one tweed suit and did not care greatly for it. With the smart fashions that her cousins had pressed on her and her elegant Lucile clothes, her high heels, and polished nails, she was a conspicuous figure in Essex County society and regarded with a certain amount of suspicion. Among her neighbours she made few friends.

There was, however, one notable exception. The Countess of Warwick, one of the most beautiful, gracious, and resplendent hostesses of that period, lived at Easton Lodge, some ten miles from Durrington, and she took the young and inexperienced bride under her wing. No one was a more capable or energetic Lady Bountiful than Lady Warwick, but though Elinor tried hard to emulate her, she found she had little vocation for the task. She did not enjoy taking port and jellies to sickly villagers and sitting with them while they told her all about their tedious illnesses and families. They, in their turn, did not altogether relish the patronage of someone so bizarre and *outré*. No county in England is more insular than Essex and they never came to regard Elinor as anything else but a "foreigner."

Lady Warwick was, however, more successful in instructing her in her social duties, for, though Elinor had often been to the great houses of England in the Cranford days, being a hostess was a new experience for her. Army or naval officers, diplomats or clergymen, it was explained, might be invited to luncheon or dinner. The vicar might be invited regularly to Sunday lunch or supper, if he was a gentleman. Doctors and solicitors might be invited to garden parties, though never, of course, to lunch or dinner. Anyone engaged in the arts, the stage, trade or commerce, no matter how well connected, could not be asked to the house at all.

Elinor had much cause to be grateful to Lady Warwick. For years she was her closest friend. She supported the young bride and championed her when others in the county were

distant and cool. The hospitality of Easton Lodge and Warwick Castle, two of the greatest centres of society at that date,
was always open to her. But though Lady Warwick's friendship was undoubtedly a great help and consolation to Elinor
in those first difficult years, we may doubt whether it was a
benefit in the long run, tending as it did to bring out and
emphasise Elinor's less lovable qualities, her class-consciousness and her arrogance.

2.

Married life with Clayton was also not quite easy. The
divergence in their tastes and interests and in their attitude
towards life became more marked now that they were living
together. The episode of the swimming-bath at Brighton
seemed to have been his last romantic gesture. Back at Durrington he picked up the threads of his normal life and he
expected his wife to take her rightful place.

She, still a little bewildered at finding herself so suddenly
the wife of a country squire, would watch him covertly from
the far end of their long dining-room table and try to suppress
her growing doubts about him.

An incident which occurred shortly after their wedding
typified the situation between them at this time, although she
recorded it much later in her diary.

Oh my heart! This evening I have been in a wood! A
wood! which for eighteen years I have longed to enter, but
it has been *défendu*. "Women must not walk there, they
will disturb the pheasants, only the feet of the keepers must
tread these sacred paths." And so it has remained a place
of mystery. I first saw it at exactly this time of year, when
bluebells were blooming and the larks singing and all nature talking of love and hope. I was very young and had

been married about a fortnight. We walked there and I remember how the beauty of it came upon me and with a
foolish little cry I rushed forward to pick the bluebells—
and it was then it was explained to me the impossibility of
an entrance. Bluebells! ridiculous! Did I not know at that
time of the year the mischief going into a wood caused! And
so we walked on round it and my pleasure in the day was
gone. And in the years that followed it always hurt when
I remembered and I never tried to penetrate among the
trees even in winter. Indeed as long as pheasants lasted it
was ever *défendu*, a forbidden corner, an unexplored land.

Once again we must discount the tone of self-pity, but in
that incident we find a microcosm of their contrasted attitudes
toward life: the ardent, passionate girl, tending to dramatise
herself, longing to enjoy the more romantic aspects of nature
in springtime; and the quizzical ex-bachelor, afraid for his
young pheasants and unable to understand why his wife
should want to run about in bluebell woods.

It would, however, be a mistake to regard Elinor as an unhappy bride. Like every other newly married couple she and
Clayton had many mutual adjustments to make. The fact
that they both declined to make these adjustments did not
affect the marriage till later. In the meantime there was much
that was new and exciting. Above all, there were the house
parties. She and Clayton were never happier together than
when they were sitting in their brougham behind their two
horses, Pair and Impair (named in memory of Monte Carlo),
driving over to Easton.

3.

Country house parties played an important part in the social
life of the time and formed the background of Elinor's first

four novels; so it is perhaps worth while to examine them a little more closely and see just what they involved.

The guests might number anything from twenty to forty, the *crème de la crème* of society—peers, senior Tory politicians, Ambassadors, sportsmen, perhaps even the Prince of Wales. They came with their valets or ladies' maids, driving up to the front door in their broughams and landaus, there to be welcomed by the groom of the chambers, that immensely competent and discreet factotum who organised the entire household. They were then ushered into one of the drawing-rooms, where their hostess was waiting to welcome them with afternoon tea. No introductions were ever made and it was tacitly assumed that everyone present already knew everyone else, an assumption which made things a little difficult for young men and girls in their first season and for brides like Elinor.

The whole house, with perhaps the exception of the hostess's private wing, was open to the guests. They were free to wander through the many rooms and galleries, admiring the furniture, the family pictures, or the rich tapestries. The effect was lush and magnificent, though by modern standards every room would have been thought overfilled with sofas, tables, and china cabinets. The walls of the front hall were invariably covered with heads which the host had brought back from his several big-game expeditions. Upstairs the bedrooms were no less luxurious than the drawing-rooms, with silk bed curtains, huge armchairs and sofas, innumerable soft cushions, and a white bear hearthrug. A dozen of the newest novels, biographies, and travel books stood on the bed table. The writing tables were equipped with every imaginable gadget from Asprey's or Webster's and every variety of stamp or writing-paper. Flowers were placed on the dressing-table every evening for the guest to wear at dinner, carnations or gardenias for the men, great sprays of stephanotis or orchids for the women. There were, of course, no bathrooms, but each bedroom contained a metal tub, painted to match the curtains, tipped up against the wall behind a screen. This was laid out, filled, and emptied by toiling housemaids with huge cans of hot water every evening.

The rooms were usually warm in winter, with big fires in the grates, but the passages were normally cold and draughty. As evening cloaks or scarves were not fashionable, ladies would scurry down them with chattering teeth. Easton Lodge was an exception in having warm passages.

The clothes to be worn at these visits were formal and picturesque. In the daytime the guests would wear whatever was suitable for the time of year and the particular sport of the moment. It was not, however, correct to lunch in tweeds and ladies were expected to change into frocks. After lunch they changed back again into tweeds if it was a shooting party, or put on full-length sealskin coats if they were to go motoring. For tea they changed again into tea gowns, seductive, diaphanous affairs with low-cut bodices, while the men wore brightly coloured velvet smoking suits; Clayton's was sapphire blue, and other popular colours were emerald green and crimson. For dinner the guests wore full evening dress, the men in white ties and tails and the women in dresses with trains, carrying ostrich feather fans. Evening bags were never used, as cosmetics were at that time almost unknown in society circles and could be bought only at a theatrical costumiers.

The food at these parties was equally sumptuous. Breakfast could be taken either in bed or downstairs from a row of silver chafing-dishes on the sideboard, the men sitting grumpily apart at their own table. Lunch was a lengthy but informal meal; often it took place out of doors at the shooting-stand, or in the lunch tent at the cricket match or the race meeting. Tea, in the drawing-room, varied from the thin bread and butter offered at some houses to the comprehensive farmhouse tea—muffins, honey, and Devonshire cream—provided by Lady Warwick at Easton.

But it was dinner that was the great moment of the day. The guests were paired off in the drawing-room and went in, arm in arm, in order of precedence. There were usually nine or ten courses to be got through, each with a different wine, and the meal naturally took a very long time. Polished tables were not then in fashion and the table was covered with a white damask tablecloth. Great bowls of flowers stood in the centre of the table and elsewhere in the room, and these were changed for each meal.

After dinner the gentlemen drank port while the ladies retired to the drawing-room. When they rejoined the ladies they would all split into pairs or groups for conversation. Good conversation at that time was not a way of passing odd moments but an end in itself. It was one of the objects of the assembly to hear and to practise witty, rapid, devastating, profound, or cynical repartee, especially if some notable figure or wit was present. For those few who did not care for conversation there was always the billiard room or the card room for bezique or whist. In certain houses, Shipley and Titchborne for instance, but not Easton, baccarat was permitted.

The object of these elaborate and costly house parties was threefold. The first was the enjoyment of the good things of life; good living, good food, good company; the exercising of the privileges of a highly exclusive society, membership of which could be attained virtually only by birth.

The second object was sport. Most of the large parties centred round a big shoot or meet in the winter, a race meeting, a cricket or a yachting-week in the summer. The men would participate, the women would listen sympathetically, watch as much as they could bear, and hope that it would soon be over.

The third object was philandering. If the etiquette was strict, the morals were light. Any husband or wife, however newly married, was fair game and large house parties were an admirable cover for clandestine love affairs. Gentlemen could whisper to ladies as they lit their candles for them at night, notes could be brought on the breakfast trays, arranging accidental meetings or rendezvous. No hostess was so expert as Lady Warwick in summing up at a glance just how alone a couple wished to be and detaching any tactless and unwanted third. There were so many places the happy pair could go to —portraits of ancestors to be seen in a gallery, books of engravings to be turned over in some small library. They could take walks through the woods to a belvedere or viewpoint. In the grounds of Easton, within comfortable walking distance, there was a small pleasure house, with the *Love Lyrics* of Laurence Hope already lying conveniently on the table in case the cavalier should become suddenly tongue-tied.

The essence of all these affairs was absolute secrecy. Everybody, in fact, knew who at the moment was interested in whom, but it was never admitted, even tacitly. In the company even of their closest friends, who knew all about the affair, lovers would remain friendly but distant. To have betrayed any sign would have been "frightfully bad form." Just as a stranger, joining one of these parties for the first time, would have found it difficult to discover who was whose husband or wife, so he would, without enlightenment, have found it impossible to know who was whose lover or mistress—unless, that is, he was sufficiently misguided as to wander about the passages at night.

They asked me why I was so sleepy, and I said because I had not slept well the last night and that I was sure the house was haunted. And so they all screamed at me, "Why?" and so I told them, what was really true, that in the night I heard a noise of stealthy footsteps, and as I was not frightened I determined to see what it was, so I got up—Agnes sleeps in the dressing-room, but, of course, *she* never wakes—I opened the door and peeped out into the corridor. There are only two rooms beyond mine towards the end, round the corner, and it is dimly lit all night. Well,

I distinctly saw a very tall grey figure disappear round the bend of the hall! When I got thus far every one dropped their books and listened with rapt attention, and I could see them exchanging looks, so I am sure they know it is haunted, and were trying to keep it from me. I asked Mrs. Smith if she had seen or heard anything because she sleeps in one of those rooms. She looked perfectly green but she said she had not heard a sound, and had slept like a top, and that I must have dreamt it.

Then Lady Doraine and every one talked at once, and Lord Valmond asked did anyone know if the London evening papers had come. But I was not going to be put off like that, so I just said, "I know you all know it is haunted and are putting me off because you think I'll be frightened; I am going to rush out and see the ghost close."

Then everyone looked simply *ahuri*. Mrs. Smith looked at me as if she wanted to poison me, and I can't think why specially, can you?*

After a week or so the house party would disperse, to re-assemble again shortly afterwards, in almost the same form, at another stately home. It was this society which Elinor entered in full flower as a bride. She had tasted it before in her Cranford days, but it had not formed so continuously a part of her life as it did now. Yet, though she was an accepted part of it, intermingling freely and naturally, she always remained distinct, watching it objectively and curiously, a little critical, a little puzzled. She relished its splendours but she recorded its shortcomings caustically in her diaries and in her novels. It was not its exclusiveness that worried her; she had as little sympathy as any other member of it for upstarts and parvenus and "colonials." But she was concerned about its ineffectiveness, its uselessness and, within the closed circle, its unkindness. The great personalities, the great hostesses she admired

* *The Visits of Elizabeth.*

warmly. She was less impressed by the spitefulness and the time-killing inactivity of the lesser fry.

4.

In August 1892 the Glyns went to St. Fillan's in Perth-shire for the grouse-shooting, which was not only the re-quired activity for August but also Clayton's favourite sport. Elinor soon discovered that it was very far from being her favourite pastime. With her high heels, her long skirts, her long gloves, her big hat and veil, her parasol she found walking across the heather a hot, tiring, and uninteresting occupation. She resented, too, the somewhat ignominious position to which women were relegated at shooting-parties; she dis-liked having to play second fiddle to mere birds. "Men," she wrote in *Letters to Caroline*, "are always hunters at heart, jealous, primitive darlings!" and it was only natural for them to be primarily interested in sport. But that was no reason why their womenfolk should have to be present on these occasions and Elinor determined that in future years she would leave Clayton in Scotland in August and go herself to visit her French relations. It was a further divergence of their ways.

From St. Fillan's the Glyns went on to a number of shoot-ing-parties, ending up at Shipley Hall in Derbyshire, where Elinor took part in some *tableaux vivants*. These amateur theatricals were a popular country-house amusement at the time, usually put on in aid of some charity in which the hostess was interested. Elinor enjoyed them very much, throwing her-self on this occasion into the part of Mary Queen of Scots with gusto and complete lack of self-consciousness.

That autumn and winter Elinor and Clayton spent at Dur-rington, and here there was no escape from shooting-parties. Though she detested walking round the covers on a cold day or tramping across muddy fields, she accepted it meekly. Her shooting manners were, of course, perfect; in her books it is only the upstarts or the villainesses who wear bright yellow at the stands or talk as the birds come over.

After a few months, however, she discovered to her joy that she was expecting a child and she was able to give up for the time the more strenuous aspects of shooting-parties and spend long hours lying on the sofa, sewing or reading. The child, a daughter, was born in June of the following year. Clayton was clearly a little disappointed that it was not a son, but Elinor was delighted. She called the child Margot after her cousin Margot Fouquet Lemaître, who was to be a godmother.

In her book of essays, *Three Things,* Elinor differentiated sharply between what she termed "animal mothers" and "spiritual mothers." Spiritual mothers, into which category Elinor enrolled herself, were interested in the child's character, thoughts, ideals, tastes, manners, and general behaviour. Animal mothers, on the other hand, were concerned almost exclusively with the child's physical welfare, with mothering its small body. For this form of motherhood Elinor had neither sympathy nor inclination. She regarded it as a regrettable form of self-indulgence on the part of the mother and she handed over the physical care of her own child altogether to a nanny, dissociating herself completely from that side of family life. The nanny was, fortunately, both kind and competent.

Clayton, for once, fully shared his wife's views in the matter. Small children did not appeal to him and he would not even travel on the same train as his daughters until they were grown-up. Special arrangements at Durrington had to be made to keep all nursery sounds and smells away from his notice.

5.

After a year of married life Elinor was reasonably happy and contented, especially when she compared it with what had been two years or ten years before. She had come to terms with life in the country and was able, within limits, to live in her own sophisticated urban way. She was able to condemn most of her future heroines to a rural life without a qualm when they married their heroes and began to live happily ever after.

The principal disappointment was Clayton. She had always known in her heart that he was not the lover about whom she had dreamed for so many years, but she could not prevent herself still wishing that he was, still hoping that one day he might become so. In fact, however, he seemed to be growing progressively less ardent as the weeks went by. To counter her disappointment she reminded herself often of his many good qualities, his kindness, his sympathy, his good humour, his grand-seigneur manner, his generosity, the way he paid her huge Lucile bills without even reading them through.

He took her to Paris two or three times a year so that she might shake the country earth off her high heels, meet her cousins, and buy even more clothes. In the coldest of winter months they, like the rest of fashionable English society, went to the Mediterranean.

It was at Hyères in January 1894 that Elinor caught typhoid and was seriously ill. She seems to have suffered from a series of misfortunes at this time, for no sooner had she recovered from typhoid than she had a concussion of the brain, the consequence of a fall while taking part in some amateur theatricals at Lord Rosslyn's house near Edinburgh.

As a consequence of her continued illnesses she gave up, with Clayton's approval, and probably at his suggestion, her losing struggle to take her full part in rural activities. Henceforward she confined herself to the house and the garden, and put her tweed suit away in moth balls. A girl who had been one of Elinor's bridesmaids came to stay at Durrington at this time and Elinor was grateful to her for taking over some of her own rustic chores; the girl, a healthy, open-air type, seemed actually to like washing dogs, rubbing down horses, and going for long walks in the rain, all the things that her hostess loathed so much, and Elinor was glad that Clayton should have her companionship on his rounds of the estate. It was not until later that she came to suspect that the association might not be entirely innocent.

The extent to which Clayton was losing interest in his wife was brought home to her forcibly by an incident which occurred that summer. A large house party was gathered at Warwick Castle and Lord Warwick himself took Elinor round the rose garden in the late afternoon of the second day of her stay. There he began to make love to her, saying that she was the fairest rose in the whole garden and that he had fallen deeply in love with her. He then kissed her.

Elinor was outraged. She drew herself up haughtily and tried to freeze him off. At that moment other guests arrived on the scene and caused a diversion. But Elinor was considerably concerned in her own mind whether she should tell Clayton or not. She half feared to do so, half hoped that the knowledge of the incident, the realisation that other men found her desirable might stir him out of his own apathy towards her.

She told him that evening after she had finished dressing for dinner. He was in his dressing-room next door, in his shirt sleeves, tying his white tie in the looking-glass, the moment of the day when he always seemed especially glamorous to her. His valet, Billingham, discreetly left the room and Elinor related the incident, both fearing and hoping for an explosion of jealous rage.

He caught her eye in the looking-glass and grinned at her. "No! Did he?" he said. "Good old Brookie!" And he went on tying his tie imperturbably.

"You see, Paul," said the lady in *Three Weeks*, "a man can always keep a woman loving him if he kiss her enough and make her feel that there is no use struggling because he is too strong to resist. A woman will stand almost anything from a passionate lover. He may beat her and pain her soft flesh; he may shut her up and deprive her of all other friends—while the motive is raging love and interest in herself on his part it only makes her love him the more."

Bayard Delaval in *The Great Moment* said, "A woman would have to be utterly mine in word and thought and look. I'd never stand any other fellow hanging around. If I gave her the whole of my heart, I'd want the whole of hers."

"Yes, I could be cruel, I expect," said Prince Gritzko in *His Hour,* "I could be even brutal if I were jealous or the woman I loved played me false . . . If ever she became my Princess she shall be entirely for me. I will not let her have a look or thought for any other man. All must be mine unshared and then she shall be my Queen."

But Clayton Glyn, learning that his wife had been kissed by another man, only laughed and said, "Good old Brookie!"

It was a bitter blow and she took it very hard. Her romance was already over after only two years. Was this what she had dreamed about? Would her passionate Frenchman have been so apathetic?

6.

It is difficult at this stage to be sure just why Clayton Glyn's affections towards his wife should have cooled so soon and so completely. Perhaps his love would have cooled equally rapidly towards any wife. He had had twenty years of aloof, self-contained bachelordom, to be betrayed for a time first by curiosity and then by infatuation; but in the end his own essential character must have reasserted itself.

Or perhaps there may have been some failure, some inadequacy on Elinor's part. In her books *The Philosophy of Love* and *This Passion Called Love,* and in many of her uncollected articles, she reiterates her belief that love could not be commanded at will. A man could not guarantee to love one woman all his life any more than he could promise to keep the wind in the south. It was up to the wife to attract and retain her husband's love, and *vice versa*. By admitting this Elinor tacitly placed the failure of her own marriage fairly and squarely on her own shoulders.

She was undoubtedly a difficult person to live with, though he must have known when he married her that he was acquiring no ordinary bride. At times, of course, he was extremely proud of her, of her beauty, her composure, and presence in social gatherings. When she was in a cynical or mischievous mood, they were very close together. But at other times, her passionate enthusiasms, her lush romanticism, her originality, her self-dramatisation, her partiality for "scenes" must have jarred on his dry, quizzical temperament. He must have been saddened by her inability to share fully in his own pursuits and interests.

Elinor firmly believed all her life in the universality and infallibility of the masculine hunting instinct. Man, she asserted, was always basically a hunter. It was the elusiveness of his lady and the uncertainty of his final success which intrigued him and challenged him during his courtship. But after marriage that was gone and "no man likes shooting tame rabbits." A wife, therefore, should be elusive, mysterious, unpredictable, so that her husband's hunting instinct would never be lulled to sleep, later to be reawakened by some new quarry.

7.

In August of that year, 1894, Clayton went, as usual, to his Scottish grouse moor while Elinor took her year-old baby Margot to meet her French godmother at Dieppe, then a fashionable watering-place. The astringent atmosphere of French society was a welcome change after Essex and consoled Elinor a good deal for the frustrations of her private life.

She was almost thirty and in the full noonday glory of her beauty. She was also, it appears, in good spirits, despite the shortcomings of her husband as a lover, if we are to judge from two portraits of her which Jacques Blanche painted on this visit. One of them was a formal portrait of great beauty; despite the colour of her hair the artist gave her a pink bow. Fifteen years later this was repainted blue at the insistence of Lord Curzon of Kedleston, who could not bear the clash of colour. The other picture, Le Chat Nelly, is a delightful and witty exposition of her feline character, painted forty years before her own interest and pleasure in the company of marmalade-coloured cats.

She returned to Durrington in the autumn, and for the next year continued the social round to which she was now accustomed; visits all over England and Scotland, the South of France in January, Paris at Easter, the London season in May and June, Cowes in July, Dieppe once again in August. In the autumn they went to Italy, and Elinor saw Venice for the first time. It made a great impression on her; no other place she had yet seen was so romantic. She ached for her dream lover, for the ardent Frenchman whose memory was still with her, for someone who would whisper words of passion and adoration in her ear as they stood in the loggia of their *palazzo* or floated down the Grand Canal in a gondola.

But Clayton had never been given to things like that, now less so than ever. He insisted on Elinor's maid, Williams, going with them in the gondola so that she, too, might have the pleasure of seeing the Grand Canal by moonlight. Elinor was utterly frustrated, but she gained a little introverted satisfaction from dashing off passionate love scenes between herself and an imaginary lover in her diary.

8.

It was during this year, 1895, that Clayton decided that Durrington was too large, expensive, and inconvenient a house for them and suggested that they should move to Sheering Hall, a three-hundred-year-old farmhouse about a mile away. Elinor never questioned her husband's decision on matters of this sort and she set herself to make Sheering as comfortable as possible. Amongst other alterations a new wing had to be built on for the nursery, so that it might be kept far away from Clayton.

The actual move into Sheering Hall took place early in 1896 and with it a new life seemed to begin for Elinor. The ill-health and emotional frustration which had dogged her for the past two years seemed to slip away. Clayton, too, seemed to rediscover that he had a passionate and beautiful wife.

They took a small flat in Sloane Street for the season and Elinor threw herself once more into the delights of social London. In May she took part in a masked ball at Covent Garden dressed, with Lady Rosslyn, as *les chauves-souris*. A few days later she was presented at court for the first time. This was long overdue but a combination of illness and other circumstances had prevented its taking place before.

It was the first time she had ever been to a court function and she wrote in her diary afterwards pages of glowing description of the splendid scenes in the throne room and the anterooms. She herself, looking radiantly beautiful, made her six curtseys faultlessly to the Princess of Wales (who was deputising for Queen Victoria) despite a train four yards long. She was, however, less impressed by the other ladies at the court. She wrote in her diary:

There were numbers of hideous women there, with Ye Gods! what skins! Brown or pimply or red and coarse! One could count on one's fingers the women who could stand being viewed in full regalia in the sunlight with impunity.

Mrs. Kennedy had by this time given up the Davies Street house to Lucy and her daughter and Clayton now installed her in a cottage near Sheering called Lamberts. Though it had recently been pebble-fronted, Lamberts was old and spacious, but further enlargements and modernisations were required before it was ready for Mrs. Kennedy.

In January 1897 the whole family, Clayton, Elinor, three-and-a-half-year-old Margot, Mrs. Kennedy, and retainers went to Italy to escape the cold months, the first of many large-scale family excursions. They went first to Rome, where they had many friends at the various embassies. Later they went on to San Remo to stay with Sir William Walrond (later Lord Waleran) who had often entertained them at duck-shooting parties in England. Sir William Walrond was at the time Government Chief Whip, but such was the tempo of the age that he was able to conduct the bulk of his parliamentary duties perfectly satisfactorily from his villa in Italy.

The rest of the year they divided between Sheering and Sloane Street. On Sunday nights they would often dine at the Savoy at a window table, looking out over the embankment. These were some of the happiest hours of Elinor's whole life.

One of the consequences of her amateur theatricals in Scotland, her close knowledge of Paris fashions, and her own beautiful clothes was her first journalistic commission. The editor of the magazine *Scottish Life* invited her to write a series of fashion articles, to take the form of a weekly open letter from Suzon to Grizelda and to contain not only a description of the latest clothes and hats but also general advice on beauty.

The first instalment of *Les Coulisses de l'Elégance by Mrs. Glyn,* as the series was called, appeared on May 14, 1898, and ran all through the summer and autumn. Elinor began a little diffidently:

I am sure you will be nice to me, Grizelda, and won't write back and tell me that from a literary point of view my letter is all wrong, my grammar horrid and my sentences not properly formed, because I confess to you I have never written a letter to be printed in my life—though upon the subject of frocks and chiffons I do claim to know a good deal.

But she soon gained her self-confidence.

I hear, Grizelda, that you are tall and lovely, but also that you stoop. I shall have to give you a tremendous lecture about this because it is of the first importance. No one, however beautiful, looks distinguished with round shoulders; I don't believe any woman (except Miss Hardcastle) ever yet stooped and conquered.

There we have in one paragraph the three principal ingredients of an Elinor Glyn article; the emphasis on poise and deportment, the admonitory tone and the crisp phrase, which were to remain unaltered throughout the hundreds of articles she was to write during the next forty years.

Les Coulisses de l'Elégance, however, caused no great stir and she herself seems to have forgotten in her later life that they were in fact her first published works.

9.

Elinor's second daughter, Juliet, was born in December of that year. It was a hard, exhausting birth, and it was feared for a time that Elinor herself might not survive it. However, she recovered slowly, nursed by her mother. Clayton was bitterly disappointed at being presented with a second daughter. He waited long enough to be sure that his prostrate and exhausted wife was not going to die and then he went off by himself to try to forget his sorrows at Monte Carlo.

He was a born gambler and believed in backing against the run of the cards or the wheel and in staking heavily to recover earlier losses. On this occasion he lost more than ten thousand pounds and he returned to Sheering in a gloomy frame of mind. Fortunately for her health Elinor did not learn about these losses till later.

Quite apart from this financial setback the birth of a second daughter had a deep and far-reaching effect upon the marriage and upon Clayton's own attitude towards life—just how far-reaching and drastic Elinor did not discover for another ten years. The immediate consequence, as far as she was concerned, was that a deathblow had been dealt to his interest in her, only so recently reawakened. Henceforward his attitude towards her was affectionate, considerate, and avuncular.

10.

During that winter a governess, Miss Mary Dixon, was engaged to give Margot her first lessons. This was a happy and auspicious event; Dixie, as she was always known, came to be dearly loved and depended upon, not only by the two children but by the whole family. She remained with them for the next thirteen years, and after that was, and still is, a close and valued friend. At first she bicycled out daily from Harlow, but later as her responsibilities increased, she lived in with the family.

Shortly after she was up and about again, Elinor was caught in a heavy rainstorm at a shooting-lunch which she had been unwisely persuaded to attend, and she developed rheumatic fever. Once again she was seriously ill and both Clayton and Mrs. Kennedy were deeply anxious about her. For a time Elinor herself was convinced that she was going to die and felt vaguely that it would be romantic and beautiful to die so young and that the world had little left to offer her. However, as she recovered her strength, her natural buoyancy and resilience came to her aid and to amuse the beginning of her convalescence she asked her mother to get out some of the diaries which she had written at the time of her first country-house visits, and her journal of her first French season with the Fouquet Lemaîtres. This journal had been in fact written in the form of letters to her mother but had not been posted; her mother was shown it at a later date.

Reading them through again now, Elinor was much amused, and the idea came to her to rewrite them in the form of a book. Everyone was considerably surprised by her plans, but the invalid had to be humoured. Apart from the fashion articles and her diary, the creative urge had lain dormant inside her for fifteen years and there was no holding it now. Lying out in a deck chair in the warm spring sunshine, too weak to be able to cross or uncross her own legs, Elinor began to write *The Visits of Elizabeth*. She wrote fast, in her fine handwriting and her incredible spelling, correcting, revising, recopying pages, drawing on incidents and characters both from the Cranford days and from her more recent experiences, shaping the raw material into a polished, rounded whole, a witty, sparkling, shrewdly observed, sometimes malicious description of society.

The work was cast in the form of letters from Elizabeth to her mother, and when it was finished Clayton took it up to London and showed it over lunch at the Garrick Club to Samuel Jeyes, then assistant editor of the *Standard*. To have a wife who had written a book was at that time and in that society a matter more for shame than for anything else, but Clayton was concerned for his wife and thought that a friendly comment from an established literary man would be a nice surprise for the convalescent.

Mr. Jeyes read the book and was sufficiently amused to read some of it aloud that evening in the club, to the accompaniment of guffaws from other members. He declined to say who the author was and it was assumed that he had in fact written it himself. The following day, Elinor, who was beginning to hobble about on two sticks, was astonished and delighted to receive a telegram from Jeyes: "Elizabeth will do. May I come and see you."

He came the following Sunday and told Elinor, now improving rapidly with the excitement, that the editor of the *World* had agreed to buy the serial rights. She asked Jeyes to make all the arrangements for her and it was decided that the book should be published anonymously.

The first instalment of *The Visits of Elizabeth* appeared in the *World* on Wednesday, August 9, 1899, and as the weeks went by, the letters caused something of a sensation. All fashionable society read the *World* and there was little difficulty in recognising most of the characters and the places described. There was a good deal of speculation about the author's identity; it was obviously someone who knew society very well. But Jeyes kept the secret well and Elinor believed that even the editor of the *World* himself did not know. One lady coming to visit the Glyns at Sheering brought a copy with her to amuse Elinor and speculated at length about who the author might be. Finally Elinor admitted responsibility, but the guest remained unconvinced.

"But, Nellie darling, it can't possibly be you!" she exclaimed. "A really clever person must have written these letters."

Society, on the whole, was much amused by it. One or two people were rather shocked and wrote letters to the paper calling it "disgraceful" and a "melange of vulgarity, nastiness, and unclean stupidity and dullness"; but the book was vigorously defended in reply by an anonymous admirer calling himself Toby Belch, and Elinor was most gratified.

II.

Under the stimulus of the success of her book, Elinor's health improved rapidly, and by the late summer she was able to resume her normal place in society. In May of the following year, 1900, she took part in a matinee at Her Majesty's Theatre arranged by Lady Arthur Paget in aid of a South African war charity. She appeared with four other red-haired society ladies, Baroness d'Erlanger, Lady St. Oswald, Mrs. Curzon, and Lady Mary Sackville, in a *tableau vivant* of an imaginary Titian picture, The Five Senses. To make the effect even more striking Beerbohm Tree, who was the producer, made them sprinkle copper dust on their hair. In a few hours it turned bright green and proved extremely difficult to get out.

For the coming winter Clayton decided that his wife would benefit from a stay in a still warmer and more dependable climate than even the South of France provided and he proposed that they should go to Egypt. The children were to be left with their grandmother at Lamberts, and in anticipation of this plans were put in hand for extensions to be built on to the old cottage, a nursery wing and a servants' wing to house the additional staff which would now be required there. Mrs. Kennedy was delighted at the prospect.

During the summer Samuel Jeyes met Gerald Duckworth, who had recently started a publishing house and was looking for new authors for his list. Jeyes, remembering with some pride the success which *The Visits of Elizabeth* had had as a serial, suggested that the letters would probably be well received in book form and sent him a copy. Duckworth's reply was received on the eighteenth of August.

My dear Jeyes,

I like very much *The Visits of Elizabeth* and think in volume form they should sell well. Will you put me into communication with the authoress? I should suggest a 15% royalty.

I am ordered to Aix-les-bains for baths and leave London on the 28th. Can it be done before this date so that I may put things "en train"?

Yours ever,
Gerald Duckworth

Jeyes accordingly came down to Sheering once more, bringing the good news, which thrilled Elinor. The letters, he explained, would need to be considerably lengthened for publication in book form. When he had gone, Elinor got out again her French journal and interposed the whole of the French section of the book, the part which may be thought to contain some of the best scenes and characters. The revised manuscript was sent off to Duckworth, and Elinor sat back with a delightful feeling of achievement and expectation, very different from the melancholy gloom of eighteen months earlier.

There was a certain amount of discussion as to whether the complete book should also be published anonymously and if not what name should be chosen. Elinor herself favoured her normal signature; since most of her friends now knew that she was the author, there was little point in concealing her identity any longer. She consulted Lady Warwick, who agreed with her, adding, "Elinor Glyn sounds like a nom de plume, anyway."

12.

The Visits of Elizabeth was published in November 1900, price six shillings, an apple-green volume with a flat back, white label, and gold lettering, a form of binding which, in varying colours, Duckworth was to use for all her books and which provided a uniform edition from the very beginning. It was very well received by the critics and seemed to appear overnight in stacks on every bookstall. It was all very surprising and unexpected for a lady of fashion.

The world of high society which Elinor Glyn satirised in her first novel has long since passed away but the gayety and the wit of *The Visits of Elizabeth* is still as fresh as ever. There is practically no plot and very little romance. Harry, Marquis of Valmond, is forward enough to kiss Elizabeth under the ear at an early stage and gets his face sharply slapped for his impertinence. He annoys her by repeatedly forcing his charming and, of course, irresistible presence upon her.

> And we made up our quarrel, and—he kissed me again—and I hope you won't be very cross, Mamma; but somehow I did not feel at all angry this time. And I thought he was fond of Mrs. Smith; but it isn't, it's Me! And we are engaged. And Octavia is writing to you. And I hope you won't mind. And the post is off, so no more.

The bulk of the book consists of Elizabeth's descriptions and experiences of her first season, recorded with neat and ingenuous frankness.

> What *do* you think has happened? Sir Dennis sat beside me on the sofa just as he did last night and well, he said I was a perfect *darling*, but that he never could get a chance to say a word to me alone, but that if I would only drop my glove outside my door it would be all right; and I thought that such a *ridiculous* thing to say that I couldn't help laughing, and Lady Cecilia happened to be passing, and so she asked me what I was laughing at, and so I told her what he said, and asked why? There happened to be pause just then and, as one has to speak rather loud to Lady

Cecilia to attract her attention, everyone heard, and they all looked *flabergasted;* and then all shrieked with laughter, and Sir Dennis said so crossly, "Little fool!" and Lady Desmond simply glared at me, and Lady Cecilia said, *"Really, Elizabeth!"* and Sir Dennis got purple in the face and Jane Roose whispered, "How could you dare with his wife listening!" and everyone talked and chaffed. It was too stupid about nothing; but the astonishing part is, that funny old thing I thought was the mother turns out to be *his wife!*

Elinor herself maintained later that the character of Elizabeth had been partly inspired by Lady Angela St. Clair-Erskine, who had been something of an *enfant terrible* at some house parties. But in fact the character of Elizabeth is a portrait in a mirror—not a complete portrait, but a demonstration of some of her most lovable qualities, her gayety and her mischievous sense of fun (the book was written in a moment of painful illness and emotional depression), her ability to combine shrewd satire with gentle warmheartedness, her observant eye and light pen, her ability to laugh at others and at herself simultaneously.

The comedy of manners, of which, of course, Jane Austen is the supreme exponent, is one of the principal currents in the great river of English fiction; and in this current *The Visits of Elizabeth* was a highly popular and not insignificant landmark.

13.

In January 1901, Queen Victoria died, and Elinor, staying the night before with Lucy in Davies Street, watched with deep emotion the funeral procession from the windows of the Berkeley. Soon afterwards, with the children safely installed with Mrs. Kennedy at Lamberts, the Glyns sailed for Egypt.

Travelling with Clayton was always a pleasure—automatically to have the best cabin, the most comfortable compartment, smiling managers, head stewards, headwaiters to greet her at every stage, specially attentive service, every plan dovetailed and smooth and effortless. This was due not only to his careful planning and generous but not excessive tipping, but also to his obvious appreciation of the finer points of service, food, and wine. Even in places which he had not visited before, his fame as a connoisseur of good living had gone before him, passed from one restaurateur to another, so that the same cordial welcome awaited him as if he had been a visitor all his life.

This was especially so in the case of these visits to Egypt, the longest journeys which he and Elinor ever made together. For Elinor this particular voyage was made especially pleasant from seeing the number of people on board who were reading *The Visits of Elizabeth.*

She was delighted by Egypt and rhapsodised in her diary about the beauty and the colour of everything, the sapphire-blue sky, the brilliant green rice fields, the picturesque buildings, the domes and minarets, the camels, the desert, the sense of endless space and endless time.

They stayed at the Savoy Hotel, and soon found themselves participating in the social life of Cairo, led by Lady Cromer, the wife of the High Commissioner, and Lady Talbot, the wife of the General Officer Commanding. The social life was quite as gay and select as in London but with fewer vices, since most of the men were usefully employed.

A pleasing incident occurred after they had been there about a fortnight. One of the pashas had been eyeing Elinor with a good deal of interest; he now approached Clayton through an intermediary and asked whether Clayton would be willing to sell the pasha his wife. Perhaps the English gentleman would be tired of his wife by now, it was explained; one tired quickly of redheads. Both Clayton and Elinor were delighted by the story, but the intermediary swore solemnly that it was a perfectly serious offer. Clayton often teased his wife in later years, threatening that he would sell her into a harem if she became tiresome; but Elinor, whenever she told the story, always left out the part about tiring quickly of redheads. It was too near the truth for joking.

On this visit they spent only a few weeks in Cairo and returned to England in March, staying in Naples and Rome on the way. Back at Sheering they threw themselves once more into the English social season.

14.

It was now that the inevitable happened—the consequence of a romantic temperament, an uninterested husband, and a gay, leisured social world. Indeed, one can only wonder that it had not happened earlier. Elinor fell, deeply, passionately, desperately in love.

Major Seymour Wynne Finch was a Guards officer whom she had met many times at parties. Even in that brilliant, fashionable throng he was a person of unusual charm and distinction. He was very handsome and his appearance was especially elegant; his smoking suit was made of Paisley shawl with black silk facings. He had a gay and ready wit: on hearing that a certain lady treated her husband "like furniture," he asked without a moment's hesitation, "Drawing-room or bedroom? It does make such a difference." He had a warm and sympathetic personality; he himself was deeply in love with Elinor.

One can imagine the happiness and the distress that must have been going on simultaneously inside her; torn not only by the unavoidable conflict of conscience and desire but by the two different halves of her own temperament. The approved solution of the time would undoubtedly have been a discreet love affair, such as most of her friends indulged in. Clayton himself might well have countenanced it, provided that it was carried out without any scandal, the *sine qua non* of all such affairs. Elinor's own cynical side, her eighteenth-century training, the Duc de Saint-Simon himself, would have found no fault in it. In *The Reflections of Ambrosine,* the French Marquis who had been the lover of Ambrosine's grandmother says, "The only vows which a lady or gentleman may break without dishonour are the marriage vows."

But the romantic side of Elinor's personality rebelled against such a thought. Even Mrs. Saunders had believed firmly in the sanctity of marriage vows and Elinor herself had not yet entirely despaired of her marriage. The correct ending for the fairy story was for Prince Charming and Cinderella to live happily ever after; not, after a few years, to go their own ways with mistresses and lovers. She placed several of the heroines of her novels in precisely the same predicament, and it is significant that (excepting *Three Weeks,* which is a special case) it is not until she reached *The Sequence* in 1912 that she allowed one of them to yield.

She said a sad farewell to Seymour Wynne Finch and never saw him again.

15.

The visit to Egypt had been such a success that it was decided to take out the whole family that winter, including the children, Mrs. Kennedy, a French governess, Mademoiselle Courtellement, and Williams. This time they remained in Cairo the whole winter and the social life seemed more sparkling than it had been before, Elinor even allowing herself to be persuaded by Lady Newtown-Butler, the leader of the "Kasr-el-Dubara" set and later the Duchess of Sutherland, to watch the 11th Hussars playing polo at the Gezireh Club.

Cairo at that time was full of interesting people. Cecil Rhodes and Dr. Jameson passed through and Elinor wrote in her diary:

> Rhodes and Jameson and those other three men were sitting together at dinner and five more ill-shapen creatures I have never seen. Dr. Jameson's back view is like that of an old rat with pink ears and a bald head!

Sir Ernest Cassel was also there and became friendly with the Glyns.

The inevitable *tableau vivant* for charity was organised and Elinor took part as the Lorelei, clad only in tights, yards of green gauze, and her hair, which she combed out to its full length. She must have been a wonderful sight. She went shopping in the mouski for *rahat lakoum* and for cheap flawed pale green emeralds to match her eyes. The High Commissioner gave a children's fancy-dress party at the Residency to which the eight-year-old Margot and the three-year-old Juliet went, looking like china dolls in hooped skirts and powdered hair.

This particular party, however, ended in wails of misery. The balloons which the children were given were filled with gas and, once lost hold of, rose rapidly to the ceiling, where they bobbed about tantalisingly. Lady Cromer had to promise to have long ladders brought and to send the balloons round to the children the next day at their own homes. At another fancy-dress ball, this time for grownups, a set of Lancers was arranged by Lady Talbot: eight ladies, including Elinor, dressed as Romney portraits and eight officers of the 11th Hussars in full levee dress.

The great ball of the winter was the Khedive's Ball. At this time the Grand Duke Boris of Russia was in Cairo and one of his suite was Prince Gritzko Wittgenstein, a young daredevil whose exploits and wildness were notorious even outside Russia. He was immensely good-looking. "I think," wrote

Elinor, "that he was the most physically attractive creature that I have ever seen." The tales of his wickedness were endless; of his orgies in his palaces; of how he would fight duels in darkened rooms over a lady; of how he would ride his favourite Arab horse up and down the stairs till its legs were broken; of how, when a gipsy girl defied him, he stripped her naked and dropped her over the balcony of the restaurant where they were dining into the soup tureen of the unsuspecting dinner party below. He was not formally presented to Elinor, but she noticed him watching her as she talked to the Grand Duke Boris. He was a striking figure in his full-skirted scarlet Cossack uniform.

Later he came and, still unintroduced, asked her to dance. Before she could wither him for his impertinence, he swept her on to the floor in a waltz, pressing her so tightly that the cartridges in his crossbelts left red weals on her white chest. Manoeuvring her skilfully into a corner, he suddenly bent and kissed her on the throat and then abruptly turned and left her blazing with cold fire, speechless with outraged haughtiness. She was to make good use of this scene later.

But the most memorable incident of the visit was an expedition to the Sphinx by moonlight on a camel. At that time the Sphinx was not surrounded by shacks and advertisement hoardings, and the beauty and mystery of the scene, the play of moonlight and sand, the aloof, brooding agelessness of the Sphinx itself touched some chord in Elinor's mind. She was deeply moved and she determined that her children, too, must have this wonderful experience.

A few days later, to their intense delight and excitement, she mounted them on camels and led them out into the moonlit desert. The other ladies in Cairo thought it very odd of her and it was long past the children's bedtime. But Elinor was indifferent to the views of such animal mothers. It was her duty to teach her children to appreciate the fine things in life, and the Sphinx by moonlight was certainly one of them. It was never too early to begin.

16.

The illness which dogged so much of the early part of her life descended on her again now in the form of painful attacks of gallstones. It would come upon her in waves of agony and she had several times to be given morphia. She lost weight, and both Clayton and her mother became once more very anxious over her.

As she got slowly better, Prince Hussein, later the King of Egypt, gave her permission to sit in his garden at Gezireh Palace. This was a remarkable place, situated on a small island; but it was so cunningly contrived with vistas and artificial mounds that it seemed to stretch for miles. It was filled with flowers, giant violets, roses, lilies of the valley; bougainvillea and clematis hung from the tree trunks. There was never any sign of a dead or dying plant, the gardeners working by night, digging up every wilting bloom and replacing it with a fresh one.

In this exotic atmosphere Elinor's spirits and health revived rapidly and, as before, her return to convalescence was marked by a desire to write a book. She lay there in the garden, wondering what would have happened if she had married the bearded millionaire eighteen years earlier. How would she have endured life, supposing she had later met and fallen in love with Seymour Wynne Finch? In the Gezireh garden, with that central situation in her mind, she began her second novel, *The Chronicle of Ambrosine.*

She did not, however, get very far with it before the moment came to leave for home. Clayton and Elinor were once again to travel back through Italy while the rest of the party went home by sea. Their arrival at Naples was marked by a scene of utter farce, the sort of third-rate bedroom comedy, which Elinor, to her great amusement, seemed fated to undergo periodically.

A liner had been delayed leaving Naples and their reserved bedrooms had not been vacated. The valet of Mr. Van Allen, a distinguished American diplomat, who had been friendly with the Glyns on board, succeeded in finding a bedroom with two single brass beds in it and it was proposed that all five should share this for the night. Elinor and Williams were to have one bed, Mr. Van Allen the other, Clayton was to be on the sofa and Mr. Van Allen's valet on a chair.

Williams was appalled at the presumption of sharing a bed with her mistress and slept on the very edge. Clayton and Mr. Van Allen undressed with difficulty behind a small screen; the valet did not even unfasten his collar. It was a disturbed night. The valet sat bolt upright on a small gilt chair, his mouth wide open, snoring hard, while his master occasionally shouted at him. At intervals Williams fell out of bed. The lamplight poured into the room through the venetian blinds and every time Elinor sat up in bed to get a breath of air, she noticed Mr. Van Allen propped on one elbow, staring at her, murmuring, "God! what a form!" Whenever she woke up during the night, he was still sitting gazing at her, muttering passionately to himself.

"Old fool!" said Clayton the next day, who was not amused by the breakdown in his travelling arrangements. "Bothering about women when we were all so tired."

Clayton seems to have been in a testy mood all that spring, for when they reached Rome, Elinor began rhapsodising about the beauties of art and architecture and he would exclaim, "For goodness' sake go and get your ebullitions over while I order lunch."

In Rome they attended a large wedding between an Austrian Prince and an Italian Princess and went on motoring expeditions in the American Ambassador's new Packard to

Viterbo, Orvieto, and Villa d'Este. Italian peasants shook their
fists at the strange new machine, with its weirdly garbed oc-
cupants, trundling slowly along. Elinor struck up a firm friendship with Lord Grey, who took her sight-seeing and tried to
fill the gaps in her Roman history which Gibbon had left. A
young attaché at the French Embassy fell passionately in love
with her and confided to Clayton during a picnic at Villa
d'Este that it made him furious to see Elinor going about so
much with Lord Grey. Clayton tried to reassure him: "Don't
worry, my dear fellow. He's only one of Elinor's antiques."

While in Rome they went to many large parties in the
palaces of Italian nobles, but she also had a recurrence of
pain and Clayton took her to see Dr. Axel Munthe, at that
time famous only as a physician. She was immensely struck
by his almost hypnotic personality and by his uncanny appearance—the soft, closely cut beard and spectacles so thick that it
was impossible to see his eyes. He was also apparently much
struck by Elinor, and he told her later that he had described
her in his casebook by the single word "siren." He was openly
contemptuous of the smart Italian ladies who flocked to see
him, but he was kind and sympathetic to Elinor and the
treatment he prescribed proved effective.

From Rome they went on to Lucerne. Elinor had never
seen Switzerland before and was quite overcome by the beauty
of the Alps and the Lake of Lucerne itself. It was springtime,
the time of year when she, in common with most of the world,
always felt especially romantic. She longed once again for an
ardent and passionate lover and turned to Clayton in hope and
desperation. But he was no longer able even to conceal his
boredom at his wife's continual ecstasies, and in deep disappointment she turned, as she had done in Venice, to her
diary, where she wrote long, passionate, imaginary love scenes.

In a fur shop near the Hotel National was a magnificent
tiger skin and Elinor was fascinated by it. She stared at it
longingly, and finally she asked Clayton to buy it for her. In

his disgruntled mood he flatly refused; his wife was already sufficiently tigerish without that. In frustrated silence they walked back to their hotel through the rain.

There she found a letter from Duckworth enclosing a large cheque on account of royalties from *The Visits of Elizabeth*, which was still selling very well. After lunch she crept out, cashed the cheque, and bought the tiger skin, paying in her eagerness about double its proper price. It was, however, a splendid beast. I have it still; even after fifty years, its hair is hardly worn.

It was brought up to their sitting-room that afternoon, and when Clayton came in later, he found his wife reclining on the floor on the tiger, stroking its fur, quivering with emotion, staring at him with smouldering, romantic eyes; looking, in fact, very like the later popular idea of herself.*

It was the last straw! It was bad enough having a siren wife who wandered round Europe in a starry-eyed dream, rhapsodising about the beauties of art and nature, with thirty-seven new dresses, a train of antique admirers, and a maid who fell out of bed—and now a tiger skin, for which a large special trunk had to be bought the following day.

17.

In July the pain returned and on Axel Munthe's advice Elinor went to Carlsbad to try a cure there. She liked the place, and even more she liked the intimate group of English people who gathered there every summer. Two of them, Sir Francis Jeune (later Lord St. Helier) and his wife were to become her most dearly loved friends. Jeune, besides being a High Court judge, was also a fine classical scholar and he

---

* In her autobiography Elinor explained that she did this mainly in order to tease her too, too solid husband.

reawoke in Elinor all her Greek enthusiasms and aspirations, which had now been dormant for some years.

They would take their slow prescribed walks through the Carlsbad woods, discussing Greek art and Greek philosophy. From him she was able to fill in some of the gaps in her haphazard education, to evolve a critical standard, and to weld the isolated items in her already comprehensive knowledge of classical art and history into a proportioned and homogenous whole.

Her favourite authors were Plato, Aristotle, Herodotus, Thucydides, Aristophanes, and Lucian. She read the tragedies but they seem to have meant less to her. One surprising omission was Homer, for one would have thought that both the *Iliad* and the *Odyssey,* with their noble, fearless heroes and their beautiful women, enslaving the men's devotion or inspiring them to greater deeds of glory, would have been exactly to her taste.

As her health improved with the cure, she took up again the manuscript of *The Chronicle of Ambrosine* and she finished it on August 20. For the next ten days she revised and expanded it, and a fortnight later she changed its title to *The Reflections of Ambrosine.* Sir Francis Jeune read it in manuscript, liked it very much, and urged her to continue to write what she wanted to write, irrespective of what her friends or the critics might think. She followed this advice faithfully; in fact, she rarely read reviews of her own books and she did not subscribe to a press-cutting agency until she went to America after the First World War.

Jeune also suggested that she should write more slowly, taking more pains over her style and her English, her grammar and spelling, even when she had cast the book in the form of a diary or letters. Sir Gilbert Parker, the novelist, who was also in Carlsbad, read the manuscript and gave her the same advice, as many of her other friends were to do in the years to come.

It was, of course, sound and well-tried advice, but one may wonder now whether it was right for Elinor Glyn. For her composition was a spontaneous effort of creation. She meditated on an idea for a long time, but when the moment came, she thought and wrote fast. She was usually prepared to alter and revise her manuscripts and to accept, though often with considerable reluctance, the criticisms and suggestions of others. The more flagrant errors of grammar or spelling she was content to leave to the printer or her friends to put right. But it may be thought that her best books are the ones which she wrote fast; the ones over which she laboured were less successful.

18.

*The Reflections of Ambrosine** was published in December 1902 and, like its predecessor, was very well received both by the public and by the critics. Now, fifty-two years later, it is of all her books the most disagreeable to read—a heavy-handed, long-winded sermon on the theme that Norman blood and the distant shadow of a coronet are worth far more than a kind heart.

Ambrosine Athelstan, a haughty, blue-blooded girl whose ancestor died under the guillotine, had been brought up in proud poverty by her grandmother (a ferocious portrait of Mrs. Saunders). The landlord of their cottage, a wealthy, amiable young man called Augustus Gurrage, was much attracted by Ambrosine. He used phrases like "snug little crib," "beastly hard luck," and "jolly fellows," and she regarded him as unspeakably common. The grandmother had a heart attack and learned that she had not long to live; and she ordered her granddaughter to accept Augustus' proposal, if and when it should materialise; otherwise she would starve. It would be

* Published in America under the title *The Seventh Commandment.*

distasteful to Ambrosine, but she would bear it with the fortitude and control which she had been trained to show. "The great honour you will do him by marrying him removes from you all sense of obligation in receiving the riches he will bestow on you."

Ambrosine could have screamed with horror at the order, but she obediently accepted Augustus' proposal.

"Darling," he said, and kissed me deliberately. Oh!—the horror of it. I shut my eyes, and in the emotion of the moment I bent the clasp on the top of the frame of Ambrosine Eustasie.

Then dragging myself from his embrace and stuttering with rage:

"How dare you," I gasped, "how dare you!"

He looked sulky and offended.

"You said you would marry me—what is a fellow to understand?"

"You are to understand that I will not be mauled—and kissed like—Hephzibah at the back door," I said with freezing dignity, my head in air.

"Hoity-toity!" (hideous expression!), "what airs you give yourself! but you look so deuced pretty when you are angry——!" I did not melt, but stood on the defensive.

He became supplicating again.

"Ambrosine, I love you—don't be cross with me, I won't make you angry again until you are used to me. Ambrosine, say you forgive me." He took my hand—his hands are horrid to touch, coarse and damp—I shuddered involuntarily.

He looked pained at that; a dark red flush came over all his face; he squared his shoulders and got over the window-sill again.

"You cold statue," he said spitefully, "I will leave you."

"Go," was all I said; and I did not move an inch.

He stood looking at me for a few moments; then with

one bound he was in the room again and had seized me in his arms.

"No, I shan't!" he exclaimed. "You have promised and I don't care what you say or do, I will keep you to your word."

Mercifully at that moment Hephzibah opened the door, and in the confusion her entrance caused him, he let me go. I simply flew from the room and up to my own; and there, I am ashamed to say, I cried—sat on the floor and cried like a gutter child. Oh! if Grandmamma could have seen me, how angry she would have been. I have never been allowed to cry—a relaxation for the lower classes, she has always told me.

My face burnt—all the bottles of lubin in Grandmamma's cupboard would not wash off the stain of that kiss I felt. I scrubbed my face until it was crimson.

It is the character of Ambrosine herself that sticks in our throats. Elinor, naturally, could not have detected the difference between Elizabeth and Ambrosine for they were both based on different facets of her own many-sided personality. It is, however, surprising that the critics should have been equally unable to notice the difference. "Mrs. Glyn's new book is very much like the letters of Elizabeth," wrote the *Spectator*. "Ambrosine is Elizabeth over again."

But Ambrosine was a very different person. For one thing she had no sense of humour.

19.

The book is worth considering for a moment here however, primarily because of the character of Sir Antony Thornhirst, the book's hero, for he appears under different names in a great number of Elinor Glyn's novels. "The *beau ideal* of a cynical gentleman, cultured, a *viveur,* gallant and brave and gentle," he was the dream hero not only to his author but to many maidens of the time. Handsome, well born, rich, elegant, a fine shot, a good man to hounds but otherwise completely idle, he was typical of his age. There were dozens of men like him at every house party, and no one thought it odd that they should have no interest in life except sport. It is only since 1939 that we have come to regard wealth and leisure with suspicion.

Naturally, many young men of the time and the class did have a profession. They were soldiers, sailors, politicians, barristers, or diplomats, and it is to be noted that Elinor's own closest friends were drawn from this group. Her "antiques" were men who had had distinguished careers in their various professions; the most cherished of her younger friends were regular soldiers. But, curiously, she never put them into her books. Her imaginary heroes joined the Army in time of war, and were sometimes killed gallantly in action, but they were never in the regular army. Out of her first fourteen novels the heroes of twelve have no peacetime occupation at all.

They were in theory landowners, and various hints are dropped through the books about the duties involved in this. One cannot, however, take this very seriously. None of the gentlemen are ever prevented from going to a house party or London or Cowes or abroad by pressure of work on their estates. Two of them, indeed, go off at short notice to Tibet or Alaska for several years to shoot bears and ease their broken hearts, without noticeably inconveniencing their tenants. In *The Sequence,* Sir Hugh Dremont comes to visit his beloved Guinevere on the pretext of seeing some new stable drains that her husband has just put in. This deceives no one, for though he is a model landowner, he has never been known to take any interest in stable drainage before. Many landowners, including Clayton, took a pride in not understanding the business of their estates and in leaving everything to the agent.

It was their position and their right, as it had been their fathers', and they accepted it unquestioningly and unquestioned. But Elinor—and here she was in advance of the general spirit of her time—did not accept it. Almost every one of her heroines chides the hero for his self-indulgent idleness and urges him not to waste all his life and his great opportunities in shooting. She did not mean that he was to go and increase his already great wealth in some money-grubbing middle-class profession, but that he should do something great for his country. Elinor's heroes usually responded by throwing themselves vigorously into politics; most of them were already members of the House of Lords.

In this we may see the pattern, not only of the time, but of Elinor's own attitude to life and to the role of women in it. The men were brave, noble, cultured, gentle, and honourable; but they were "sound asleep to the fine" in life, to their potentialities and responsibilities. It was the duty of women to awaken them, to inspire them with noble ideals, to urge them on to great deeds and great causes. In the words of her favourite quotation from Kingsley's *The Heroes*:

I am Pallas Athene, and I know the thoughts of all men's hearts and discern their manhood or their baseness. And from the soul of clay I turn away; and they are blest, but not by me. They fatten at ease like sheep in the pasture, and eat what they did not sow, like oxen in the stall . . . But to the souls of fire I give more fire, and to those who are manful I give a might more than man's. These are the heroes, the sons of the Immortals who are blest, but not like the souls of clay, for I drive them forth by strange paths, Perseus, that they may fight the Titans and monsters, the enemies of gods and men. Through doubt and need and danger and battle I drive them, and some of them are slain in the flower of youth, no man knows when or where, and some of them win noble names and a fair and green old age.

She allotted the role of Pallas Athene to the heroines of her English novels, and to herself in real life, not seeing the essential conflict between this and her other role, that of siren. It was to her no contradiction to seek to be at once a driving-force and a magnet.

20.

On the eleventh of June, 1903, the King and Queen of Serbia were assassinated. The whole world was shocked, none more so than Elinor, for whom regicide was the vilest of all crimes. The thought of the death of Queen Draga upset her particularly; it was the first time since Marie Antoinette that a Queen had died by violence. She brooded long over it, with results that will be seen later.

She had benefited so much from her cure at Carlsbad the year before that she determined to return there again this year and, accordingly, she left London as soon as the season was over in company with Lady Arthur Paget.

Once again there was pleasant company assembled at the spa, amongst them Lord Milner, resting after his arduous and prolonged efforts in South Africa. Elinor and he took to each other at once and their friendship was cemented by a common love of Greek writing and philosophy. Once again she took the measured walks through the pine forests, discussing the Greek contribution to art and knowledge and, once again, with enormous benefit to her own critical standards. She was deeply impressed by Milner. "I always thought," she wrote, "that he must be the reincarnation of Socrates."

On the terrace in the evening he would read Plato aloud.

To the end of her life Elinor never ceased to be surprised by the number of eminent men who chose to express their friendship and pleasure in her company by reading Plato and Aristotle aloud to her. It was a curious tribute to one who was so often regarded, not without reason, as a siren. But it should be remembered, when we consider her vanities and egotism, her follies and foibles, her astonishing financial incapacity, that her closest and most faithful friends were the ablest men of her generation and they regarded her as being in her own way their intellectual equal. Two of them, Lord Curzon and Lord Milner, were never men to suffer fools gladly.

21.

Elinor, Lady Arthur Paget, and Milner returned to England together, stopping for a while in Nuremberg to see the sights. As a farewell present Milner gave Elinor an inscribed copy of Henley's poems.

Back in Essex she found that Clayton was proposing to move house once again. He had never been very happy at Sheering Hall and he thought it was too near the river to be good for his wife's health. Ever since their return from Egypt the children had spent most of their time at Lamberts with their grandmother, who adored them and who was always at hand to give them the motherly care she had withheld from her own daughters. Clayton's idea was that he and Elinor should move in to Lamberts, too, thereby reuniting the whole family under one roof.

Elinor, as always in matters of that sort, acquiesced without argument. For her Sheering Hall was associated with pain and illness and she would be glad to leave it. There was room in the actual cottage itself for Clayton's bedroom and study but a new annex would have to be built on for Elinor's rooms.

Work on this was begun the same autumn and the house began to resemble in plan a game of dominoes.

Elinor's annex was joined to the main house by only a glass-roofed passage. The rooms were for herself alone and she was able to give her artistic taste full rein in their decoration. Outside the annex's appearance was unprepossessing, but inside she decorated it to resemble Marie Antoinette's rooms in the Petit Trianon at Versailles. Her drawing-room was filled with French furniture, with cushions and beautiful stuffs and brocades. She would rearrange it in different colours to suit her mood or the mood of the book she was writing. Her bedroom was filled with hundreds of pink silk roses, on the canopy of her bed, on the bed curtains, on the bed ends, on the covers and bedspreads; they were sewn indefatigably by Elinor herself, with considerable assistance from Margot, Dixie, her maid, and anyone else who might be induced to lend a hand. In her bathroom next door she decided, rather surprisingly, to put in a sunken Roman bath. It is still there, a monument to the originality and unpredictability of her tastes.

The whole annex she called her Pavilion in the Garden, or, more usually, her Trianon; and here she could retire when she wanted peace or privacy.

At this time she was almost always writing—novels, diaries, journals, notebooks, commonplace books, letters, anything which would provide an outlet for her boundless creative energy. She did not in any sense regard herself as a professional author and in her diary she always differentiated between "working" and "writing." "Working" to her meant sewing. She was merely a society lady who wrote books to amuse herself. Apart from Duckworth and Jeyes, and a slight acquaintance with Sir Gilbert Parker, she knew no one at all in the world of letters. She was a complete amateur whose books people happened to enjoy.

She wrote always with a stylo pen, either in her "rose-bed," as she termed it, or curled up on a sofa with a lot of cushions.

In the summer she liked to write out in the garden. In the middle of the lawn there was a large old apple tree. She had a seat and a platform built up in the tree, and there, with rugs, cushions, and her block, she would retire on a summer afternoon and be undisturbed by the vicar, if he should call. Another hide-out was in the ha-ha, where the trees met overhead, forming a cool green tunnel. Here she had a bench put and commanded Monk the gardener to grow flowers all about so that she might see them as she wrote. He, however, said there was too little sun for flowers and he felt, in any event, disinclined to co-operate with such idiosyncrasies.

When her novels were finished, she would take them up herself to Gerald Duckworth at 3 Henrietta Street, Covent Garden. She was by this time on extremely cordial terms with her publisher and he encouraged her to read her books, or large portions of them, aloud to him. Her books, she maintained, were intended to be read aloud and lost their proper effect if they were read in silence. She herself was extremely proud of her reading voice; she would read slowly, with long dramatic pauses, and Duckworth would meekly put aside all other work and listen, while Margot often waited patiently in the hansom outside.

When Duckworth had had enough, he would take her to lunch at the Savoy, where they would eat steak, fried onions, and boiled lettuce, before returning to the office and a further instalment of the work. Sometimes he would come down to Lamberts for a Saturday-to-Monday (it was never called a week end in that society) and would retire with her to the house in the tree or the Trianon to hear the new book. He was, it will be seen, prepared to give a great deal of time and trouble to the books of Elinor Glyn not only because they were proving extremely profitable, but because he was also personally fascinated by their author.

22.

Elinor's next novel, *The Vicissitudes of Evangeline,** was published in March 1906. After the sour tone of her last two books, it is a relief to find that in the new one she is back again in her happiest mood. Evangeline herself is the most enchanting of all her heroines, even including Elizabeth—a merry girl of twenty with red hair, green eyes, and long black eyelashes, from under which she gazes at young men to see what the effect will be. It is invariably devastating.

The book starts splendidly:

> I wonder so much if it is amusing to be an adventuress, because that is evidently what I shall become now. I read in a book all about it; it is being nice-looking and having nothing to live on, and getting a pleasant time out of life—and I intend to do that! I have certainly nothing to live on, for one cannot count £300. a year—and I am extremely pretty, and I know it quite well, and how to do my hair, and put on my hats, and those things, so, of course, I am an adventuress!

Unfortunately for her chosen career, she has a warm heart and rapidly falls in love with Lord Robert Vavasour. "He has great big sleepy eyes of blue and rather a plaintive expression and a little fairish moustache turned up at the corners and the nicest mouth one ever saw. And when you see him moving and the back of his head, it makes you think all the time of a beautifully groomed thoroughbred horse." She is persuaded not to go and stay at Claridge's all alone, (the only hotel she knows of) as she at first intended, but to visit some relatives of hers for a while until something more permanent can be arranged.

* Published in America under the title *Red Hair*.

The relatives are rather shocked by her.

Lady Katherine and Mrs. Mackintosh came into my room on the way up to bed. She—Lady Katherine—wanted to show Mary how beautifully they had had it done up, it used to be hers before she married. They looked all round at the dead-daffodil-coloured cretonne and things, and at last I could see their eyes often straying to my nightgown laid out on a chair beside the fire.

"I do not think such a nightgown is suitable for a girl," said Lady Katherine in a grave duty voice.

"Oh! but I am very strong," I said. "I never catch cold."

Mary Mackintosh held it up with a face of stern disapproval. Of course it has short sleeves ruffled with Valenciennes and is fine linen cambric nicely embroidered. Mrs. Carruthers was always very particular about them and chose them herself at Doucet's. She said one never could know when places might catch on fire.

"Evangeline, dear, you are very young," Mary said, "but I consider this garment not in any way fit for a girl—or for any good woman either. Mother, I hope my sisters have not seen it!"

I looked so puzzled.

She examined the stuff, one could see the chair through it beyond.

"What *would* Alexander say if I were to wear such a thing!"

The thought seemed to suffocate them both.

"Of course it would be too tight for you," I said humbly, "but otherwise it is a very good pattern and does not tear when one puts up one's arms."

"I hope, Evangeline, you have sufficient sense to understand now for yourself that such a—a—garment is not at all seemly."

"But why not, dear Lady Katherine?" I said. "You don't know how becoming it is."

"Becoming!" almost screamed Mary Mackintosh. "But no nice woman wants things to look becoming in bed!"

The whole matter appeared so painful to them I covered up the offending nightie with my dressing-gown and coughed. It made a break and they went away, saying good-night frigidly.

And now I am alone. But I do wonder why it is wrong to look pretty in bed—considering nobody sees one too!

Evangeline is, however, befriended by a Lady Verningham, who loves her ingenuousness, the only snag being the discovery that Lord Robert is Lady Ver's "special friend," which, of course, puts him out of Evangeline's reach for ever. Lord Robert encounters Evangeline sobbing on a bench in a fog in Hyde Park (she cannot help such a vulgar exhibition since one of her grandmothers was, regrettably, a housemaid, and breeding will tell). There is a charming love scene; she explains why she has been freezing him off and he tries to reassure her. But there is a further difficulty. He is heir to his half brother's dukedom and fortune and the Duke would never tolerate Evangeline, because of the housemaid's blood. Evangeline, however, takes the bull by the horns and succeeds in persuading the Duke that she will herself, in due course, make an admirable Duchess. All ends happily, Evangeline snuggled against her Robert, Robert bewitched by the amount of red hair he has suddenly acquired, and only Evangeline's maid a little sad that she will not be able to embroider coronets on her mistress's lingerie just yet.

It is a light, frothy soufflé of a book, to be read at a sitting and not be taken too seriously.

It is both a beguiling entertainment and another self-portrait of the authoress in her gay, mischievous mood. Indeed, the miniature of Evangeline which forms the frontispiece to the book was a portrait of Elinor, painted by Miss May Dixon, Dixie's sister, to Elinor's exact specification of expression. The novel was dedicated, affectionately and triumphantly, "to the women with red hair."

23.

The Vicissitudes of Evangeline marks the definite end of the first stage of Elinor Glyn's literary progress. The *Sphere* wrote at this time: "She is, at this moment, our leading novelist of modern manners." She was still very far from being the Queen of Passion or the High Priestess of Romance, as she was later termed, and for which she is now chiefly remembered.

But she was already moving in that direction. Robert's and Evangeline's love scene was handled with more warmth and tenderness than anything in her first two novels. In her next book, *Beyond the Rocks,* she took a long stride forward towards romance. Her cynical vein, for the moment, had worked itself out; her innate romanticism was beginning to take hold. One may detect the change in the new form of title and in the fact that she took the precaution of calling her new book "A Love-Story." It was the first time, too, that she wrote in the third person.

She started with the same situation she had already explored in *The Reflections of Ambrosine,* the situation which was so close to her own predicament, and which held at this time a special fascination for her. Theodora Fitzgerald, blonde, blue-eyed, and sweet, marries a rich Australian to save her charming ne'er-do-well aristocratic father's broken fortunes. But the characters this time are entirely different. Josiah Brown, the Australian, though vulgar, is elderly and ailing and Theodora loyally does her best to be a good wife to him. However, she meets Lord Bracondale, a handsome, well-bred, elegant man of her own class, and falls in love with him. They have many pleasant but innocent meetings at Versailles, where the first half of the book takes place. Later the scene moves to the familiar house parties of England. Finally Theodora decides that she and Lord Bracondale must part. Happening to be alone at a house party for the moment, she writes a long, passionate letter of farewell to him and a short note to Josiah about her return to London. Her enemy, Morella Winmarleigh, who is jealous of Theodora's success with Lord Bracondale, changes the letters over and Josiah learns that his wife's affections belong elsewhere. He behaves with great dignity at this moment; Lord Bracondale goes off to Alaska to shoot bears, consoled with a bust of Psyche, and Josiah slowly dies of a broken heart.

Beyond the Rocks is a sentimental little story, too slight in plot for its length, but it has some charming moments, especially the love scenes and the day in the woods at Versailles when Lord Bracondale tells Theodora a fairy story. The effect on his worldly, sophisticated attitude of the girl's innocence and purity is skilfully touched in; the social background, the balls and house parties, are drawn with greater mordancy than usual, almost with venom; there is hardly a character who is not immoral or spiteful or vindictive, and there is a terrible picture of everyone closing ranks to exclude and humiliate Josiah and Theodora.

But despite this *Beyond the Rocks* is a minor work of Elinor's, remarkable mainly because it provides the bridge between her comedies of manners and her romances. There is none of the wit of *Elizabeth* or *Evangeline* but, equally, there is none of the sour self-pity of *Ambrosine*.

24.

Seymour Wynne Finch's place in Elinor's affections had by now been taken by Lord Alastair Innes-Ker, Royal Horse Guards. He, too, was charming, elegant, and amusing, a perfect specimen of the breed. He was often at Lamberts, and both Clayton and Mrs. Kennedy were much attached to him.

Margot was due to go to school in France that autumn and the whole family, including Innes-Ker, went to Paris that September for a holiday and to see Margot installed (together with a copy of *The Reflections of Ambrosine*, which she was enjoined to keep in a locked box beside her bed, a circumstance which the school regarded with the gravest suspicion). Before the family returned, Elinor took Innes-Ker out to Versailles. She made him walk with his eyes shut across the great terrace, so that his first sight should be the full façade of the palace stretched out in its splendour. When they reached the top of the steps, above the *tapis vert*, she said, "Now! Turn round and look."

His immediate comment—"Gosh! what a lot of lightning conductors!"—deflated her completely. Later she would tell the story as an illustration of how completely the young gentlemen of her generation were sound asleep to the fine things of life. But in fact it seems more likely that he was teasing her for her dramatic gesture.

Even after this episode Elinor remained very fond of him. When he went away to India the following year, he gave her a copy of Laurence Hope's *Love Lyrics from India* as a farewell present, and Clayton, a typical Edwardian husband, told his children to be specially kind to their mother.

25.

In August 1906 the Glyns went to stay with Lord Kintore near Glamis. The focus of this particular house party was fishing, and Elinor spent one uncongenial day sitting beside the river in the pouring rain, watching the male members of the party failing to catch salmon. At teatime they abandoned the sport and went home to bath and change. After tea they sat round the fire, Elinor idly watching a young man, a member of the party, lying on the hearthrug in his velvet smoking suit, playing with his rough-haired terrier. He was yet another perfect specimen of the breed, well born, educated at Eton and Oxford, handsome, virile, a sportsman, "intellectually and emotionally sound asleep." Elinor wondered vaguely what would happen if he were suddenly awakened to life, if he were to meet and fall in love with some intense, passionate woman, someone like Sarah Bernhardt in *Theodora*.

A picture seemed suddenly to form inside Elinor's brain. A number of unconnected impressions and longings of the past dropped into place like pieces in a jigsaw puzzle—her imaginary love scenes in Lucerne and Venice, the murder of Queen Draga of Serbia, the tiger skin, the handsome boy lying on the hearthrug, Andreas and Theodora, Lancelot and Guinevere, Tristram and Yseult.

Someone suggested that Elinor, the storyteller, should amuse them as they sat there; and she complied by telling them the story of her new novel, which had been born that moment in her brain. It was a very different affair from the stories of country-house philandering which had previously occupied her.

The moment the party dispersed she hurried back to Essex and there, in her Trianon, she began to write the novel which was to send her fame ringing round the world. Her inspiration was white-hot. "It seemed as though some spirit from beyond was guiding me," she wrote in a later article. "I wrote breathlessly for hours and hours on end, hardly conscious at times of the words which were pouring into my brain, until I came to read over the chapters and found that what I had written was exactly what I had hoped and meant to say. The original manuscript shows this, it flows on with hardly a correction or alteration."

She felt intensely as she wrote; often she was in tears. The two warring elements inside her had clashed and exploded; her ardent romanticism had burst into flame, breaking through the barriers of self-control and repression that Mrs. Saunders and Elinor herself had so carefully built up in the earlier years. All the time she was writing her new book she lived as one who had seen a vision. She saw again Lucerne in springtime, the *palazzi* of Venice by moonlight, Sarah Bernhardt caressing her lover. In a little over six weeks the book was finished.

26.

The story of *Three Weeks* is simple and dramatic. Paul Verdayne, the handsome and athletic son of Sir Charles and Lady Henrietta Verdayne, broke his collarbone in a hunting-fall and was looked after by Isabella Waring, the parson's daughter, who washed his dog Pike and read the sporting papers aloud to him. She had large red hands and was fond of hockey and running with the hounds. One regrettable afternoon Paul kissed her large, pale lips just as his mother came into the room.

It was a most unfortunate entanglement. As soon as he recovered he was sent abroad so that he might forget Isabella. Paul went grumpily sight-seeing in France, decided Versailles and Fontainebleau were "beastly rot," and longed to break his promise and write passionate love letters to Isabella, from whom he was being so cruelly parted. In a furious temper he reached Lucerne in the pouring rain. He cursed the waiters for the smoking fire and resented the elaborate attention which the hotel staff were bestowing on a lady at the next table. He drank four glasses of port and stared at her with hostility.

He fancied he smelt tuberoses and perceived a knot of them tucked into the front of her bodice.

A woman to order dinner for herself beforehand, to have special wine and special roses and—special attention too! It was simply disgusting!

An elderly dignified servant in black livery stood behind her chair. She herself was all in black and her hat cast a shadow over her eyes. Her face was white, he saw that plainly enough, startlingly white, like a magnolia bloom, and contained no marked features. Yes—he was wrong, she had certainly a mouth worth looking at again. It was so red. Not large and pink and laughingly open like Isabella's, but straight and chiselled and red, red, red.

The white lids with their heavy lashes began to irritate him. What colour could they be? those eyes underneath. They were not very large, that was certain—probably black too, like her hair.

He could not say why he felt she must be well over thirty. There was not a line or wrinkle on her face—not even the slightest nip in under the chin, or the telltale strain beside the ears.

After dinner he sat on the terrace and smoked a cigar.

A vague feeling of oppression and coming calamity passed through him. The woman and her sinuous and sensous black shape filled the space of his mental vision. Black hair, black hat, black dress—and of course black eyes. Ah! if he could only know their colour really.

He started violently, and brusquely turned and looked up. Almost indistinguishable in the deep shadow he saw the woman's face. And looking down into his were a pair of eyes—a pair of eyes. They seemed to draw him—draw something out of him—intoxicate him—paralyse him. Were they black, or blue, or grey, or green? He did not know, he could not think—only they were eyes—eyes—eyes.

The lady did not come into lunch the next day but he encountered her unexpectedly that afternoon on the Burgenstock; almost immediately she disappeared again. He returned to his hotel, baffled, and found a letter from Isabella all about his horse and his dog, which thrilled him less than it ought to have done. The lady was again at the next table at dinner, and afterwards, as he sat on the terrace, he saw her go across to a little gate, a private entrance to her suite. He waited for a while, and just as he despaired of seeing her again, there above the ivy he saw her face looking down upon him.

He jumped on to the bench. Now he was almost level with her face. Was he dreaming or did she whisper something? He stretched out his arms to her in the darkness, pulling himself by the ivy nearer still. And this time there was no mistake:

"Come, Paul," she said.

The apartments of the lady (she is anonymous throughout) were presumably the best suite of the hotel, but they had been transformed by her. There were masses of flowers, roses, tuberoses, lilies of the valley. The lights were low and a great couch covered with a tiger skin filled one side of the room. It was piled with pillows of all shades of rich purple velvet and silk. She reclined on it and teased Paul, in a voice which was like rich music, about why he was so upset and drank so much port.

Suddenly she sprang up, one of those fine movements of hers full of catlike grace.

"Paul," she said, "listen," and she spoke rather fast. "You are so young, so young—and I shall hurt you—probably. Won't you go now while there is yet time? Anywhere away from me."

She put her hand on his arm and looked up into his eyes. And there were tears in hers. And now he saw they were grey.

He was moved as never yet in all his life.

"I will not!" he said. "I may be young, but tonight I know—I want to live! And I will chance the hurt because I know that only you can teach me—just how——"

Then his voice broke and he bent down and covered her hand with kisses.

The next day they went on the lake together and talked of many things, and in the evening he forced himself to write a farewell letter to Isabella. As he walked through the streets of Lucerne, he saw a tiger skin in a shop window and he bought it for the lady. That evening he was again admitted to her sitting-room.

A bright fire burnt in the grate, and some palest orchid-mauve silk curtains were drawn in the lady's room when Paul entered from the terrace. And loveliest sight of all, in front of the fire, stretched at full length, was his tiger—and on him—also at full length—reclined the lady, garbed in some strange clinging garment of heavy purple crepe, one white arm resting on the beast's head, her back supported by a pile of the velvet cushions, and a heap of rarely bound books at her side, while between her red lips was a rose not redder than they—an almost scarlet rose.

Paul bounded forward but she raised one hand to stop him.

"No! you must not come near me, Paul. I am not safe today. Not yet. You bought me the tiger, Paul! Ah! that was good! My beautiful tiger!" And she gave a movement like a snake, of joy to feel its fur under her, while she stretched out her hands and caressed the creature where the hair turned white and black at the side and was deep and soft.

"Beautiful one! beautiful one!" she purred. "And I know all your feelings and your passions, and now I have got your skin—for the joy of my skin!" And she quivered again with the movements of a snake.

"Oh! Good God! If you knew how you are making me feel—lying there wasting your caresses upon it."

She tossed the scarlet rose over to him—it hit his mouth.

"I am not wasting them," she said, the innocence of a kitten in her strange eyes. "Indeed not, Paul! He was my lover in another life—perhaps—who knows?"

"But I," said Paul, who was now quite mad, "want to be your lover in this!"

Then he gasped at his own boldness.

With a lightning movement she lay on her face, raised her elbows on the tiger's head, and supported her hands.

"Paul—what do you know of lovers—or love?" she said. "My baby Paul!"

A rage of passion was racing through Paul, his incoherent thoughts were that he did not want to talk—only to kiss her—to devour her—to strangle her with love if necessary.

He bit the rose.

She talked to him about love, which must be paid for in tears and cold steel and blood. Then she read to him Apuleius in Latin, and finally she sang to him to a guitar.

"*You* mustn't be teased. My God! it is you who are maddening me!" he cried, his voice hoarse with emotion. "Do you think I am inanimate like that tiger there? I am *not*, I tell you!" and he seized her in his arms, raining kisses upon her which, whatever they lacked in subtlety, made up for in their passion and strength. "Some day some man will kill you, I suppose, but I shall be your lover—first!"

The lady gasped. She looked up at him in bewildered surprise, as a child might do who sets light to a whole box of matches in play. What a naughty, naughty toy to burn so quickly for such a little strike!

But Paul's young strong arms held her close, she could not struggle or move. Then she laughed a laugh of pure glad joy.

"Beautiful savage Paul," she whispered. "Do you love me? Tell me that."

"Love you!" he said. "Good God! Love you! Madly, and you know it, darling Queen."

"Then," said the lady in a voice in which all the caresses of the world seemed melted, "then, sweet Paul, I shall teach you many things, and among them I shall teach you how—to—LIVE."

They went to stay across the lake on the Burgenstock, where they could be alone. Everything was discreetly arranged by the lady's servants, Dmitry and Anna. There their honeymoon began.

"Oh! darling, do not speak of it," cried Paul. "I worship, I adore you—you are just my life, my darling one, my Queen!"

"Sweet Paul!" she whispered, "oh! so good, so good is love, keep me loving you, my beautiful one—keep my desire long to be your Queen."

And after this they melted into one another's arms, and cooed and kissed, and they were foolish and incoherent, as lovers always are and have been from the beginning of time.

The spirit of two natures vibrating as One.

At the first glow of dawn, he awoke, a strange sensation almost of strangling and suffocation upon him. There bending over, framed in a mist of blue-black waves, he saw his lady's face. Its milky whiteness lit by her strange eyes —green as cat's they seemed and blazing with the fiercest passion of love—while twisted round his throat he felt a great strand of her splendid hair. The wildest thrill that yet his life had known then came to Paul, he clasped her in his arms with a frenzy of mad, passionate joy.

Her voice grew faint and far away, like the echo of some

exquisite song and the lids closed over Paul's blue eyes and he slept.

The light of all the love in the world seemed to flood the lady's face. She bent over and kissed him, and smoothed his cheek with her velvet cheek, she moved so that his curly lashes might touch her bare neck, and at last she slipped from under him and laid his head gently down upon the pillows.

Then a madness of tender caressing seized her. She purred as a tiger might have done, while she undulated like a snake. She touched him with her finger-tips, she kissed his throat, his wrists, the palms of his hands, his eyelids, his hair. Strange subtle kisses, unlike the kisses of women. And often, between her purrings she murmured love-words in some fierce language of her own, brushing his ears and his eyes with her lips the while.

And through it all Paul slept on, the Eastern perfume in the air drugging his senses.

Paul had now gathered that his lady was a Balkan Queen and he was considerably disturbed when Dmitry asked him to carry a pistol the whole time. Gradually he learned about her husband.

Then at last she looked up at him and her eyes were black with hate. "I would like to kill one man on earth—a useless vicious weakling, too feeble to deserve a fine death —a rotting carrion spoiling God's world and encumbering my path! I would kill him if I could."

"Oh! my Queen, my Queen!" said Paul, distressed. "Don't say such things——"

Later they moved on to Venice, the lady, Dmitry, and Anna going on ahead to make the arrangements. Here their honeymoon reached a new phase.

Her expression too was altered. A new mood shone there;

and later, when Paul learnt the history of the wonderful women of *cinquecento* Venice, it seemed as if something of their exotic voluptuous spirit now lived in her.

This was a new Queen to worship—and die for, if necessary. He dimly felt, even in these first moments, that here he would drink still deeper of the mysteries of life and passionate love.

"*Beztzenny-moi,*" she said, "my priceless one. Ah! I must know it is really you, my Paul!"

They were sitting on the tiger by now, and she undulated round and all over him, feeling his coat, and his face, and his hair, as a blind person might, till at last it seemed as if she were twined about him like a serpent. And every now and then a narrow shaft of glorious dying sunlight would strike the great emerald on her forehead, and give forth sparks of vivid green which appeared reflected again in her eyes. Paul's head swam, he felt intoxicated with bliss.

"This Venice is for you and me, my Paul," she said. "The air is full of love and dreams; we have left the slender moon behind us in Switzerland; here she is nearing her full—the spring of our love has passed. We will drink deep of the cup of delight, my lover, and bathe in the wine of the gods. We shall feast on the tongues of nightingales and rest on couches of flowers. And thou shalt cede me thy soul, beloved, and I will give thee mine——"

But the rest was lost in the meeting of their lips.

As they travelled about Venice in their gondola, they became aware that they were being followed, and presently another of the lady's servants, Vasili, arrived to say that the *Imperatorskoye* was in danger.

"Shall I kill the miserable spy? Vasili would do it this night," she hissed between her clenched teeth. "But to what end?"

A tumult of emotion was dominating Paul. He understood now that danger was near—he guessed they were being watched—but by whom? By the orders of—her husband? Ah! that thought drove him mad with rage—her husband! She—his own—the mate of his soul—of his body and soul—was the legal belonging of somebody else! Some vile man whom she hated and loathed, a "rotting carrion spoiling God's earth."

"Queen," he said, his voice hoarse with passion and pain, "let us leave Venice—let me take you away to some far land of peace. You would always be the empress of my soul."

She flung herself on the tiger couch and writhed there for some moments, burying her clenched fists deep in the creature's fur.

"*Moi-Lioubimyi*—my beloved!" she whispered in anguish. "If we were lesser persons—yes, we could hide and live for a time in a tent under the stars—but we are not. They would track me and trap us, and sooner or later there would be the end, the ignominious end of ordinary disgrace——" Then she clasped him closer, and whispered right in his ear in her wonderful voice, now trembling with love.

"Sweetheart—listen! Beyond all of this there is that thought, that hope ever in my heart that one day a son of ours shall worthily fill a throne, so that we must not think of ourselves, my Paul, of the Thou and the I, and the Now, beloved. A throne which is filled most ignobly at present, and only filled at all through my birth and my family's influence. Think not I want to plant a cheat. No! I have a right to find an heir as I will, a splendid heir who shall redeem the land—the spirit of our two selves given being by love, and endowed by the gods. Ah! think of it, Paul. Dream of this joy and pride. It must quiet this wild useless rage against fate."

All that was noble and great in his nature seemed rising up in one glad triumph-song.

A son of his and hers to fill a throne! Ah! God, if that were so!

The following night they celebrated the feast of the full moon.

The lady was the most radiant vision he had yet seen. Her garment was pale green gauze. It seemed to cling in misty folds round her exquisite shape, it was clasped with pearls. A diadem confined her glorious hair which descended in the two long strands twisted with chains of emeralds and diamonds. Her whole personality seemed breathing magnificence and panther-like grace. And her eyes glowed with passion, and mystery, and force.

Paul knelt like a courtier and kissed her hand. Then he led her to their feast.

The whole place had been converted into a bower of roses. The walls were entirely covered with them. A great couch of deepest red ones was at one side. From the room chains of roses hung, concealing small lights. The dinner was laid on a table in the centre, and the table was covered with the tuberoses and stephanotis, surrounding the cupid fountain of perfume. The scent of all these flowers! And the warm summer night! No wonder Paul's senses quivered with exaltation. No wonder his head swam.

Throughout the repast his lady bewildered him with her wild fascination. Never before had she seemed to collect all her moods into one subtle whole, cemented together by passionate love. It truly was a night of the gods and the exaltation of Paul's spirit reached its zenith.

"My darling one," the lady whispered in his ear, as she lay in his arms on the couch of roses, crushed deep and half-buried in their velvet leaves. "This is our souls' wedding. In life and in death they can never part more."

In the early morning, before Paul was awake, the lady,

shaken with fierce, dry sobs, tiptoed away, wrote him a fare-well note, and was gone. The three weeks were over.

When Paul awoke and found that she had indeed gone, he collapsed and was unconscious with fever for days. In his delirium the whole story came out and his father, who had been sent for, learned everything. Paul crawled back to life at last, to his beloved Queen's last letter and her last gift to him, a gold collar for his dog, over which he cried like a child. His father took him back to England, but he was a changed man. He studied earnestly in preparation for a political career and all the time he watched the calendar in gnawing anxiety.

At long last the letter came, containing a tiny curl of golden hair, and written on the paper: "Beloved, he is strong and fair, thy son."

Meanwhile his father and a friend, Captain Grigsby, man-aged to discover who the lady was. Paul, by arrangement, met Dmitry again in Paris. The lady would be at her villa on the Bosphorus later that year, and if the Excellency could come, he might be able to see her again. The cry of a sea gull three times would show him it was safe to land.

He set off at once with his father in Grigsby's yacht, landed, but was promptly sent away by Dmitry, who told him there was danger. He must return in two days' time, if the flag was flying. Two days later he returned, desperately anx-ious; but the flag was not flying. Later, in a letter from Dmitry, he learned the awful truth. The King had entered suddenly and in a drunken rage had stabbed the Queen to death, say-ing, "It will be a joy to kill thee," only to have his own life throttled out a moment later by Vasili.

Paul, almost mad with grief, travelled the world for five years, searching in vain for consolation. At last he realised that he was wasting his life; he mastered his sorrow and longed to see his little son. He wrote to the Regent, who replied, inviting him to be present at the celebration for the little King's fifth birthday.

It was in a shaft of sunlight from the great altar window that Paul first saw his son. The tiny upright figure in its blue velvet suit, heavily trimmed with sable, standing there proudly. A fair, rosy-cheeked, golden-haired English child.

And as he gazed at his little son, while the organ pealed out a *Te Deum* and the sweet choir sang, a great tenderness filled Paul's heart, and melted for ever the icebergs of grief and pain.

And as he knelt there, watching their child, it seemed as if his darling stood there beside him, telling him that he must look up and thank God too—for in her spirit's constant love, and this glory of their son, he would one day find rest and consolation.

27.

We cannot now quite take *Three Weeks* in the spirit in which it was written. Its voluptuousness, its exotic setting, its full-blooded passion, its uninhibited idiom, its use of the second person singular, its exclamation marks are no longer fashionable. But the intensity of the inspiration still comes through. Elinor was convinced when she was writing it that she was creating one of the great love stories of the world, which would be remembered long after she was forgotten. And it is the love scenes which are the glory of *Three Weeks*.

Oh! the divine joy of that night!

"Paul," she said, "out of the whole world to-night, there are only you and I who matter, sweetheart. Is it not so? Remember, Paul," she whispered when, passion maddening him, he clasped her violently in his arms—"remember —whatever happens—whatever comes—for now, tonight, there is no other reason in all of this but just—I love you— I love you, Paul!"

"My Queen, my Queen!" said Paul, his voice hoarse in his throat.

And the wind played in softest zephyrs, and the stars blazed in the sky, mirroring themselves in the blue lake below.

Such was their wedding night.

Oh! glorious youth! and still more glorious love!

28.

Three Weeks was published in June 1907 and fell like a thunderbolt on the unsuspecting world.

"An exceedingly difficult work to know how to review," wrote the *Onlooker* rather helplessly. "It is perhaps better written than anything Mrs. Glyn has done before. It is emphatically not *pour les jeunes filles.*"

The *Bystander* put up a cautious umbrella against the storm to come:

> Mrs. Glyn has chosen to write of a passionate and beautiful love episode between persons who have not previously been married. That is her offence and for it, of course, she must suffer the abuse of those most trustworthy of Mrs. Grundy's spokesmen—the daily reviewers.

The *Sunday Times,* almost alone, came out on Elinor's side.

With the exception of the *Times Literary Supplement,* which maintained a pained silence, all the other critics were unremittingly hostile.

29.

Critical response seemed to have little effect on the public, however, for as fast as Duckworth reprinted, he was barely able to keep pace with the demand. It is not possible now to give an exact figure of the total sales of *Three Weeks* to date. In 1916, nine years after publication, and immediately before the production of the first cheap edition, the sale in Great Britain, the British Empire, and America was just short of two million copies. The book was translated soon after publication into virtually every European language, the sales being particularly heavy in Scandinavia, Spain, and South America. We must also include the flood of cheap editions which began in 1916; in Great Britain no less than three separate publishers brought them out. In 1933 an article in *Everybody's* stated, on information supplied by the author, that the total world sales were then five million copies. If we can accept this figure—and it is just possible—then *Three Weeks* must take its place among the Himalaya of world best sellers.

Three Weeks brought in, as was to be expected, a very large quantity of fan mail from all parts of the globe. This had been coming in a quiet stream ever since *The Visits of Elizabeth;* now it burst into full flood. Kings and Queens sent messages; Australian bushmen, Bishops, Klondike miners, Roman Catholic priests all wrote letters of appreciation. There were also a large number of abusive letters, but Elinor noticed that these only came from English-speaking countries, just as it was only British and American reviewers who did not admire the book unreservedly.

A more substantial form of fan mail arrived over the years in the form of tiger skins, presented by various admirers, known and unknown, including one each from Lord Curzon and Lord Milner. It was at this time, too, that the rhyme, which caused Elinor much amusement, first appeared; and which helped to contribute to her reputation as a scarlet woman.

> Would you like to sin
> with Elinor Glyn
> on a tiger skin?
> Or would you prefer
> to err
> with her
> on some other fur?

30.

The book sold sensationally fast, but even faster went its reputation for immorality. Lady Warwick had read the manuscript and sternly advised Elinor not to publish it, as, if she did, none of her friends would ever speak to her again. It was bad enough for a society lady to write novels at all, without perpetrating books of that sort.

Despite her warning Elinor was surprised and bewildered by the extent of the hostility engendered by *Three Weeks*. Among her friends in society she was abused and reviled, called an immoral woman and a glorifier of adultery. This hurt her extremely and she felt that such criticism was, from that source, pure hypocrisy; the members of Edwardian society, with their lovers, mistresses, and illegitimate children, were, she felt, the very last people to cast stones.

Even Professor Thomas Lindsay, the Principal of Glasgow College, coming to spend the week end at Lamberts, scolded her for having produced such an offensive book. She asked him whether he had himself read it, and on learning that he had not, she gave him a copy and sent him up to his bedroom to read it. He did not come down to lunch, and she found him later that afternoon in tears, sobbing that he had grossly misjudged it. Elinor was much gratified.

She gradually came to believe that those who were most shocked by the book were those who had not themselves read it; or if they had read it, had missed the point, Paul's regeneration, by not bothering to read on after the lady's death. This view was strengthened by a further episode. *Three Weeks* had been banned at Eton, as at most schools, and the Headmaster, Dr. Edward Lyttelton, wrote to her (beginning, formally, "Madam") to inform her of this. She replied spiritedly, challenging him whether he had himself read it, to which he was obliged to reply that he had not. She sent him a copy, and later he wrote to her again (beginning "My dear Mrs. Glyn") to say that he had enjoyed the book and had been misled by its reputation. The ban, however, must stay.

In her distress and bewilderment at the reception of the book into which she had poured her whole heart, she was much comforted by the fact that those whose opinion she really valued saw the point of the story and appreciated it. The Duchess of Abercorn and Lady Arthur Paget both wrote charming letters, and she specially treasured the letter that Lord Milner wrote her.

Three months after its English publication the book was published in America, and there it raised the same storm. It was banned altogether in one state. It was not allowed to be sent through the post. It was boycotted in Boston and banned in most schools and libraries. Though it found many champions, American high society was in general shocked by it. These strong feelings lasted for many years. Twenty-five years later, in 1932, a Mickey Mouse cartoon was banned altogether in the state of Ohio because it showed at one moment, a cow, reclining in a field, reading *Three Weeks*.

A consequence of the book's sales and fame was, not unexpectedly, the appearance of several works purporting to be by her and trying to pirate her idea. One of these, called

One Day, which Elinor regarded as a travesty of her own inspiration, achieved a certain success, siphoning off some of her own sales in the process and damaging her own literary reputation. In 1915 a film appeared called *Pimple's Three Weeks (without the option).* It was a burlesque of such crudity that Elinor brought an action for infringement of copyright against the film company.* Mr. Justice Younger, in the course of his judgement, said:

> But there is another, and from the public point of view, a much more important aspect of this case which in my judgment entirely debars the plaintiff from obtaining relief in this court. The episode described in the plaintiff's novel, which she alleges has been pirated by the defendants, is in my opinion, grossly immoral both in its essence, its treatment and its tendency. Stripped of its trappings which are mere accident, it is nothing more nor less than a sensual, adulterous intrigue. And it is not as if the plaintiff in her account of it were content to excuse or palliate the conduct described. She is not even satisfied with justifying it. She has stooped to glorify the liaison, both in its inception, its progress and its results and she has not hesitated to garnish it with meretricious incident at every turn. Now, it is clear that copyright cannot exist in a work of a tendency so grossly immoral as this; a work which, apart from its other objectionable features, advocates free love and justifies adultery where the marriage tie has become merely irksome.
>
> We are constantly hearing of the injurious influence exercised upon the adventurous spirit of our youth by the "penny dreadful" which presents the burglar in the guise of a hero. So is a mischievous, glittering record of adulterous sensuality, masquerading as superior virtue, such as we find in this book, calculated to mislead, with consequences as

* Glyn v. Western Feature Film Co., Ltd., 21st December, 1915.

certain as they are sure to be disastrous, into the belief that she may without dishonour choose the easy life of sin, many a poor romantic girl, striving amidst manifold hardships and discouragements to keep her honour untarnished. It is enough for me to say that to a book of such a cruelly destructive tendency no protection will be extended by a court of equity. It rests with others to determine whether such a work ought not to be altogether suppressed.

This remarkable judgement still stands in law. It is curious to think that if judicial precedent be followed, no modern book, play, or film which deals with adultery, no matter how tragically but without direct censure, is protected by the law of copyright.

31.

It appears strange that *Three Weeks* should have inflamed such high feeling, for it seems now a very mild and inoffensive book. There is not a salacious word in it. Many modern novels contain descriptions far more intimate and detailed than *Three Weeks*. Elinor herself was not much interested in sex; she thought it unromantic, animal, earthy. She was interested in love, in the romantic disguise which enveloped more material thoughts and feelings, and the maintenance of which was the great ideal of her life.

There was nothing crude about her pattern of love-making, which she repeated many times in her later novels. The man, passionate and strong, would master the woman with his strength and the intensity of his love; then, suddenly, all the mastery would be gone and he would be on his knees before her, offering worship and homage. Further than that Elinor did not go. It may have been a little unrealistic, her own wishful thoughts finding expression, but it was certainly not lascivious.

One is struck, too, in reading *Three Weeks* now, by its high moral tone. A very large part of the book is devoted to the lady's lectures to Paul on being worthy of his name and race. And the final scene in the cathedral, with Paul on his knees in joy and thanksgiving, is not what one would expect in a vulgar and offensive "shocker."

For the first American edition Elinor wrote a preface, in which she defended her book and hoped to temper the wind in advance. She later wrote a longer and more detailed defence, which she had privately printed, and which she incorporated into an article in the *Grand Magazine* of March 1920, called "Why I Wrote *Three Weeks*." Her defence rested on a number of points: that the lady was a Slav and must not be judged by English standards; that her marriage to her husband was a marriage in name alone, and for this he was solely responsible; that she was accustomed, being a Russian Imperial Highness as well as a Queen, to ordering anyone who amused her into her sitting-room, a performing monkey, a street singer, a carpet seller, or Paul; that the love between Paul and herself was overwhelming and perfect on every level, body, mind, and soul; and, lastly, that the lady, having offended against the laws of man, duly paid the supreme price of her life.

Elinor also printed, for private circulation, Mark Twain's defence of *Three Weeks,* in which he argued that so great a love was divine and beyond human control or law.

None of these arguments, however, had any effect at the time. Only the passing of years, which, ironically, has spoilt the flavour of the prose, has been able to acquit *Three Weeks* of an immoral purpose.

32.

The astonishing and sustained sales of *Three Weeks* cannot be wholly attributed to its immoral reputation though this, of course, played a considerable part. To be banned was then, as now, to be assured of a certain curiosity value. But the sales of *Three Weeks* were just as heavy in countries where its reputation was blameless, and something further is required to explain its success.

We may perhaps attribute it to its being unashamedly and sumptuously a romance. A great love story fills a crying need of the human heart and it had been many years since there had been another one in the class. The fact that so many of the love stories of the world—Paris and Helen, Antony and Cleopatra, Lancelot and Guinevere, Tristram and Yseult, Sigurd and Brynhild, Nelson and Lady Hamilton, Paul and his lady—cut across the marriage ties was, in Elinor's view, an unfortunate outcome of the conflict between the laws of God and the laws of man. She was in later years to devote much thought to the reasons why domesticity should so often prove fatal to great love, and to proving that the two need not necessarily be mutually exclusive. It should be possible, she argued, given sufficient skill and wisdom on both sides, not only to generate but to maintain inside marriage the degree and quality of love that Paul, and others, had found only outside it. It was to providing this skill and wisdom that she gave so much of her later time and energy, with, as will be seen, considerable success.

Another reason for the popularity of *Three Weeks* may perhaps lie in the fact that it coincided with the great wave of feeling which sought to sweep away the restrictive and unimaginative barriers of Victorian puritanism, and which washed up on the beach such a curious mixture of treasure-trove and flotsam. Elinor herself would have been both surprised and indignant if she could have realised the company she was in, if she could have seen that *Three Weeks* appealed to the same renascent and manumissive instinct that had also welcomed, for example, Freud. She and Freud, of course, were poles apart in ideals, in methods, in aspirations; they were united on one count only, a hatred of repression for repression's sake.

And, lastly, seeking to account for the success of *Three Weeks*, we must not forget the book itself. It had, and still has, something over and above its fulfilment of the widespread longing for romance, its embodiment of the general distrust of restrictive prohibitions, its appeal, if indeed there ever was any, to the salacious-minded. *Three Weeks* was written in a white heat of inspiration. The heat is not yet cooled. The book is by no means the best of Elinor Glyn's novels, but alone of them it flickers and glows with the rare fire of genius.

33.

The book's success had one further consequence, which was again not entirely unexpected. The rumour went about that it was, in fact, a true story. Several men announced that they were Paul; one man in America called himself Prince Paul, thereby showing that he had not read the book. It was also reported that the Czar had mentioned *Three Weeks* as being a book about his wife.

Elinor regarded these reports indulgently, the inevitable consequences of the book's popularity. The story, she maintained, was wholly imaginary; she had made it up on a wet afternoon in a Scottish castle.

A little more fully documented, however, was the story of a man she met the following year in America. He said that the Dowager Empress of Russia, despairing of an heir, had sent her daughter-in-law off on a yacht with "Paul" nine months before the birth of the Czarevitch; and the Czarevitch's haemophilia was transmitted, as always, through the mother. The American insisted on the story, asserting that the "Paul" was an Englishman and had in fact died in his arms.

Elinor was interested, but once again disbelieving. The book, she assured him was entirely imaginary; it had no connection with the Romanoffs.

It was not until 1910, when she went to Russia, that she came to realise that she might, in writing *Three Weeks,* have stumbled on something dangerously close to the truth.

BOOK THREE

American Journey

1907–1908

I.

During the summer of 1907, Clayton Glyn decided that it was time his family saw more of the world, and he planned to take them that winter on a trip which would encompass the globe. In July, Elinor went to France to collect Margot from her school, and, while in Paris, she stayed with Mrs. Kate Moore, a well-known American hostess, who suggested that she should visit America that autumn. Elinor was considerably more attracted by America than by Ceylon or Japan and she accepted gladly. She paid herself for Mrs. Kennedy and Dixie to travel with the family in her place and it was arranged that she should meet them in San Francisco and that the whole family, reunited, should travel back across America together.

In the autumn, just before her forty-third birthday, Elinor sailed for America in the *Lusitania*, armed with a sheaf of introductions from Mrs. Moore and Lady Arthur Paget. She was a striking figure in a purple overcoat, a purple toque, and a purple chiffon veil, which she could wrap round her face; the whole effect was reminiscent, not altogether without design, of the *Imperatorskoye*. She took also sixty pairs of high-heeled shoes for her beautifully shaped, tiny feet.

She was enjoying herself immensely. Travelling with Clayton had been very pleasant and luxurious, but it was agreeable for a change to be on her own, to be Elinor Glyn the famous authoress rather than the odd-looking wife of Clayton Glyn, the well-known traveller.

She had one friend on board, Consuelo, Duchess of Manchester, a fascinating American* who was a close friend of King Edward and Queen Alexandra, and the Duchess warned Elinor that the reporters would fall on her like wolves in New York. Elinor did not altogether credit this. She had not yet got used to the idea that she was a famous personality and that anyone outside society circles might be interested in reading about her. She had, in the past, been interviewed by reporters only once or twice at most, and she had been then, unwisely, a little brusque.

She was taken aback now by her reception in New York. Reporters boarded the ship from launches as soon as she entered New York Harbour. Elinor was interviewed, photographed, interviewed again on the quay, followed to the Plaza Hotel, and interviewed again there. She had had no idea of the methods of the American press and she was amazed at the barrage of personal questions fired at her.

Was it true that *Three Weeks* was her own life story? Who was the real Paul? What did she think of America? What did it feel like being famous? What did she think about American divorce? What were her early struggles like? How long was she going to stay?

Elinor thought at first that they were joking, especially when she read in the previous day's paper a list of possible Pauls, culled probably from Debrett. But as soon as she realised that they were serious, she did her best to answer carefully and fully. She attributed afterwards the kindness with which the American press invariably treated her, both then and later, to the good impression she succeeded in mak-

* She was the daughter of Antonio Yznaga de Valle of Ravensnood, Louisiana.

ing in those first interviews in New York. Though they naturally portrayed her as the siren to end all sirens, they never indulged in the bitter personal attacks which she had often later to endure in the British press.

New York astonished her—the height of the buildings, the hurry and the bustle, above all the noise. People seemed always to be shouting at the top of their voices, even in private rooms; usually, Elinor observed, they were shouting that they knew what you were saying already; however, she went on, such was their capacity for absorption that they no doubt did, soon after they finished speaking.

After London and Paris the "democratic" manner of porters, waiters, chambermaids, and shopgirls pained her. It required a thick-skinned determination to make a purchase in a shop. However, when she next returned to America four years later, she found that once again the Americans had learnt fast and the New York shopgirls were now level with, if not ahead of, their London and Paris counterparts in subtle, flattering salesmanship.

2.

Together with Mrs. Fritz Ponsonby (later Lady Ponsonby) and the Duchess of Manchester, Elinor went, soon after her arrival in America, to stay with Mrs. Frederick Vanderbilt at her stately home at Hyde Park on the Hudson. Elinor had known Mrs. Vanderbilt in Paris and had found her a kindly lady, completely human and natural; she was utterly unprepared for the imperial grandeur of Mrs. Vanderbilt's manner at home.

A long flight of marble steps led from the drive to the front door, and on every third step was a footman in knee breeches and with powdered hair, drenched in the pouring rain. The guests were received in the hall by a pompous English butler and led through a series of salons to the great drawing-room, where their hostess was waiting to receive them, magnificently gowned and wearing some fifty thousand pounds' worth of pearls and long white kid gloves. The drawing-room was furnished with fine cabinets and chairs, the cream skimmed from the antique dealers of the world.

Tea in English country houses was an informal meal, dispensed by the hostess, but here it was evidently a highly formal occasion, with rows of footmen waiting as if it were a state banquet. The ladies sat in a line on a series of valuable but rather uncomfortable sofas; the gentlemen, silent and ill at ease, sat opposite them on a row of hard gilt chairs with their backs to the wall. It was as if everyone present were about to take part in some parlour game.

The conversation was slow and platitudinous, until suddenly Mrs. Stuyvesant Fish, whose caustic tongue was famous, remarked:

"They say in Europe that all American women are virtuous. Well, do you wonder? Look at those men!"

The line of men sitting meekly on their gold chairs fidgeted awkwardly and accepted this sally in docile silence. Elinor reflected that Clayton or Wynne Finch or Innes-Ker would not have allowed such a quip to go unanswered.

Dinner that night was an amazing meal, twice as large and magnificent as anything Elinor had previously experienced. She was particularly astonished by the flowers; the American Beauty Roses, each one of which would have won a prize in a flower show, were so enormous as to seem artificial. The food was wonderful, and the whole company dined, of course, off gold plate.

Only the conversation seemed a little below the standard, with everyone speaking slowly and loudly, rarely pausing to listen for an answer. A pleasant and refreshing feature, however, was the absence of *double-entendres,* which were such a feature of English society conversation.

One thing is noticeable and nice. The conversations everywhere are all absolutely *jeune fille,* never anything the least *risqué* though it is often amusing.*

The bedrooms were fully as palatial as the downstairs salons. Each room had at least two Louis Quinze suites. The curtains, the dressing-table covers, the pillow cases, even the edges of the sheets themselves were embroidered with real Venetian lace. The *pot-de-chambre* had a lace cover; the lavatory chain a large blue satin bow on it. There were no books or any evidence that the room had ever been slept in before.

Mrs. Vanderbilt's own bedroom, where she received Elinor the following morning, had a balustrade separating the bed from the rest of the room, as in Louis XV's state bedroom at Versailles.

"I suppose," murmured Elinor reminiscently, "that only Princes of the Blood are allowed behind the balustrade."

"*Elinor!*" said Mrs. Vanderbilt, deeply shocked. "You must not say such things in America."

It was with a certain relief that Elinor discovered that the Vanderbilt standard of living was not typical of the whole of American society. She spent week ends with the Ogden Mills at their house on the Hudson, and with the Bryces and the Greswolds on Long Island, and there she found an atmosphere more nearly approximating that of an English country house.

In between these week ends she lived at the Plaza Hotel and saw the sights of New York: Central Park, the Stock Exchange, a big newspaper being put to press, and even an opium den in Chinatown, though she discovered later to her chagrin that this had been arranged specially for her.

* *Elizabeth Visits America.*

3.

America, even in 1907, was a very different place from England. Elinor found it difficult at first to reconcile herself to the different attitudes towards life which she found in New York. The domination by the female sex she found particularly hard to accept. In her view man must always be the master; women might be the inspiration, the consolation, the ideal, even the goal in themselves, but they could never be the masters. A matriarchy seemed to her a topsy-turvy world.

Almost equally odd she found the lack of interest of the sexes in each other. The men seemed to be married to Wall Street, the women to their clubs.

And what with the smell of the innumerable flowers and the steam-heated rooms, and the cigarettes, I can't think how they have wits enough left to play bridge all the afternoon, as they do—with never a young man to wake them up. Of course it is amusing for Octavia and me to see all this as we are merely visitors, but fancy, Mamma, doing it as a part of one's life! Dressing up and making oneself splendid and attractive to meet only *women! !**

And why, she wondered, should the men, even the sons of millionaires, who had no need to work, rush downtown early every day to spend their best hours in a masculine bedlam like Wall Street, when they could be enjoying the company of beautiful women at home?

This point troubled her a good deal, and she finally attributed it to the gold-digging propensities of American women. It was they who drove their menfolk on in the eternal pursuit of the Almighty Dollar. It was the mothers, wives and daughters, she decided, wanting enough furs, new cars, jewels, ali-

* *Elizabeth Visits America.*

mony, not only to keep up with the Joneses but to go one better, who drove their men to stupefied exhaustion, platitudes, sentimentality, and too many cocktails. Money in England was not a subject of much interest in high society; either you had it or you did not, in which case you might be forced into taking up some profession. But if you had it, there was no earthly reason why you should bother to make any more; it was not as if it had any great virtue in itself. In America the opposite view seemed to prevail.

Elinor was, of course, meeting for the first time a society of men earning their daily bread, a society which is now universal and commonplace; and she was meeting it in a drastic form. Here was an upper class which did not regard estate ownership, sport, and opening bazaars as an adequate life occupation, and who equally seemed to take little interest in public service or public affairs. It was rarely that politics were discussed at meals or in drawing-rooms; the masculine talk was always of finance, the feminine of culture or of bridge. Elinor herself at no time in her life took any interest in any form of finance and was accordingly specially unimpressed by this great interest of the American male; nor did she ever play bridge; and she regarded the type of culture purveyed by American women's clubs as highly superficial.

In her diaries, her memoirs, and her book, *Elizabeth Visits America,* she was particularly severe on the "fluffy little gold-diggers" she found in New York society. Everything seemed to be on a tit-for-tat basis. A girl would only give a kiss in return for an engagement ring, a wife would only allow her husband his marriage rights in return for flowers or furs. Everything had to be bought by the man; love was never bestowed as a free gift for the joy of its own sake or for the sheer pleasure in giving. It was not even parted with on credit terms.

It is ironical that when Elinor came to America after the First World War, she found herself attempting to push the pendulum the other way, urging greater restraint and fastid-

iousness in the relations between the sexes, less casual pawing
and petting and kissing. But in 1907 there was certainly no
need for such advice.

Elinor found regrettably little romance in New York, with
the two sexes living in their own worlds. When they did meet,
it seemed to be more on a brother-and-sister basis. The women
seemed to have very little desire to make themselves mysterious or elusive, to arouse the men's hunting instinct, and indeed, she wondered if the men had a hunting instinct for
anything except dollars.

> The dance was such fun, a *bal blanc*, as only young peo-
> ple were asked, and they all came without chaperones, so
> sensible, and all seemed to have a lovely romp and enjoy
> themselves in a far, far greater degree than we do. It was
> more like a tenants' ball or a children's party, they seemed
> so happy, and towards the end lots of the girls' hair became
> untidy and their dresses torn, and the young men's faces
> damp and their collars limp.*

Elinor smiled indulgently but was deeply puzzled. She
would never have allowed a man to ruffle her hair.

Elinor was prepared to give full credit to American women
for their *soigné* appearance, their beautiful clothes worn with
style, their well-groomed heads; the all-pervading influence of
the beauty parlour put them well ahead of their English or
French counterparts. In this, she observed, they certainly gave
their husbands value for money.

She was, however, deeply pained by the drinking habits of
American society, especially the younger members of it. She
found it distressing to go into a ladies' cloakroom and find girls
of nineteen or twenty laid out "like salmon on a slab." At one
dinner party which Elinor attended a young man became extremely drunk and disgraced himself. In England he would
have had to resign from his clubs, possibly from his regiment,

* *Elizabeth Visits America.*

too, if he had one; but in New York this course was apparently not necessary. He was only being gently teased for being "overfull" when Elinor met him again at a dance two nights later. But there were compensations even in drunkenness, one vice driving out another.

> She says the young men now in New York nearly all drink too many cocktails and that is what makes them so unreserved when they get to their clubs. So the women can't have them for lovers because they talk about it.*

Elinor reserved her full scorn for the pretensions and snobbery of high society, those members of the Four Hundred who informed her continually about their own ancestry.

> If people are nice in themselves how can it matter who they are, or if "fashionable" or not? The whole thing is nonsense and if you belong to a country where the longest tradition is sixteen hundred and something, and your ancestor got there through being a middle-class puritan or a ne'er-do-well shipped off to colonise a savage land, it is too absurd to boast about ancestry or worry in the least over such things. The facts to be proud of are the splendid, vivid, vital, successful creatures they are now, no matter what their origin. Nearly everyone tells you here their great-great-grandfather came over in the *Mayflower*. (How absurd of the Cunard Line to be proud of the *Mauretania!* The *Mayflower,* of course, must have been twice the size.)*

> Among the "smart set" (do forgive this awful term, Mamma, but I mean by that the ones who are "in the swim" and whose society is the goal of the other's desire) they don't often tell you about the *Mayflower* and their ancestors —though on Wednesday a frightfully rich person who has only lately been admitted into the inner circle because both her daughters have married foreign Princes, said to me, she

* *Elizabeth Visits America.*

loved the English, and was, indeed, English herself and
some distant connection of our King, being descended from
Queen Elizabeth!!! It was unfortunate her having pitched
upon our Virgin Queen, wasn't it, Mamma? But, perhaps,
as she had rather an Italian look, it was the affair of the
Venetian attaché—and when I suggested that to her,
she gazed at me blankly and said: "Why, no, there never
has been any side-tracking in our family, we've always been
virtuous and always shall be!!"*

And again:

The talk of equality is just as much nonsense in America
as in every other place under the sun. How can people be
called equal when the Browns won't know the Smiths! And
the Van Brounkers won't know either and Fifth Avenue
does not bow to Riverside Drive and everyone is striving
to "go one better" than his neighbour?*

It should not, however, be imagined that Elinor found only
subjects for carping criticism in the New World. Her eighteenth-century upbringing had taught her to pay great attention to outward form and etiquette, and many customs of
America startled and jarred on her. Nor was there, at any
rate in the environs of New York, a rosy aura of romance to
compensate and appeal to the other side of her nature. But
once the first shock of America had worn off, she found much
to admire and appreciate—the frankness, the kindheartedness,
the generosity, the abundant hospitality.

These few days in New York have confirmed our opinion
of everyone's extraordinary kindness and hospitality. All
their peculiarities are just caused by being so young a nation, they are quite natural whenever their real feelings
come out. As children are touchy, so are they, and as chil-

* *Elizabeth Visits America.*

dren boast, so do they, and just as children's hearts are warm and generous, so are theirs. So I think this quality of youth is a splendid one, don't you, Mamma?*

She also strongly admired their determination:

I felt obliged to ask them [some boxers] if they minded at all having their noses smashed in, and black eyes, and if they felt nervous ever—and the little coloured gentleman grinned and said he only felt nervous over the money of the thing!! He was not anxious about the art or fame! He just wanted to win. Is not that an extraordinary point of view, Mamma, *to win?* It is the national motto, it seems, *how* does not matter so much, and that is what makes them so splendidly successful, and that is what the other nations who play games with them don't understand. They, poor old-fashioned things, are taking an interest in the sport part, and so scattering their forces, while the Americans are concentrating on the winning. And it is this quality which, of course, will make them the rulers of the world in time.*

The only thing she really missed in America was romance, and she was to find this further west.

4.

Elinor returned to her suite at the Plaza Hotel one day to find that Mark Twain had called while she was out. She was flattered that he should have come all the way from his house in Washington Square just to see her, and she returned his call the following day.

He is a dear old man with a halo of white silky hair and a fresh face, and the eyes of a child which look out on life

* *Elizabeth Visits America.*

with that infinite air of wisdom one sees peeping sometimes from a young pure soul. To find such eyes in an aged face proves many things as to the hidden beauties in the character. Mark Twain was dressed in putty-coloured—almost white—broad-cloth, very *soigné* and attractive looking. We sat on a large divan, and he gave orders that we were not to be disturbed.

She stayed for an hour and a half, and for most of that time they discussed *Three Weeks,* which he greatly admired, both in matter and in style.

As she was leaving Elinor said she would write down a summary of their conversation and send him a copy to read; it is this summary which forms the basis of the paper already referred to and which is quoted above. She duly sent him the summary and Mark Twain, clearly a little afraid that she might publish it, which would be a breach of his contract with his publisher, replied:

21 Fifth Avenue,
Jan. 24, 1908.

Dear Mrs. Glyn,

It reads pretty poorly. I get the sense of it, but it is a poor literary job; however, it would have to be because nobody can be reported even approximately except by a stenographer. Approximations, synopsized speeches, translated poems, artificial flowers, and chromos all have a sort of value, but it is small. If you had put upon paper what I really said, it would have wrecked your type-machine. I said some fetid and over-vigorous things, but that was because it was a confidential conversation. I said nothing for print. My own report of the same conversation reads like Satan roasting a Sunday School. It, and certain other readable chapters of my autobiography, will not be published until all the Clemens family are dead—dead and correspondingly indifferent. They were written to entertain me, not the rest of the world. I am not here to do good—at least not to do it intentionally. You must pardon me for dictating this letter; I am still sick a-bed and not feeling as well as I might.

Sincerely yours,

S. L. Clemens

They met again later that winter when they were both guests of honour at a dinner given by Daniel Frohman. Mark Twain made a kind and most entertaining speech about Elinor. Also at the dinner was John Barrymore, who made a point of telling her how much he had himself enjoyed *Three Weeks*.

Elinor remained in New York all through the winter.

I used to have ovations wherever I went, and began to think that the role of a famous authoress was a most delightful one. The air of America is rightly compared to champagne—exhilarating, delicious, but most intoxicating, and fatal to good judgement and capacity for self-criticism!*

5.

In the spring she set out on her coast-to-coast trip. She started by going to Philadelphia, which she found quieter and more old-fashioned than New York; but she regretted that the finest site in the city should have been used for a cemetery. She was fascinated by a reporter who described it as a "cunning place to take your best girl on Sunday to do a bit of a spoon." Love in a cemetery was a new aspect of romance for Elinor.

From Philadelphia she went, via New York, to Niagara, where she stayed at the honeymoon hotel. There were four honeymoon couples there at the time and she was surprised to

* *Romantic Adventure.*

find them all breakfasting downstairs in public. None of them spoke. One couple, who had been married three days, read the morning papers propped up against their cups, at the same time furtively holding hands under the table. The second couple, "mere children," had been married only the day before and the girl blushed crimson when she had to ask her husband whether he took sugar in his coffee. The third, married a fortnight, were obviously already very bored with each other; and the fourth, married three days, bolted down their breakfast as fast as they could before rushing out to play tennis. As honeymoons went, it was a very different atmosphere from *Three Weeks*.

On the train from Niagara to Chicago, Elinor met the millionaire who made such a deep impression on her.

He had "raised" two young men in his office, and as proof of their wonderful astuteness from his teaching—"I give you my word, Ma'am," he said, "either of them could draw a contract now for me, out of which I could slip at any moment!!!"*

Detroit she thought the most perfectly laid out city she had ever seen; Chicago itself she found "an immense, busy place with colossal blocks of houses and some really fine architecture; all giving the impression of a mighty, prosperous, and advancing nation, and quite the best shops one could wish for, not too crowded and polite assistants. (Even at the ribbon counter!)"*

The further west she went, the more she seemed to like America.

One of the strangest things is, that no one is old, never more than sixty and generally younger, the majority from eighteen to thirty-five and also something we have remarked everywhere, every one seems happy. You do not see weary,

* *Elizabeth Visits America.*

tired, bored faces, like in Europe, and no one is shabby or dejected, and they are all talking and drinking and laughing with the same intent concentrated force they bring to everything they do, and it is simply splendid.*

And here, too, she was struck by the chivalry and consideration of men for their womenfolk.

The cold in the wife's head could be heard quite plainly even where we were, and the host shouted so kindly, "Say, Anabel, be careful of that draught."

Fancy an English husband bothering to think of a draught after a catarrh had been there for fifteen years!*

6.

The next section of her journey led through the mining-camps and ranches of Nevada, and here at last she found the romantic America which she had been seeking. When she reached the town of Goldfield, a deputation of miners awaited her, saying that they had all greatly admired *Three Weeks* and would Mrs. Glyn come and visit their new camp at Rawhide, nearly a hundred miles away. Elinor accepted gladly, and that visit to Rawhide was to remain one of the happiest memories of her life; indeed, one may regard it as a turning-point in her spiritual progress.

Rawhide was not at first sight an inviting place. It was in the middle of a desert, without a blade of grass or any greenery. For hundreds of miles on either side there was nothing but earthy sand and sad grey sagebrush. The camp itself had been built only some two months before, but there were dance halls and a rough board hotel with a gambling-saloon, a bar on the ground floor, and about thirty bedrooms above. These had cheap, ill-fitting, plank partitions, in some cases papered

* *Elizabeth Visits America.*

with old newspapers, and the doors consisted of a few boards nailed together, with only a lift latch for fastening. Round the camp rattlesnakes were plentiful and the continual wind blew the dust about in sandstorms.

It was the miners themselves who impressed Elinor so deeply. They seemed to have stepped straight out of the pages of Bret Harte. They all carried guns openly—it was an offence to have them concealed. Many of the qualities and traditions of the old covered-wagon days had survived; the courage, the endurance, the respect for women, the modesty, the rough but real sense of justice. In physical appearance, too, they were very different from the more thickset types of the eastern seaboard or the Middle West. Here in Nevada they had the slim, loose-limbed, well-bred appearance of thoroughbreds.

There were, of course, those who did not come up to the standards set by the others, "the bad men," "the dirty yellow dogs," and at intervals these were rounded up and dealt with in a suitable way. There was also Scottie.

Scottie was a desperado, an outlaw who lived near by in a lair called Death Valley, a humid place below sea level, where he was guarded by his gang. In the sack of fan mail about *Three Weeks* which Elinor had found awaiting her at Goldfield was a letter from Scottie, saying how much he had enjoyed the book and would she come and spend an evening with him, when he would show her the real Wild West. He gave details of the rendezvous and the point where she was to leave her escort and go on alone; and he promised "on the honour of a bandit" that she would be returned to her friends safe and unharmed. Elinor was keen to accept, but her hosts, the sheriff and deputy constables, flatly forbade it and in deference to them she had to decline, writing that she had no time on this trip, and enclosing the signed photograph for which he had asked.

The miners showed her all round the camp. She was taken down a gold mine and suffered agonies of claustrophobia. She watched them playing poker in the gambling saloon, wearing green talc eye shades, which gave the gamblers' faces a strange, livid glow; a felt-slippered bartender silently padded round with drinks. The usual stake was a thousand dollars, and some of the men had twenty-five thousand dollars in front of them. The guns were all put up on a shelf, because, as the proprietor told Elinor, "They so often got to shootin' one another when they played as high as that." He found it "more conducive to a peaceable evenin' if their guns were handed out before they began." At the other end of the saloon there was singing and dancing.

The etiquette towards women, Elinor found, was strict and formal. A miner's wife was perfectly safe at any hour of the day or night with anyone; but any woman who wished to be flighty was fair game and she would live in a special part of the camp with "Katie" or "Polly" written over her door.

There was one pleasant incident when a deputation of miners, led by Governor Hutchinson, came to present Elinor with a gun.

"We give you this here gun, Elinor Glyn," said one of the miners, "because we like your darned pluck. You ain't afraid and we ain't neither."

Then Governor Hutchinson pinned the badge of deputy-constable on her breast and told her she could now arrest "any boy in the state." Elinor replied happily that she would like to arrest the lot, they were all so delightful. Everyone cheered wildly.

They also gave her a banquet. The long table in the saloon was specially covered with white oilcloth and about twenty of them sat down on plain, backless benches. Once again Elinor remarked the perfect, unaffected manners of the miners. Those sitting at the other tables glanced up and smiled as she came in; after that they never looked her way again. She was a strange, unaccustomed sight in that, or indeed in any, community, but they never stared. She might have been at Easton or Cranford.

The drinking-water had to be brought six miles. The food had come a hundred miles by wagon, the champagne from a good deal farther off. One man had ridden ninety miles across the desert to fetch some yellow daisies, the only flowers procurable, to decorate the centre of the oilcloth-covered table. Elinor was almost in tears. Ninety miles, there and back, across the desert, just to fetch her some flowers, and she never even knew which man it was.

She had always vaguely considered the phrase "nature's gentleman" to be a polite fiction, but now here he was before her eyes, the living proof that gentle manners and aristocratic behaviour were dependent, not on birth, or on the acquired traditions of centuries of authority, or on education, but on character. It was a shattering discovery. Mrs. Saunders would have accepted it with the utmost reluctance; Ambrosine would have died rather than admit it. But Elinor Glyn, faced with its actual presence, accepted it unconditionally.

> Nowhere in the world, whether in the houses of the rich, or in the courts of Kings, have I found such chivalry, such a natural sense of the fitness of things, such innate aristocracy as in the mining camps of Nevada.*

She never forgot the Rawhide miners. They seemed to her the embodiment of everything that was best in the New World. She set the climax of two of her novels in the Nevada gold fields; and the deputy-constable's badge and the gun—a small pistol mounted in mother-of-pearl—were for the rest of her life her most cherished possessions.

* *Romantic Adventure.*

7.

From Nevada she went, via Denver, to San Francisco, and there she found herself back in the hectic socialite atmosphere. Her hosts, Mr. and Mrs. Miller Graham, had not yet arrived from Santa Barbara, and she lunched by herself in the Fairmount Hotel. At the next table were six ladies, who were evidently the hostesses of a ball being given that evening for the officers of the fleet.

They were arguing in loud voices about whether one of their guests should be "thrown down" that night. The advantages and disadvantages of this action were fiercely debated. Another lady, joining the party late, strongly advised against such a course, as the guest in question was a personal friend of Mrs. Vanderbilt and Mrs. Stuyvesant Fish, no less. Elinor realised that it was she who was under discussion.

She attended the ball that night for which Admiral Long had sent her a special invitation. She was not "thrown down," and she was a little disappointed to find that the hostesses did not seem to recognise her as the lady at the next table at lunch. She thanked them politely for inviting her, to the amusement of Admiral Long, who had heard the whole story.

Three Weeks seemed to have aroused greater hostility in San Francisco than anywhere else in the world; Elinor suspected that, once again, most of the book's principal critics had not themselves read it. She was accustomed by now to receiving whole sacks of fan mail at each of her halts across America, the larger and masculine part of it favourable, the smaller part, almost entirely from women, abusive. But in San Francisco even the men seemed to be shocked by its reputation.

It is not altogether surprising that Elinor liked San Francisco the least of all the American cities she visited, though she attributed this not so much to its hostile reception of her book as to something sinister and discordant in the atmosphere. Most of the town had been destroyed by earthquake and fire only two years earlier, the disaster which had shown up the graft of the original building contractors and revealed so many apparently solid walls as mere shells filled with rubble. This seemed to be a cause more for pride than for shame, and Elinor was astounded by the number of San Franciscans who told her, a visiting stranger, the full details and drove her about so that she might herself see as much as possible of the evidence of corruption.

In San Francisco she found a message from Clayton from Japan, saying that he was unable to get passages across the Pacific and was taking the family home instead across Siberia.

On the first stage of her own journey home she travelled south from San Francisco to Los Angeles, then only a small California town, and eastward to Salt Lake City, where she saw the Mormons. The idea of sharing a man with several other women was yet another new aspect of romance to her, but one which did not appeal greatly.

From Utah she went on to St. Louis, where Mr. James Hackett was arranging to produce a dramatic version of *Three Weeks*, which Elinor had written herself in New York a few months previously. However, when she finally reached New York again, she unwisely allowed herself to sign a contract allocating not only the stock repertory rights of *Three Weeks* but, as was afterwards discovered, the whole dramatic rights east of the Missouri to a Miss Marbury for a mere one hundred pounds. All her life Elinor suffered from an inability to refrain from signing any contract laid before her, and the result of this sale was to prevent the stage production of *Three Weeks* not only in St. Louis, but in New York, too.

8.

Elinor returned from America with a number of new ideas and theories about life. The chief of these was the so-called "New Thought," which at that time was sweeping America and whose literature was to be seen on so many bookstalls. With her rejection of the teachings of the Church and her deep curiosity about the causes and reasons behind life and human behaviour, she was specially vulnerable to influences of this sort; and after nearly a year of adulation and lionization her critical faculties were a little blurred.

The language with which the teachings of "New Thought" were veiled, quasi-Biblical with quotations from the New Testament, made it only too easy for Elinor to believe that here was the true Christian teaching undistorted by centuries of ecclesiastical misinterpretation.

The conception of the mind's influence over matter was, of course, basic to her Saunders upbringing, but Mrs. Saunders would never have approved, or even understood, the methods of the newly discovered "thought-force" and the ends to which it was applied. Those who practised this cult were beyond doubt more prosperous and successful than those who did not and there were apparently thousands of Americans who spent hours every day willing themselves to receive large sums of money, exceptionally profitable contracts, or new fur coats. Elinor herself spent much time reading the publications, especially Richard Ingalese's *The History and Power of Mind;* it seemed to fit in, in so many ways, with her own instinctive beliefs and disbeliefs, and it provided an authoritative explanation for many of the points which troubled her. She would sit—her sense of humour for the moment in abeyance —for more than an hour a day concentrating in the approved manner, doing the prescribed exercises, and visualising the power and the riches which she was teaching herself to desire.

In due course she sloughed off the greedier and more materialistic aspects of New Thought and she came to consider them evil, verging almost on black magic. But she never abandoned her belief in the power of thought-force. She had been taught that the atmosphere was full of good and evil thoughts, magnetic and unmagnetic vibrations, radiating like wireless waves, and the human mind, by regulating its own thoughts, could "tune in" and receive whatever good or bad influences were present in the surrounding atmosphere. To think evil thoughts, to break one's promise, to lie were not only wrong in themselves; they would tune her mind to receive only evil or unmagnetic vibrations, which would probably bring disaster in their wake. She extended this theory to cover her own personal inclinations; to save for a rainy day, she contended, was inevitably, by the power of thought-force, to attract that rainy day—a financial doctrine which was to drive her relatives and advisors almost to despair.

Apart, however, from this special application, this later, modified conception of New Thought was both harmless and appealing. I myself can remember her sitting in the garden under a purple parasol, her eyes closed as she concentrated upon golden light.

She also returned from America with a new philosophic jargon, the chief item being "The New Religion of Common Sense." Her eighteenth-century rationalism had always prized this quality and she herself used the term to describe indifferently both the sensible and the incredible. Part of this enthronement of common sense was a series of laws—"The Law of Cause and Effect," "The Law of the Boomerang," "The Law of Periodicity"—laws whose universal application she sought to establish, not always successfully, by scientific or logical method.

Yet another acquisition in America was "The Secret of El-Zair," a form of the elixir of eternal youth. Over the next two

years Elinor carried out at carefully regulated intervals the
prescribed treatment, partly mystical, partly medicinal, and
kept a full account of her progress in a notebook specially
bound to resemble a copy of *Beyond the Rocks*. She averred
that she benefited considerably from the treatment, adding
drawings and data to prove her point; it not only rejuvenated
the skin, the muscles, and the eyes, but also removed neural-
gia, neuritis, and rheumatism. She succeeded in persuading
a number of friends, including Lucy, her new husband, Sir
Cosmo Duff-Gordon, and Lord Redesdale to try it, though
Lord Redesdale, who was then seventy-two, was too old to
benefit fully except in "his youthful exaltation of mind."
Lucy's actual health improved:

> . . . but I am more than ever sure, from one case I have
> closely observed, that if used with doubt and grumbling,
> the effect is only half as good and the youthful effect nil.

Far more serious and fundamental than these theories and
experiments was Elinor's belief in reincarnation, which came
at this time to full flower. This was not a new discovery in
America; she had been thinking deeply on the matter for years.
She herself attributed her first interest in the subject to a visit
she made to Paestum in Italy on the occasion of her first return from Egypt. It was there that she had a very definite
sensation of having been in the place before, of being linked
in some way with the past. This sensation was to return to
her several times in her life and in widely different places,
amongst them St. Petersburg, Versailles, and Shepherd's Market in London.

The more she thought about reincarnation, the more it appealed to her as an explanation and a pattern of life. It provided a satisfactory reason, a "common sense reason," for so
many of the perplexities, the seeming unfairnesses of life. It
fitted in, too, with her conception of a supreme, benevolent

and rather negative Deity, occasionally overriding the laws of nature to help and comfort some repentant sinner.

During Elinor's stay in America and in the years that followed she meditated a great deal on the subject, eventually clarifying her theory and restating it in a number of articles and essays. In later years, as her views became more widely known, she would elaborate her own earlier lives in more detail. She would even claim that she could, in certain moments of insight, see glimpses, half-seen pictures, of the earlier lives of her friends. They found this a bewildering gift, uncertain whether she was serious or joking.

In fact, she was sometimes one, sometimes the other, depending on her mood. For, like the rest of the English nation, she had the ability to make jests on occasions of the things she held most sacred.

BOOK FOUR

The Breadwinner

1908–1914

I.

Elinor arrived at home in June 1908, very pleased with herself and with life, with her success in America, with the new sights and scenes of her travels, with the large sums of money which all her books were now bringing in. She was utterly unprepared for the reversal which awaited her.

Her family had arrived back some three weeks previously and were full of the wonderful time they had had on the long journey, which had even included a mild train crash on the Trans-Siberian Railway. The children had grown and developed considerably under the stimulus of new sights and sounds, while Mrs. Kennedy declared that she had had her happiest six months since her first husband died.

But Clayton seemed to have changed considerably for the worse. Seeing him every day, Elinor had been less aware of his physical deterioration; now, after an interval of nearly a year, she was shocked by the change. He had grown very much stouter and there was about his face a purple tinge indicative of heart trouble. He had always been a little asthmatic and this, too, seemed to be worse.

For years his doctors had been urging him gently to give up smoking twelve cigars a day, to eat less rich food, to drink less port, to cut down the numbers of turkish baths, journeys in hot countries, long August days on grouse moors—all the things which he loved most in the world. He had steadily ignored the doctors' advice, even when Elinor had joined them in urging him to treat his no longer youthful constitution with more consideration. Now it seemed that he was paying the price for his own self-indulgence.

After a while Elinor noticed that the trouble was not only physical. His gayety, his merry smile had gone; there was a pathetic hangdog look about him. She realised with a sinking heart that there was something else, other than his health, worrying him. It was several weeks before she discovered what it was.

He came into her room one day—one of the few occasions on which he ever entered her Trianon—and handed her, without speaking, a letter from his solicitors. For a while she could not grasp its meaning. Then the terrible truth dawned on her.

Clayton had been living all these years not on his income, but on his capital; and the capital was now exhausted. Worse than that, he had been borrowing money everywhere he could find it. The property was mortgaged to its full extent; he was deeply in debt to the bank, to his friends, and to money-lenders. And now his creditors were demanding repayment. The crash had come.

In later years Elinor blamed herself severely for not realising that in the first sixteen years of their marriage they must have been living far beyond their possible maximum income. But, in fairness, she must be exonerated from this charge. Clayton never took her into his confidence about his financial affairs; indeed, he would have avoided discussing them with her even had she shown any desire to. He had never suggested that their standard of living, their long luxurious journeys were too costly. He had virtually encouraged her to spend as much as she liked on clothes. His only efforts at economy, their successive removal to smaller houses, he always camouflaged by giving some other reason for the change.

Elinor herself had never been of a frugal nature and she had spent her own earnings freely. However, so large were the royalties which her books were now bringing in that she had, almost without intention, accumulated a considerable fortune in her bank account. She did not hesitate to give the whole of this to Clayton, but large though it was, it was only sufficient to meet the more pressing of his creditors, and after a few weeks it became apparent that if he was to be saved from bankruptcy, she would have to sign away her marriage settlement, too. Once again she agreed, preferring to part with her last financial resources, the sole bulwark between her and destitution in the years to come, rather than that Clayton should be publicly disgraced. She also undertook, with rather a heavy heart, the support and maintenance of her husband and children, since she alone was capable of earning her own living. From now onwards, she realised, the whole family would be dependent upon her earnings. Her pen alone stood between them all and starvation.

It was her responsibility now to reorganise the family finances. In one way there could have been few people less fitted for the task. Her own lack of financial acumen, her spasmodic but unpredictable and irresistible extravagances, her dislike of petty restrictions did not assist her to impose a more economic pattern of life upon the family.

She had, however, two enormous assets to help her at this moment of crisis. One was her own innate courage and the other, almost equally great, was her capacity for making money.

2.

It was not till after Clayton's death in 1915 that Elinor was able fully to understand the reasons which lay behind the purblind, cruelly short-sighted attitude towards life that he had adopted. Then, going through his papers, she was able to learn enough of his early life to understand, if not to excuse, his later behaviour.

His father had died while he was a child and he had been brought up by his mother to expect every luxury and, at the same time, to live on an allowance small compared with his ultimate expectations. He had wanted to go into the family regiment, the Rifle Brigade, but she had persuaded him out of this. He was called to the bar, but she did not encourage him to practise. By the time he came to his full inheritance, the damage was done; he was by then fully accustomed to luxury, idleness, and debt. Even at Oxford he had got into the hands of moneylenders and he remained in their clutches for the rest of his life.

The property was already heavily mortgaged when he married Elinor, but he made, reluctantly, one or two efforts at economy so that there might be some of his estate left to bequeath to his son. It was the birth of a second daughter and the loss of ten thousand pounds at Monte Carlo that settled the pattern of his future life. There was now to be no son and so there was now no point in saving any of his estate for the next generation.

The alternative before him had been clear-cut and had been presented, no doubt, in a most cunning light by the moneylenders, who were the evil geniuses of his life. Either he could economise and live out a dreary but probably much longer life, or he could continue the way he was going, the way of the lotus-eater, and have a shorter but a gayer life. He chose unhesitatingly the second course.

His doctors had assured him that he was killing himself with his present manner of living and he continued in that way, even stepping it up further, gayly and deliberately undermining his health, smoking not twelve but sixteen cigars a day. Suicide itself was vulgar and unthinkable, but it seemed only too likely that he would be naturally dead before his money ran out.

After that his widow would have her marriage settlement, and judging by the number of her admirers, she would have little difficulty in marrying again. His children, too, were provided for under the settlement; so too was Mrs. Kennedy, who was at this time drawing a fair income from her founder's shares in Lucile's. The only losers would be those who had lent him money and who now, his widow's settlement being untouchable, would never recover it; but Clayton, like so many others of his generation, had little sympathy for disappointed creditors, even his own! He had only himself to think of and he was, according to his lights, perfectly entitled to choose for himself the swift and easy path to destruction. One can exonerate his doctors, who knew nothing of the financial reasons for his way of life and who continued to urge much greater austerity upon him; but one cannot avoid wondering at those who knew the truth and who acquiesced meekly in such an egoistical and disastrous policy.

By ending his married life with his wife Clayton could be certain of never having a son, the contingency which would upset his plans. But he could never be certain that he would die before his money and his credit were finally exhausted. That must always be a gamble and, as such, it attracted him, a born gambler. As always, he lost—lost by seven long, pitiful years.

3.

Even though she did not know the full truth at that time, Elinor never blamed her husband for bringing them, without a twinge of conscience, to their present pass. He was still for her the grand seigneur, and whatever his other faults and shortcomings, she never ceased to look up to him and admire him, even when no points of mutual contact remained, even when he seemed almost to delight in adding to her burdens rather than in diminishing them. Indeed, on looking back, her principal reaction was of astonishment at his gayety and cheerfulness all the years when the gaunt spectres of death and disaster were approaching remorselessly nearer, all the time that he was hugging his terrible secret to himself. She took the attitude that it was his money to do with as he pleased. While he had had it, he had spent it freely upon her. Now it was her turn to repay his generosity.

For Clayton, as for many others of his generation, debt was no special matter for shame. It was perfectly natural to borrow money, even from personal friends, without any hope of repayment. It was only actual bankruptcy which was a disgrace.

Upon this point Clayton and Elinor had, once again, a totally different attitude. She detested borrowing money, but, if she was forced to do so, it was inconceivable not to repay it at the first opportunity. In the years that followed, she was several times forced to ask some of her friends, especially her cousin Geoffrey Glyn and her sister Lucy, for assistance. But she always repaid them as soon as possible in full.

It was not easy to economise at Lamberts. Elinor disliked it, Clayton resisted it. Mrs. Kennedy adored Clayton; in her eyes he could do no wrong. Her character was always at its weakest when there was a male influence in her life, and now she connived at his extravagances, she indulged his luxuries at a time when she ought to have been resisting them and urging retrenchment.

The six years that followed were a continual struggle for Elinor to pay the household bills, to bring up and educate her children, and to maintain a reasonable standard of life for her family. They were years of almost unremitting financial crisis. Over and over again she was saved from ruin by an unexpected cheque from her publishers, or if this was not forthcoming, by the proceeds of hastily written novels and short stories. Sometimes the weight of the burden upon her seemed to be almost overwhelming, but she was always just equal to it.

4.

The immediate necessity was to increase the family income. Over a year had elapsed since the publication of *Three Weeks* and there had been nothing since then, apart from a slim anthology of quotations and aphorisms derived from the early books, principally *The Reflections of Ambrosine,* called, *Sayings of Grandmamma,* and this clearly was not going to bring in any very large sum in royalties.

She began at once to write *Elizabeth Visits America,* the gayety of which she was very far from feeling, but it was to be nearly another year before that work appeared on the bookstalls.

The Grand Duchess Kiril of Russia, whom Elinor had met the previous summer in Paris, had suggested that a good way of vindicating the morals and reputation of *Three Weeks* would be to stage a private performance of a dramatic version to which the whole of London society could be invited. Elinor remembered this suggestion now. It seemed to her that by putting on such a performance at the present time she would not only clear the name of her book, but she might well also interest a manager in a commercial presentation. The dramatic version of the novel was already written and Elinor threw herself energetically into the preparations for the performance.

It took place, as an invitation matinee, on the twenty-third of July, 1908, at the Adelphi Theatre. In order to make the presentation still more attractive Elinor was persuaded to act the part of the Queen herself. She had, apart from *tableaux vivants,* charades, and some amateur theatricals, no dramatic experience and there was no time to do more than teach her her lines. But the part, being a portrayal of yet another aspect of her own personality, demanded little more of her than that she should recreate once again her own passionate, intense mood. As her model, there was always in the back of her mind Sarah Bernhardt as Theodora.

The rest of the cast was professional. Paul was played by a handsome young actor, Charles Bryant. C. Aubrey Smith (later Sir Charles Aubrey Smith) was Paul's father, and the play was produced by Sir Charles Hawtrey. Lucile's provided the dresses for the one sumptuous performance to which most of London society came.

Even with an amateur in the principal part it was a considerable success, and it seemed for a time that both Elinor's objectives might be achieved. The play was a straightforward rather melodramatic tragedy, without a single indecent line, and many of Elinor's friends confessed to her later that they now understood the motives which had impelled her to write the book. Hawtrey himself began to make plans for a West End presentation, with a professional actress in the leading part, and the contract was signed, giving Elinor handsome terms. The play was submitted to the Lord Chamberlain for approval.

It was turned down flat. No explanation was given and all requests for information as to which lines or scenes might be thought objectionable were ignored. Elinor and all her friends were astonished, for there seemed nothing censorable in the version as played at the private performance. However, there was nothing to be done about it, and the contract was cancelled.

It was a heavy blow, for the mounting of the private performance, financed personally by Elinor, had been costly and, apart from increasing the reputation of the book and of Elinor's own resource and versatility, the outlay had yielded no dividends. It was not until later that Lord Redesdale gave Elinor to understand that the ban had been instigated at the request of the Foreign Office.

5.

One of those who came to the matinee was Lord Curzon of Kedleston. His distinguished but controversial viceroyalty of India had ended three years earlier, unmarked by any public recognition, and he was now living, a disappointed widower, in partial retirement. She had met him on one or two previous occasions and had been a little in awe of him. Now he wrote her a charming letter of appreciation of *Three Weeks,* of her acting, and above all, of her courage in trying to vindicate herself in such a bold way.

Elinor replied suitably, much cheered and comforted by the kind words from someone whom she hardly knew and whom she had previously supposed to be reserved and rather inhuman. She was not to know, when she wrote, that she was entering into what was to be the great romance of her life.

It is at first a little puzzling to see just why Lord Curzon and Elinor should have been so strongly attracted to each other. Curzon had, it is true, a penchant for romantic women novelists; he had for years kept up a desultory correspondence with Ouida. He much admired Elinor's physical beauty and he gave her later a miniature Della Robbia bust of Venus, which he thought she strongly resembled. But at first glance he and Elinor would seem to have been so different—the cold, aloof, intellectual statesman, dedicated, industrious, contemptuous of feminine charms and failings, and the ardent, passionate novelist, capable on occasions of those exaggerations and follies which he admired least.

Yet if we examine both characters more closely, we find that they were, even on the surface, surprisingly similar. Lord

D'Abernon has said of Curzon that "he was born and died in the faith of an aristocrat of the English eighteenth century," and the same may be said of Elinor, substituting "French" for "English." They were both of ancient patrician breeding, with a more immediate provincial and impoverished background. They were both lonely, both felt themselves ill-used by the British public, and both bore their moments of adversity and disappointment with courage and dignity. They were both excessively class-conscious, self-assertive, and egotistical; they both lacked a sense of proportion; they were both energetic and idealistic; they shared a common love of the classics.

There were, of course, matters in which she and Curzon differed sharply; Curzon's meticulousness, particularly over cash accounts, had no counterpart in Elinor. But in general their characters and their attitudes towards life were such as to make us believe that the bond between them was the mutual attraction, not of opposites, but of equivalents.

6.

Elinor decided that Margot's education should be finished by a stay in Dresden and Elinor herself went there later in the summer of 1908 to find a suitable *pension*. On her return journey she met Curzon at Heidelberg and he showed her the sights of the city.

Margot and Dixie went to Dresden in the autumn, but almost at once Margot caught scarlet fever and was removed by the German authorities to an isolation hospital, where, Elinor maintained, she would inevitably have died but for Dixie's devoted attendance. There was only one nurse and one wardmaid for the whole ward of thirty beds and the nurse was on duty day and night.

Elinor rushed out to Dresden again but she was not allowed

even to have a glimpse of Margot and had to content herself with receiving daily reports from Dixie. Elinor was treated, apparently, by the authorities with crude and autocratic brutality, and from this episode we must date her lifelong detestation of Germany and the German race.

She returned to England as soon as Margot began to improve. In due course Dixie brought Margot to Monte Carlo to convalesce and Elinor motored out to join them. However, a new financial crisis at this time, the one which involved Elinor in having to sign away her marriage settlement, cast a grey shadow over the gathering.

They all returned together in the new year, 1909, and Elinor started to make arrangements for ten-year-old Juliet to go to school at Eastbourne.

7.

Elinor's concern that her children should have a better education than she had had was well within the terms of reference of spiritual motherhood. She had also to guide their tastes and ideas. She made them read the books which meant most to her and chose the pictures for their bedrooms, reproductions of eighteenth-century portraits, which she mounted herself, so that her daughters might look upon good art first thing in the morning and last thing at night.

Otherwise her care for her children was a little haphazard. At times she would take immense trouble over them, particularly in cases where her own ideas of entertainment and theirs coincided. She herself had painted the bill of Juliet's duck a brighter orange so that it might win a prize at a gymkhana. She had gilded the horns of Margot's cow, Wilhelmina, and hung its neck with garlands so that it might be a worthy centrepiece for the children's *fête champêtre,* an entertainment in which Marie Antoinette herself would have delighted.

Elinor loved picnics. She would take the children and Dixie to a nearby field and there over an open fire she would cook curry for tea and everybody present would wolf it down with glee. Clayton would sometimes wander down from the house, wrinkle his nose with distaste at the smell, observe drily that they had all had a large lunch and were about to have an even larger dinner, and wander back again.

At such moments Elinor was a delightful mother. The unpredictability and unusualness of her tastes appealed strongly to children sated with nursery or schoolroom routine. But at other times she was casual and indifferent, wrapped up in her own world, not knowing whether they were happy or not. She was, of course, engaged for much of the time in writing the books which paid for their meals. But she tended too easily to think that they were brimming over with happy animal spirits whilst she was bearing the sorrows and burdens of the world alone. She had never understood the mind of a child; the special problems and unhappinesses of adolescence were equally beyond her.

It was as well for the children that Mrs. Kennedy was always at hand to provide a stable background, to give that continuous love and sympathetic companionship which they received only intermittently from their mother. Mrs. Kennedy all through those years gave the two girls all the love and devotion which she had not been able to give her own children, and both Margot and Juliet responded by considering her as being virtually their mother.

8.

Even apart from the financial crises life at Lamberts was not very easy during these years. Clayton and Elinor had for some time had very few points of mutual contact; there were practically none left now. She did not reproach him for his part in bringing about their financial ruin, but they had very little else to talk about.

The position was not made any easier by Mrs. Kennedy's own attitude towards the situation. Lamberts was her house, given to her as a present by Clayton, and it never occurred to her for one moment that she might abdicate in favour of her daughter. It was she who sat at the head of the table, with Clayton opposite her at the other end. It was she who ordered the long, elaborate meals which Clayton enjoyed so much.

Lunch never lasted less than an hour and a half, dinner two hours, and the only permitted topic of conversation was food, a conversation carried on entirely by Clayton and Mrs. Kennedy. Elinor would sit at the side of the table, silent, abstracted, almost in a coma of boredom. Her interest in food was confined to certain favourite dishes in which she revelled and liked to eat as often as possible. But it was not, in the abstract, a topic which she wished to discuss at length.

Often she would have meals sent across to her own sitting-room on a tray and she always left her husband and her mother to breakfast alone together. In the evening, after dinner, Elinor would retire at once to her Trianon—the only part of the house which seemed to her like home—while Clayton and Mrs. Kennedy would go to the drawing-room and play patience or piquet.

A stranger to the household would have guessed that it was Clayton and Mrs. Kennedy who were the married couple and that Elinor, who was in fact the breadwinner for the whole family, was a poor relation who had outstayed her welcome.

9.

In the summer of 1909 a fresh financial crisis broke on
the family, born as usual of Clayton's refusal to economise,
Mrs. Kennedy's weak indulgence of his wishes, and Elinor's
own feeling that it was not for her to refuse him anything
after all the money he had spent upon her so ungrudgingly.

A diary entry of this time gives some idea of the weight of
the burden upon her and the amount of fortitude she had to
summon to meet it. The entry also illustrates the extent to
which her private thoughts were now dominated by Curzon.

It has come. Now I must face the inevitable and call all
my forces to give me courage. Before me, humanly speaking, there is nothing to be seen but a weary life of work.
Immense worries, the responsibilities of all my dear ones
on my shoulders, the watching ever of one who suffers.

Away weakness and repining! Away concentrated absorbed thought of and for one person! Call common sense.
Say, "Your duty lies in using your brain and force for your
sweet ones and your family. It does not lie in undesired
and idolatrous obsession over the sun, moon and stars." Re-
assert your personality which was once a potent factor in
your life. Take the gifts fate throws in your way. Your idol
will not value you the less because you are successful and
gay. He is too busy over his own great aims to care for your
worship.

Cease brooding for hours if his little finger aches. Cease
praying for his glory and happiness and health from morning to night, and instead be joyous when you do see him,
and between whiles concentrate upon your affairs for the
benefit of your sweet ones and those dependent upon you.
Be true to yourself and not the miserable slave of an obses-

sion. He—your Idol—never wished you to be a slave or imposed any single thing upon you. He is great, he only desires your welfare—so away with worship!

10.

Later that summer Elinor went to Carlsbad, where she underwent not only the prescribed cure but also the secret treatment of El-Zair. Her maid, Williams, had had to give up service through ill-health, and on this trip Elinor was accompanied by her new maid, Maria Fielder,* who was to be with her for more than ten years. On her return Elinor, together with Margot, went to stay with Count Cahen d'Anvers at Champs for a shooting-party. While there, she received a telegram from the Grand Duchess Kiril of Russia asking if she could meet the Grand Duchess and her mother-in-law, the Grand Duchess Vladimir, in Munich.

Elinor accordingly went and met both ladies, who invited her to spend that winter in St. Petersburg with a view to writing a book about the Russian court. They had been much impressed by the grasp of the Russian character which Elinor had shown in *Three Weeks* and thought that she would be able to make a sympathetic study of their home life.

The Grand Duchess Vladimir, a magnificent, stately Princess, said, "Everyone always writes books about our peasants. Come and write one about how the real people live."

Elinor accepted eagerly. She loved travel and new sights, and she loved court society. Moreover, it was now becoming urgent for her to write another novel and she had no desire at the moment to return to her earlier fields, English country house parties. The Grand Duchess Vladimir advised her to

* Both Williams and Maria had red hair, and this coincidence gave rise to the story that Elinor only engaged red-haired maids because they understood her temperament.

bring plenty of dresses as it was rumoured that the Czar and the Czarina were about to emerge from their seclusion at Tsarskoe Selo and there would be court balls and much gayety. On the strength of this Elinor ordered an entire new wardrobe from Lucile's and a number of new hats from Reboux to go with Lucy's masterpieces.

Elinor arrived at St. Petersburg on the twenty-eighth of December, 1909 (English calendar), and went at once to the Hôtel de l'Europe, where she was to stay. It had been explained that she would have more liberty staying there than at the Vladimir Palace. She learnt that the Grand Duke Michael had just died in Cannes and that the court was in mourning for two months. Elinor had only two black frocks with her, one for day and one for evening, and she realised that she would have to wear these, day in, day out, for the next two months, while her beautiful new Lucile dresses remained in their trunks.

She found on taking tea with Lady Nicholson, the British Ambassadress, that afternoon that even her new black Reboux hats were unacceptable and that Lady Nicholson had already ordered her a black crepe mourning bonnet with a long flowing veil.

The following day Elinor attended church with the Grand Duchess Vladimir and was much impressed by the weird singing and the magnificent robes of the priests. Afterwards there was a salon, at which she was presented to most of the Imperial family and the various court equerries and ladies-in-waiting. She noted that the men, though otherwise fine-looking, seemed very pasty-faced, the result, she supposed, of living in steam-heated rooms without much fresh air. The Grand Duke Boris recalled their meeting in Egypt but he seemed to have aged a lot and to be very bored with life. The Grand Duke André and the Grand Duchess Helène (Princess Nicholas of Greece) examined Elinor's eyes closely to see if they were really as green as they were reputed to be.

After this they took *zacouska,* the famous Russian *hors d'oeuvre,* and eventually sat down to a banquet, the conversation being conducted in several different languages, but always in English or French whenever Elinor was within hearing.

The following day she watched the Grand Duke Michael's funeral procession from the windows of the British Embassy and wrote in her diary a vivid account of it: the Czar and the Grand Dukes marching resolutely behind the coffin, in terror of assassination; the Czarina cringing in her carriage; the priests' magnificent vestments trailing in the slush; the double line of soldiers lining the route, facing both the procession and the crowd; the blind-shuttered windows from which no one, except at the British Embassy, was allowed to watch; the sullen, ungrieving crowds. As a state funeral she could not help contrasting it with Queen Victoria's. In Russia death seemed to have no real meaning.

She attended the Grand Duke's funeral the next day, to find herself in the front row of the foreign guests, only ten feet from the Czar himself, and she was struck by his resemblance to his cousin, the Duke of York, who was later King George V, yet his face was so unnaturally composed as to seem like a mask. The Czarina had refused to be present. The service lasted for four hours and there were no chairs. With the uniforms and candles it was a fine spectacle but Elinor felt herself getting very tired towards the end. At least, being a Protestant, she did not have to hold a heavy candle throughout; nor, like the Czar and the members of the Imperial family, did she have the ordeal of kissing the dead man's face.

For the next two months Elinor lived in St. Petersburg, seeing the sights, observing the habits and customs of the Russian court, and being entertained royally. Wherever she went she was greeted by bowing officials; the policemen knew her carriage by sight and held up the traffic for her. The Czar gave orders that the Winter Palace was to be opened specially so

that she might see it, and she was shown over it, rather overcome by the honour, by two Grand Dukes and a host of lesser
royalty. Without having been there before she seemed to know
her way round the Winter Palace well, and she explained to
the startled Grand Duke André, when he commented on it,
that she was herself the reincarnation of Catherine the Great
and remembered the palace quite well, adding, for corrobora-
tion, some details about Catherine's death which were not at
that time supposed to be known outside Russia.

She was also making notes for her novel, working out scenes
and plots. She was, however, in difficulties about the character
of her hero. The Russian nobles whom she had met seemed,
for all their urbanity, a little charmless. Though they would
make admirable subsidiary characters, none of them inspired
her sufficiently to be the hero of the story that was growing
in her mind.

Finally, at tea one day in Elinor's suite, the Grand Duchess
Helène suggested that she might describe Prince Gritzko Wittgenstein, who had been killed in a duel recently. Memories of
Cairo and the Khedive's Ball flooded back into Elinor's mind,
and at once she saw her way clearly. She would start the book
in Egypt, with the Sphinx by moonlight and the Khedive's
Ball; then she would move the story to St. Petersburg. She
would put in all Gritzko's exploits, of which all the court were
now busily reminding her, even the story of the gipsy girl.

She wished to begin the book straightaway, but her Egyptian diary, with her descriptions and memories of Gritzko, was
at Lamberts and she wanted to reread it before starting. She
had also received that morning a disturbing letter from her
lawyers; Clayton had apparently been borrowing money again
and the creditor was pressing for repayment.

She decided to travel to England, ostensibly to fetch the
diary, pacify the creditor, and then return to Russia. Everyone
was deeply impressed by her conscientiousness and asked her
to be back quickly, as court mourning was just ending and

there would be balls and great festivities in honour of the King of Bulgaria, who was about to visit Russia. Elinor promised faithfully that she would be back within a week.

It was suggested that she should return to England via Moscow, which she needed to describe in her novel, and plans were made accordingly. A court official called on her in her suite and explained the arrangements for the journey. In Moscow the keepers of the palaces and museums had been instructed to give her special facilities for seeing them. A sleeper had been reserved on the night train from Moscow to Warsaw. She was to spend the following night at the Hôtel de l'Europe in Warsaw, where a room had been reserved, and catch the Berlin train the next morning. A carriage had been ordered to meet her in Warsaw, as it would be late in the evening and there might be no cabs. The official gave her her ticket and sleeping-car reservation and explained that the tickets and reservations for the part of the journey onwards from Warsaw would be awaiting her at the Hôtel de l'Europe.

The meticulousness of the arrangements was typical of the care and thoughtful planning which Elinor had experienced ever since she arrived in Russia. She thanked the official for the great trouble he had taken in ensuring her a comfortable journey. He bowed, kissed her hand, and left. Only after he had gone did she realise that she had never seen him before, although she now knew almost all the court officials by sight.

The following day she set out. Ever since her arrival in St. Petersburg, Maria had been the victim of continuous stomach upsets, which she attributed to the contrast of hot rooms and cold air outside. Elinor, however, had suspected appendicitis and had sent her back to England, her place being temporarily taken by a sulky Russian maid. Elinor thought it an unwarrantable expense to take this maid with her and she was therefore on this journey, for the first and only time in her life, travelling completely alone.

11.

The arrangements went as smoothly as clockwork. In Moscow, Elinor was treated with the same elaborate consideration which she was used by now to expect in St. Petersburg. She saw over the palaces and museums and was struck by the city's contrast with St. Petersburg. St. Petersburg was a wholly westernised city—it could have been London or Paris or Vienna. But Moscow, barbaric and oriental, could have existed only in Russia.

She caught the night train to Warsaw, as planned, and was not disturbed on crossing the Polish frontier. She reached Warsaw the following evening after it was dark. There were no porters about and she was forced to carry her own dressing-case—fortunately, on this occasion, she was travelling unusually light. Nor were there any cabs waiting outside the station, except for a single carriage with two good horses and two men on the box. This was evidently the carriage which had been ordered to meet her.

The man beside the coachman climbed down, bowed gravely, and enquired, "Madame Glyn?"

Elinor nodded and climbed in, feeling tired after the train journey and appreciating the excellence of the travelling arrangements made for her. The man climbed back on the box and they drove off.

After a while Elinor realised that they were driving very fast, and moreover that they were travelling through poor, mean streets which she was sure could not lead to the Hôtel de l'Europe. She vaguely wondered if there had been some mistake, but everything had worked so smoothly so far and the carriage had clearly been ordered expressly for her. The man on the box had said her name.

She opened the window and shouted, "Hôtel de l'Europe!"

The coachman gave no answer but instead whipped up his horses into a gallop. In the dim snow-light Elinor could see that they were almost out of the city; soon they would be in open country. With a sickening qualm of apprehension she realised that she was being kidnapped.

They were travelling too fast for her to be able to get out without serious injury. She leaned out of the window and screamed again and again as loudly as she could. The horses galloped faster than ever; the bitter wind stung her cheeks and blew her cries away across the fields. There was no sign of anyone and she felt desperate.

Suddenly she heard shouts behind her. Two riders overtook the carriage—Polish police she imagined—and forced it to a halt. There followed a long altercation in Polish, with Elinor interjecting "Hôtel de l'Europe" at intervals. At last the man who had greeted her climbed off the box and one of the policemen took his place. He made the coachman turn round and drive back into the city while Elinor sat in the carriage, weak and gasping with relief at the narrowness of her escape.

All sorts of new thoughts struck her now. Maria's stomach upsets—were they really appendicitis? Elinor had often returned to her rooms in St. Petersburg to find them in some disorder. Might that not be because someone was systematically searching them? The court official who had made the arrangements for her journey, who was he really?

They reached the Hôtel de l'Europe and the policeman helped Elinor down. She was feeling weak about the knees and glad of his support. He gave her a significant look, put his finger to his lips enjoining silence, and mounting the box, drove off. She had clearly never been intended to reach the Hôtel de l'Europe and she was hardly surprised to find that no reservation had been made for her. Indeed, the whole hotel was completely full and there was no room vacant; nor were there any tickets or sleeper reservations awaiting her. Further, the surprised night porter explained that the Berlin Express went out the same night and not the following morning.

Elinor hurried back to the station, where to her joy she found a friend, Sir Savile Crossley, also waiting for the train. She flung herself upon him, begging his protection for the rest of the journey. He made his valet give up his sleeper, and Elinor in due course arrived in London without further incident.

There she saw Duckworth and obtained an advance against her Russian novel, which she had not yet begun. She visited her lawyers and paid them the advance, for onward transmission to the creditor, and then she went to lunch with Curzon. She told him of her Polish experiences, and he strongly advised her not to return to Russia, as there was clearly someone there who wished her out of the way. But Elinor would not consider this. She was now committed to finishing her Russian novel, and in any event she despised those who were deterred from a reasonable objective by the thought of physical danger. She rejected the same advice from Lord Redesdale, who recommended her not to mention her experiences to anyone at all inside Russia, even the Grand Duchess Vladimir. He himself would ask the Foreign Office to look after her on her return journey.

She went down to Lamberts, saw her family, collected her Egyptian diary, and began again the long journey back to St. Petersburg. On the way she meditated upon the incident in Warsaw. The plot had clearly been deeply laid and meticulously planned. To have disposed of her in St. Petersburg itself under the noses of the British Embassy would not have been easy. But in Warsaw, where no one knew she was, it was a different matter. If she had disappeared mysteriously there, it would have been days before anyone noticed. Clayton would have imagined her detained in Russia, the British Ambassador in Russia would have thought her safely in England. By the time the disappearance was noticed, the trail would have been cold.

What was the motive, she wondered. She had clearly a deadly enemy in Russia. Did someone imagine that she was dangerous, that she perhaps knew too much? Elinor remembered the story that the Czar had spoken of *Three Weeks* as being a book about his wife; she remembered the American's tale about the Czarina; and she came to the conclusion that the plot against her life had been hatched in Tsarskoe Selo and that her enemy was someone in the Imperial entourage.

But the suggestion that Elinor should travel via Moscow had been made by her friends at the Vladimir Palace and the arrangements for her to see Moscow had been made on the orders of the Grand Duchess Vladimir herself, whom Elinor refused to think even as a possible accessory before the fact. Who had made the arrangements for the rest of the journey?

We may well wonder now whether the whole invitation to Russia was not part of the trap, whether her magnificent reception by the Imperial court was not window-dressing designed to cover up her later, inexplicable disappearance, with the Grand Duchess Vladimir and the Grand Duchess Kiril acting, unwittingly and innocently, the part of decoys.

Elinor was back in St. Petersburg exactly a week after her departure. Everyone expressed surprise that she should have succeeded in making such a long and arduous journey so quickly. Elinor, gazing round at their friendly smiling faces, wondered exactly how surprised some of them were.

12.

With the lifting of court mourning and the arrival of the King of Bulgaria court life in St. Petersburg was now a whirl of gayety, and at last Elinor was able to wear her beautiful new dresses. The pomp and ceremony, the glittering uniforms, the magnificent jewels, the gorgeous court balls fulfilled all the Cinderella dreams of her childhood. Even more enjoyable were the numerous private balls and parties, with their atmosphere of hectic enjoyment and irresponsible hilarity.

In the middle of the night everyone would suddenly rush out, tumble into sleighs, and drive across the frozen Neva to the Islands, there to continue the party. No one dreamt of going to bed before four or five in the morning.

She came to realise that the Russians were, for all their veneer of sophistication, due mainly to their clothes and to their mastery of foreign languages, still very primitive underneath. They were not yet grown-up; children who put on their best drawing-room manners to go downstairs and meet guests, and upstairs romp wildly by themselves. The same unaccountable waves of gayety and depression would sweep through a party as through a nursery, to be followed by yet another exhibition of high spirits.

Elinor watched it all with acute, fascinated eyes, and one can only be amazed that she should have retained enough energy not only to participate in the nightly festivities, but also to write her novel.

She needed for one scene to describe a typical Russian country house, and the Grand Duchess Vladimir arranged for her to see one at Peterhof, three hours' journey away, which had belonged to Potëmkin, the friend of Catherine the Great. At a private ball given the same night by the Countess Shuvalov for the King of Bulgaria, the Minister for Foreign Affairs came up to Elinor at about five in the morning and presented a handsome young officer who had been instructed by Her Imperial Highness to show Elinor the country house. "If they are to be back before dark," the officer explained, "they must start almost at once."

Elinor had just time to change out of her ball dress and they set off. The road was appalling and their troika, a picturesque but uncomfortable vehicle, bumped mercilessly. The young officer clasped Elinor tightly to shield her from the bumps and reassure her. She was very tired when they finally reached the house but she insisted on seeing over it, much to the surprise and annoyance of the young officer. The house itself had been extensively renovated in the worst Victorian manner and only the astoundingly inadequate sanitary arrangements made any real impression on Elinor.

Soon after they started on the return journey a terrible snowstorm broke. The light disappeared and the troika was thrown in every direction while the horses floundered on through the deep drifts and the driving snow. Elinor and the officer huddled under the fur rug, and once again he tried to console her by clasping her tight in his arms and murmuring French love words, interspersed at the worst jolts by Russian swear words. Elinor was too cold and weary to care. She fell fast asleep in his arms and she was quite surprised to find, when she woke, that they were safely back at her hotel.

The Grand Duchess Vladimir summoned Elinor at the unusually early hour of half past nine the next morning to be reassured that Elinor had come through the experience safely. The Grand Duchess was lying in bed, having her ankle massaged, and Elinor related her experiences.

Had the officer behaved well, she was asked.

"*Comme un ange, Altesse,*" replied Elinor serenely.

Beside the bed was an enormous showcase filled with thousands of pounds' worth of diamonds and white and black pearls. The Grand Duchess explained that since she was still in mourning for her husband she could not look upon any coloured jewels.

"*Quelle délicatesse, madame!*" murmured Elinor, hiding her smile.

Elinor was given neither facilities nor encouragement to see anything of Russian life other than the life of the court and she felt that it would be an abuse of the warm hospitality which she received to try to do so. But one morning she happened to glance out of her window at about nine o'clock, long before anyone normally stirred, and she saw about thirty wretched men and women, barefoot and in rags despite the bitter weather, being driven along by Cossacks with whips. She asked the hall porter later who they were, and he answered that they were only foolish people who had come into the city without passports and he advised Madame that it was wiser for her not to look from her window in such a treacherous climate.

13.

In April 1910, Elinor travelled to London, returning once more to Russia in May, this time taking Margot with her. She was astonished at the change that had come over the Russian countryside with the abrupt arrival of spring. Russia had seemed to her a land of snow—it was strange to find it green and smiling.

The gayety of St. Petersburg, however, had been closed down once again by court mourning, this time for King Edward VII, and even Margot was obliged to go about in a long black veil looking like a widow. Once again Elinor was warmly welcomed by the whole court and once again her rooms were searched continually by some unknown agent.

Elinor's Russian novel, *His Hour,* was now complete, and she read it aloud to the assembled court in her beautiful, low, clear speaking voice of which she was so proud. The readings went on for ten days, at the end of which the Grand Duchess Vladimir expressed her unqualified approval and the book was dedicated to Her Imperial Highness "with grateful homage and devotion."

14.

His Hour, which was published in October of the same year, is one of the most characteristic and one of the best of Elinor's romances. Tamara Loraine, a prim missish young English widow, visiting Egypt with relatives, encountered a strange young man while she was seeing the Sphinx by moonlight. She later discovered him to be Prince Gritzko Milaslavski. At the Khedive's Ball he behaved towards her exactly as the real Gritzko had behaved towards Elinor, and he was again on the ship going to England, where the incident with the gipsy girl took place, in a very mild and fully clothed version.

Later she went to Russia to stay with her godmother, Princess Ardacheff (the Grand Duchess Vladimir), and took part in the social life of St. Petersburg. Here she met Gritzko again, who was obviously much attracted to her and with whom she rapidly fell in love. But she held him firmly at arm's length, feeling, not without reason, that he was merely trifling with her affections. Princess Ardacheff tried to throw them together but Tamara remained haughty and reserved.

Gritzko did many of the wild deeds of his real prototype. He was slightly wounded in a pistol duel he fought in a darkened room with Count Boris Varishkine over Tamara. He broke his favourite Arab horse's legs by riding it up and down the stairs of his palace. Tamara, like all Elinor's other heroines, reproached him for wasting his life and his opportunities so flagrantly; but whereas the English heroes would have flung themselves enthusiastically into politics at this point, Gritzko—a shrewd touch this—when it was suggested that he might do something about his serfs, merely shrugged his shoulders, hopeless and Russian.

Before she returned to England, it was arranged that the

whole party, including Tamara, should see Gritzko's country house near Moscow, spending the night in Moscow. On their return from visiting the house there was a fearful snowstorm and Gritzko contrived to lose the way in his sleigh, so that he and Tamara were benighted in a shooting-hut, deliberately provided in advance with food and champagne. There, faced with the prospect of dishonour, Tamara snatched the pistol from Gritzko's belt, held it to her head, saying that she would blow her brains out if he approached any nearer. After an hour or so of this, however, she fainted, and when she came to she knew by her disordered clothing and Gritzko's triumphant expression that the worst must have happened.

Gritzko proposed to her formally by letter, and poor Tamara, disgraced and anxious about the possible consequences of Gritzko's misdeed, had no choice but to accept. The wedding took place soon afterwards, quietly because of Lent, Tamara's English relatives being greatly astonished and disapproving strongly.

That night, in his palace, Gritzko showed Tamara his mother's room and the sanctuary with the lamp swinging before the Ikon, which no woman since her death had been allowed to see. There he confessed eternal love for Tamara, and she, deeply moved, responded by breaking down the icy reserve which had encased her for so long. She forgave him freely for his misdeed towards her, and only then did he confess that in the shooting-lodge, in the hour when he had had her at his mercy, he did but kiss her little feet.

15.

His Hour undoubtedly owed its great popularity to the character of Gritzko—masterful, tempestuous, passionate, untameable. It was his picture, and not Tamara's, which was shown on the frontispiece. Young ladies would lie on their beds reading *His Hour,* wondering if such a fascinating, romantic man could possibly exist and would ever come into their lives.

But for those readers who find Gritzko's irresponsibility and wildness a little tedious, the charm of the book lies in the amazingly vivid picture of the Russian court of 1910. We are a very long way from the imaginative backgrounds of Marie Corelli or the notorious inaccuracies of Ouida. Elinor's keen eye, her gift for descriptive writing served her in good stead in Russia. Over and over again the book is illumined by some little vivid touch which lights the scene in our eyes:

> Then her attention was diverted, as it always was each time she saw the blazing braziers and heaped up flaming piles of wood at the corners of the streets, since she had been in Russia. "How glad I am there is something to make the poor people warm," she said.
>
> "When it gets below twelve degrees it is difficult to en-joy life, certainly," the Prince agreed. "And, indeed, it is hard sometimes not to freeze."
>
> It was a strange lurid picture, the Isvostchiks drawn round, while the patient horses with their sleighs stood quiet some little distance off.

The romance of Gritzko and Tamara was full-blooded enough to satisfy Elinor's greediest admirers, but when we think of *His Hour* now, we think, not of them, but of the vanished splendours of Imperial Russia, the pomp and cere-mony, the balls and banquets, the uniforms and the jewels, the endless court mourning, the endless games of bridge, the feverish, irresponsible gayety, the hot rooms and the icy wind, the polonaises and the mazurkas, the sleigh bells and the snow.

Gritzko and Tamara settled down at Milaslav, but for once we can be certain that they did not live happily ever after. They can have had only seven years at most of tempestuous married life before the Revolution swept them away.

Elinor, in her descriptions of Russian life, did not venture any criticism, apart from Tamara's pep talk to Gritzko. Indeed, with the Grand Duchess Vladimir and most of the Russian court virtually looking over her shoulder as she wrote, she was hardly in a position to do so. She had misgivings about the value and the ethics of the life she was describing, but it is doubtful if she foresaw that it must end so soon in violence. And such a prophesy would hardly have been welcomed by her hosts, who had suggested the book and who had given her such opportunities and such help in writing it. Elinor could only record what she saw objectively and, as far as possible, sympathetically. It is, for that reason, all the more devastating an indictment.

16.

Elinor and Margot returned to England in June in company with a newly acquired Siberian cat, and Elinor picked up again the threads of her normal life at home.

Tonight we have dined with Field-Marshal Sir Evelyn Wood, rather deaf, seventy-two and as active as a two-year-old! He began by saying he enjoyed the rare pleasure of a long chat with me, that I was so intelligent and he loved *listening to me!!!* He said that he adored my books and wished to hear all about my Russian trip. I opened my lips to speak, but was not allowed to get the words out, as he had a number of long stories and remarks to make himself. I remembered Sterne—"I take heaven to witness that I never once opened the doors of my lips"—and remained perfectly silent, only nodding and smiling at intervals. He told my husband I was such a witty person!! and my Russian trip must have been extremely interesting!!!

For most of the summer of 1910, Elinor seems to have been

in a depressed frame of mind; partly due, no doubt, to reaction after the excitements of Russia, partly to a particularly
dismal spell of wet weather, and partly to the endless financial
struggle and the frustrations and aimlessness of life at home.
She was also grieving and worried over Clayton—and increasingly preoccupied with the painful intensity of her feelings for Curzon.

How dark! how cold! Leaden skies and damp lawns.
Glorious roses spoilt, tears in the air, a wild rebellion in me.
Day after day the same life, incomplete, hungry, with no
aim or end, only to get through with it. A strange nameless
excitement is in my veins. There is a magnet here in England and I am a needle, and between the two are all sorts
of paltry obstacles and some great ones, and I feel I could
scream to the night, "Tear me a path, sweep them aside,
let me be free to follow my bent."

In August she and Margot went to Cowes, which, with
King Edward so recently dead, was a very quiet affair that
year. Later they went on to stay with Billy Grant at Hillersdon. They returned to London at the beginning of September
and Elinor was visited by Milner.

I have seen him, my old friend. I wonder why in the
past I never loved him. He loved me and loves me still.
His stern face grew soft when his eyes rested upon me.
We talked for hours in the firelight and he forgot his duties
and his dinner. We visited past scenes—Stephaniewartz and
the new moon! I gave him a new moon out of the tiniest
diamonds—Cartier I remember designed it and made it into
a pin—he wears it still! We spoke of Nuremberg and our
joyous day there; of pine woods; of forests; of walks high
up the mountain where, gay as children, we used to wander;
and he reminded me of our playful afternoon when we got
lost and I was childish and pretended there were bears com-

ing out of the dark trees to eat us! and how I held his hand
and made him run down into the open early moonlight.
I had forgotten it all. We talked of that time seven years
ago. His face at last was full of wistful pain—it touched
me. And at last he went away and I fear he will not come
again. I cannot love him—I love only one. But even though
he will not see me, we shall write. That side of me he can
safely have, the intellectual. He shall be the friend of my
ideals.

In September she and Margot went to stay with Curzon
at Crag Hall, Derbyshire. It was a pleasant family party.
Curzon's daughters were much the same age as Elinor's, the
eldest, Lady Irene (now Baroness Ravensdale) being just
three years younger than Margot. Elinor mercilessly drove the
whole family out to picnic in the woods, cooking over an open
fire boiled bacon and potatoes for tea. Over more formal meals
in the house the assembled families would play the history
game. Curzon would describe in splendid, orotund language
some historical event and then ask one of the girls present to
identify it. In the evenings Curzon, like so many others, would
read Aristotle aloud to Elinor.

It was a happy party, but it seems to have added fuel to
the raging fires inside Elinor. She wrote in her diary on her
return to London:

O thou great one, calm and wise, accept this my cry of
worship. Know that for me thou canst do no wrong. Thou
art the mainspring of my life, for whom I would die, for
whom I would change my character, curb my instincts,
subjugate every wish, give my body and soul, worship
blindly. Maimed or sick, well or strong, thou art adored,
my arms for thy comfort, my soul for thy assuagement.

And a little later on she wrote:

I wrote and wrote and read and worked, then I went

alone into the garden. A great bed of white roses drew me, pale stars, more pure than in June. This is the Indian Summer, the first we have had of any sort this year, and it is calling me and mocking me, I am wild with unrest and pain. Oh night! with your black wings, enfold and soothe me, give me sleep, heavy and dreamless. Blunt my longing, give me peace.

But later her spirits began to improve and on October 17, her forty-sixth birthday, she wrote:

I have seen a vision. Away with all sorrow or weariness or despair! Away with all sad and depressing things! The glory of it has gilded all the horizon. All is well. Never again can dark thoughts come to me. High above all earthly things shines the light. To thee eternal God I cry aloud in praise and thanksgiving. Shadows are passed. All is well.

She and Margot spent all Halloween staying with Lord Ormonde at Kilkenny Castle in Ireland. On her return she stayed with Lady Jeune (now Lady St. Helier) at her house in Portland Place. She had been accustomed to stay with the Jeunes whenever she was in London, first at their house in Harley Street and later in Portland Place. But she decided that it would be more convenient now if she had her own *pied-à-terre* in London and she took a small suite at the Ritz, which, despite financial crises, she retained for the next two years.

17.

Clayton longed to winter again in the South of France, and Mrs. Kennedy encouraged this wish. Elinor, remembering all the trips abroad he had given her, acquiesced. A warmer climate, too, might be good for his asthma. Accordingly he, Mrs. Kennedy, and Margot set out for the Mediterranean in November to look for a suitable hotel. They went first to Bormes before finally deciding on the Hôtel Beau-Rivage at St. Raphaël.

Elinor joined them later in the year, stopping for a while in Paris.

I am better. There are angels of some kind of peace around me. I seem to feel no sorrow. I seem to realise that all things have phases and the pendulum swings both ways. The atmosphere of Paris suits me. Here, and in Russia, there are no quaintly jealous women. They understand and appreciate what they are good enough to call my "esprit." I have my place, conceded with homage. All the great ones of the earth who are here for the time do me honour. And although honour will not lift the ache from my heart, it will soothe one's self-esteem.

Then she motored on to St. Raphaël, stopping, as was her habit, to look in the antique shops she passed for good French furniture, and finding on this occasion the lovely piece of silk brocade whose design she adopted for her bookplate.

Also staying in the Beau-Rivage was Professor F. H. Bradley, the most distinguished metaphysician of his age. He had come to St. Raphaël for peace and especially to get away from children, whom he detested. But he was apparently intrigued by Elinor, for he came up soon after her arrival and introduced himself as a fellow author. With him she struck up one of those faithful and incongruous friendships which were such a feature of her life.

They would walk together through the pine woods round St. Raphaël and Valescure discussing philosophy in general and reincarnation in particular. Like Jeune and Milner he helped to fill in some more of the gaps in her education, in particular the nature of philosophy since Aristotle, which was still largely a closed book to her. "And there were some things," she wrote in her memoirs, "which I really believe I might have taught him too, had we met earlier in both our lives."

They exchanged signed copies of their works and sat side by side in the sunshine, Bradley reading *His Hour*—he had already read *Three Weeks*—and Elinor working her way doggedly through *Appearance and Reality*. Bradley also spent a good deal of time in trying to improve Elinor's spelling, an impossible task, for though she was by now a willing pupil, it was too late for her to alter her own individual ideas about the way words should be spelt.

Elinor returned to England at the beginning of 1911 and paid a brief visit to America, seeing friends in and around New York and discussing her books with her American publisher, Appleton. She was back again in England shortly before Easter, collected Juliet from her school at Eastbourne, and took her out to join the family at St. Raphaël.

At the end of April, Clayton, Mrs. Kennedy, and Juliet returned home, while Elinor and Margot went on for a motor trip through Italy. The financial cloud had for the moment been blown away by the large sales of *His Hour,* and the Italian trip was a specially happy experience. Elinor was at the time enthralled by the Renaissance and she and Margot spent many enjoyable days exploring Perugia and San Gimignano. They remained in Italy for six weeks, returning to England at the beginning of June.

18.

During Elinor's absence in Italy, Clayton had supplemented the regular allowance which she made him by borrowing a thousand pounds from a friend against an IOU, which he had neither the resources nor the intention to redeem. The IOU came into Elinor's possession on her return from Italy and she was not only exasperated but humiliated; humiliated especially, because Clayton had got the loan from Curzon, the one person from whom, in Elinor's mind, it was utterly unthinkable to accept money. She saw herself placed in a position unbearably mortifying.

At all costs the IOU must be redeemed at once. But after the expenditure of the winter and the spring, the heavy travelling expenses and hotel bills incurred in St. Raphaël and Italy, the family exchequer was almost empty. There was not a thousand pounds in it.

In her shame and desperation Elinor went to R. D. Blumenfeld, the editor of the *Daily Express*, who was not only a friend and neighbour but also an admirer of her works. She asked him if he could help her to earn a thousand pounds as quickly as possible. He replied that he would willingly pay a thousand pounds for the first British serial rights of a new Elinor Glyn novel—provided that it was delivered before the serial at present running in the paper finished in three weeks' time. The new novel, he added, should be at least ninety thousand words. Elinor murmured something about a half-finished novel in her drawer which might be suitable and hurried back to Essex.

There was, of course, no half-finished novel in her drawer. She had at that moment not even an idea for one. Back at Lamberts she retired at once to bed, with a stack of blocks and her favourite stylo, now badly worn down on one side. She instructed Maria that she was not to be disturbed and she settled down to write the opening chapters of *The Reason Why*.

For the next three weeks she hardly got out of bed at all. Meals were brought to her on trays—in between whiles she was fortified with coffee and brandy. She wrote most of the day and far into the night. Beside her on the bed table was the terrible IOU, haunting her, driving her on even when she felt tired out. She finished the novel in eighteen days, and the first instalment appeared in the *Daily Express* on Monday, July 3, 1911, exactly three weeks after her commission to write it. She received the cheque for one thousand pounds the same day, as promised, and was able to redeem the IOU. Then she lay back, saddened and utterly exhausted.

She seems, strangely enough, to have felt no resentment against either of the two men, the borrower or the lender, who had placed her in such an invidious position, from which she had extricated herself only by straining her creative energy to its utmost limit. All her resentment at the episode was concentrated upon the unfortunate book itself. In dashing off a potboiler in such haste, without thought of style, construction, plot, or grammar, she had prostituted her art and forfeited for ever in the minds of all right-thinking people her literary reputation. For the rest of her life she always considered *The Reason Why* the very worst book she ever wrote. "My only choice on this occasion," she wrote, "seemed to lie between the degradation of myself or of my pen. *The Reason Why* is my witness that I chose the pen."

19.

Elinor's three principal literary advisors, Curzon, Milner, and Bradley, urged her continually to take more pains and trouble over her books. Curzon was especially severe on her for her "cursed facility." He wanted her to take her time and write a book which would do full justice to her literary gifts and of which she could be justifiably proud.

The opportunity to write this book seemed to present itself at this moment. *The Reason Why* was not yet out and there was no cause to hurry with a new book. And by writing such a book she would not only give herself deep satisfaction, but regain her literary standards and reputation, damaged by recent potboiling. The book was to be her *credo*, the embodiment, in the form of a love story, of her beliefs and attitude towards life. She would distil into it her love for classical

Greece. She would call the book and the heroine Halcyone, after the fairy maiden, the daughter of the beach and the wind, described in Kingsley's *The Heroes*.

She wrote the novel that autumn and winter at the Hôtel des Réservoirs at Versailles, while the rest of the family gathered once again at St. Raphaël. When the book was finished, Elinor went on herself to St. Raphaël and gave the manuscript to Bradley, who was also wintering there. He read it carefully, suggested some revisions and alterations, and provided her with the Greek quotations she required. He also corrected her myriad spelling mistakes in a handwriting so vile that even the printers could not read it.

20.

*Halcyone,** published in June 1912, and dedicated to the memory of Sir Francis Jeune, was Elinor's own favourite among her books. She prized it higher than *Three Weeks* or *The Visits of Elizabeth,* or *His Hour,* and for this reason it deserves special consideration in the canon of her works. It was also, we may note, the first of her novels in which the hero had a career to follow.

The story of *Halcyone* is almost unbearably poignant in view of what was to come later. Halcyone La Sarthe lived alone with two impoverished aunts in the dilapidated La Sarthe Chase. She was a strange solitary child, pure, innocent, loving, darting about the woods like a will-o'-the-wisp, communing with nature, uneducated but with a naturally cultivated taste and mind, revering almost to idolatry a bust of Aphrodite which she had found in an attic, herself in love with ancient Greece.

A retired professor came to live in a cottage outside the gates. Halcyone made friends with him, nicknamed him

* Published in some American editions under the title *Love Itself*.

Cheiron, and persuaded him to teach her Greek and to give her an extensive classical education. There one day she met another of his pupils, John Derringham, now a rising politician, ambitious, egotistical, with a tendency to deliver rather pompous lectures on the necessity for aristocratic government. He was at this stage not the least interested in Halcyone.

Many years later, when she was grown-up, she met him again at Cheiron's house. It was necessary for his political career that he marry someone with money and he was now wooing a rich American widow, Mrs. Cricklander, who had leased a house near by. Mrs. Cricklander had her culture purveyed to her daily, predigested, by an English companion specially employed for that purpose, and by this resourceful means she was able to keep her head above water in a company whose conversation was almost exclusively classical and even, apart from a few lapses such as confusing Cheiron with Charon, to impress John Derringham, himself a fine scholar.

John Derringham, however, met Halcyone and fell in love with her, although he had always scoffed at love.

The moon was growing brighter and a strange mysterious shimmer was over everything, as though the heat of the day were rising to give welcome and fuse itself with the night.

He was alone with the bird who throbbed from the copse, and as he sat in the sublime stillness he fancied he saw some does peep forth.

But where was she—the Nymph of the Night?

His heart ached, the longing grew intense until it was a mighty force. At last he buried his face in his hands; it was almost agony that he felt.

When he had uncovered his eyes again he saw, far in the distance, a filmy shadow. It seemed to be now real, and now a wraith, as it flitted from tree to tree, but at last he knew it was real—it was she—Halcyone! . . .

All reason, all resolution left him. He held out his arms.

"My love!" he cried. "I have waited for you! Ah, so long!"

And Halcyone allowed herself to be clasped next his heart.

They had such a number of things to tell one another about love. He who had always scoffed at its existence was now eloquent in his explanation of the mystery. And Halcyone, who had never had any doubts, put her beautiful thoughts into words. Love meant everything—it was just he—John Derringham. She was no more herself, but had come to dwell in him.

She was tender and absolutely pure in her broad loyalty, concealing nothing of her fondness, letting him see that, if she were Mistress of the Night, he was master of her soul.

He would marry her at once, though the marriage would have to be kept secret, since if it was known that he had a wife, he would have to keep her in the stately splendour his position demanded, and which he could not afford. Halcyone, loving and trustful, agreed simply. Coming to meet her at the arranged rendezvous a few days later, he fell, a little unromantically, into the ha-ha and knocked himself out; and Halcyone, distraught at his failure to appear, was taken off herself to London by her legal guardian.

John Derringham was nursed slowly back to health by Mrs. Cricklander, at the end of which time he found himself engaged to her. Too late he came to his senses and realised that she wanted him only for his position; by then he was in honour bound to her. Halcyone, heartbroken at seeing the announcement of his engagement in the paper, and Cheiron, who now knew everything and despised John for his ignoble conduct towards Halcyone, went off together for a trip to Italy, taking the bust of Aphrodite, from which she was never separated.

Mrs. Cricklander, however, discovered that the government was about to fall and, having no wish to be for years

the wife of an opposition leader, she dropped John and trans-
ferred her attentions to a Radical. John, fearful that he might
have lost Halcyone for ever, pursued her and found her on
top of a tower in Perugia. There on his knees before her he
begged her forgiveness and love. They were happily married
soon afterwards.

21.

The book was in many ways the most ambitious Elinor had
yet attempted—a study in pure and simple love, trusting, openhearted, scorning all tricks, all prevarications, all flirting,
despised, unshakeable, and finally triumphant. Halcyone herself is, of course, yet another self-portrait of the authoress,
this time as she wished to see herself, idealised almost to the
point of incredibility. Halcyone, the fey child, is frankly un-
believable, the dream child of one who never for a moment
understood children. Grown-up, she is a little more solid, a
little more three-dimensional. But she is absurdly overpraised;
her natural purity of soul, nobility of mind, and cultivation
of taste are emphasised to the point of satiety. Yet the evident
sincerity with which the character was conceived and the devotion with which she was described are strangely moving in
their intensity.

Cheiron, the professor, was a loving portrait of Bradley. And
we are given many indications of the personage who inspired
John Derringham. Like Curzon, he was a fine scholar and
had been Captain of the Oppidans at Eton. His aristocratic
descent was, like Curzon's, partly obscured by a more immediate background of poverty. Like Curzon he was an ambitious politician. Like Curzon he had already been Foreign
Under-Secretary.

We cannot think that Curzon, when he read Halcyone,
failed to recognise himself; and, equally, we cannot think that

he can have been very pleased at the character displayed there, a selfish, egotistical man who was prepared to put his own aims and ambitions before anything else; who believed, at any rate initially, that only the male sex could have souls; and who was told forcibly by the professor at the end that he was not worthy of Halcyone. The letter which Curzon wrote to Elinor after she sent him a copy has not been preserved, but she said in later years that he merely acknowledged the receipt of the book and pointed out two spelling mistakes in her covering letter.

The critics viewed the book with qualified approval and Dr. Edward Lyttelton, endeavouring to atone for his incivility over *Three Weeks,* wrote a letter of appreciation. But the rest of the great public—the thousands all over the world who loved Elinor's books—were deeply disappointed. After the strong situations and the brightly coloured passions of her last three novels they were puzzled by the gentle story and the quiet half-tones of the new book. They were bewildered by the feyness, by the unleavened mixture of piety and paganism, and by the continual classical allusions. They were frightened away by the unpronounceable title, by the Aphrodite on the frontispiece, and by the awe-inspiring inscription on the cover:

$$\text{ΔΡΑΣΑΝΤΙ ΠΑΘΕΙΝ}$$

which they were expected to translate for themselves.* Financially, the book was an almost complete failure.

22.

Margot was now eighteen, and in the summer of 1912, Elinor took a little house in Green Street, Park Lane, for her first London season. Elinor redecorated the house lavishly,

---

* "To him that doeth, so let it be done." Aeschylus, *Choephoroe.*

and there was hardly enough money left at the end for taxis, much less to give a dance. House decorating was fast becoming Elinor's ruling passion, amounting almost to mania, and while it was upon her, all thoughts of economy, never very strong, were thrown to the winds.

Margot, however, was duly presented at court and was entertained a good deal, and Elinor was able to look at society through her daughter's eyes and observe how it had changed and relaxed its formalities since the days when she had been a debutante. The summer was clouded by Clayton's health, which was now very poor, and Margot would usually go back to Lamberts for the week end to look after him.

In taking the house in Green Street, Elinor had a second purpose besides launching Margot; that was to repay some of Curzon's hospitality, and he did in fact come to dine several times, though not as often as she hoped. Her feelings towards him had not weakened in the least with the passing of the years. Despite his frequent letters and his present of a magnificent diamond and sapphire ring—the only jewels she ever accepted from an admirer—she had the inescapable feeling that their romance was not advancing towards any very happy outcome. On receiving a letter from him about this time she wrote in her diary:

> The writing always makes my heart beat. Why are we such slaves to emotion, that the sight of traced words on paper causes sudden physical sensation of thumping pulse, and heat or cold? Alas! the power of the Loved One, even at a distance! When shall I be able to dominate these things! Alas, when? One can obtain dominion over all outward demonstration with a strong will, but who can crush the soul's ache—I wish I knew.

It was only to be expected that she would be considerably influenced by Curzon's political views. Her own convictions were, by nature, high Tory and many of his opinions confirmed and crystallised her own instinctive but less explicit thoughts. Amongst other things she disapproved deeply of the suffragette movement, thinking it both undignified and unfeminine.

And as women by their greatness, tact and goodness influence affairs and governments and countries, through men, a thousandfold more than the cleverest suffragettes could influence these things by securing votes for women— I do implore you, Caroline, when your turn comes to be the inspiration of some nice young husband, to use your power over him to make him feel truly the splendour of his inheritance in being an Englishman, and his tremendous obligation to come up to the mark.*

But women were not only the inspiration and the guiding light; they were also, in the last resort, the end in themselves. She wrote in her notebook:

If a women excites a man's senses but remains a problematic possession, the man will skimp his duty, neglect his friends and snatch even hours from sleep to spend them in her company.

To Elinor there was nothing illogical or mutually inconsistent in this dual conception of the role of women. Nor at the time did she see the irony in herself being a stern opponent of the emancipation of women—she who had shocked society by earning her own living and by doing so had helped to blaze the trail towards feminine independence.

23.

In the course of the season Elinor and Margot went once again to Cowes and in the Squadron Gardens there Teresa,

* *Letters to Caroline.*

Marchioness of Londonderry, related to Elinor the story of a woman she knew. This story struck Elinor forcibly and she used it, with very little alteration, for the plot of her next novel, *The Sequence*.

After Cowes they went to Paris, where they stayed, as usual, at the Ritz. They were welcomed warmly by Olivier, the headwaiter, who was now an old friend. For lunch every day they ate lobster, raspberries, and cream; it was Elinor's favourite meal and she saw no reason why she should have to eat something she liked less well every second or third day merely for the sake of variety. Olivier called the meal, "Comme d'Habitude," and gave them a special reduction.

From Paris they went on to Carlsbad, returning at the end of the summer to the Hôtel des Réservoirs at Versailles, where Elinor finished *The Sequence*. In December they returned to England to prepare for the usual family migration to St. Raphaël.

In the new year, 1913, Elinor and Margot went first to stay with Curzon at Hackwood; then they went on to Paris and Cannes. Mrs. Kennedy went direct to St. Raphaël as advance party. Clayton was due to join her there, but he never came.

He was far from well physically, and by now his moral disintegration was almost complete. He had been living on his wife's charity for almost five years and he could bear the humiliation of his position no longer. He gathered up his remaining possessions, including some of his family silver, and disappeared into the blue. No one knew where he was until a letter, addressed not to any of the family but to Dixie, about his clothes, disclosed that he was in Constantinople. The marriage had been a long time a-dying, but it was dead at last.

One may be tempted to think that Elinor's marriage to Clayton Glyn brought her little except disillusion and disappointment and heavy financial burdens. From a bright start it had declined, at first slowly, with occasional lifts back into the sunlight, and then with an increasing acceleration down into the shadows. But to represent her marriage only as a story of decline and frustration is to present a convincing but incomplete picture. There were times, especially in the early years, when Clayton made her very happy; and while he still had the power he gave her everything she asked for—except romance. Above all, he gave her her position as his wife.

Had he not married her, her life would have been very much harder than it was. As a spinster, her place in society every year more difficult, mortified by the fact that for all her beauty no man apparently wanted her as a wife, hard up, a burden to her friends and relatives, she would only have been Poor Nellie, consumed even more with frustrated romantic longings and self-pity. As a spinster, her articles upon love and marriage, her position as an acknowledged authority on the subject, which she became in the twenties, would have been less acceptable. She would probably have written books, but they might have had to be rather different books. She might well have made money, but without the advice and re-straining influence of her daughters and sons-in-law she might easily have ended friendless and destitute like Ouida.

In marrying her Clayton Glyn gave her that essential possession, a place in the world, which she was never to lose, and for that she forgave him everything. And it was a debt which she repaid in full.

24.

As soon as the news came through, Elinor and Margot joined Mrs. Kennedy in St. Raphaël and there they waited for further developments, which did not, in fact, materialise. Early in the spring they returned to England, and arrangements were made to sell Lamberts. Essex was Clayton's home county, but now that he was gone there was no need for

Elinor to remain there any longer. The family moved for the moment into the Green Street house.

The final breakup of Elinor's marriage was, of course, her private affair only. Life must go on. Books must be published, her position in society retained; and that summer she went as usual with Margot to Cowes and to Carlsbad. On the way to Carlsbad news came that Clayton, now coming slowly home from Constantinople, was lying ill at a hotel in Interlaken and Margot went there to nurse him. When he recovered, he returned to England, where he took a small house in Richmond. Here he lived quietly for the next two years, alone but not unhappy, visited at intervals by Elinor and his daughters.

The Green Street tenancy was now up, and Elinor decided that henceforward she and her family would live mainly in France. Accordingly she took a long lease of No. 5 Avenue Victor Hugo, Parc des Princes, outside Paris, and proceeded to redecorate it in her usual extravagant style. Precautionary thoughts were brushed aside: beautiful brocades were specially woven; she did not even ask for estimates for the alterations she planned and the builders' bill alone for the house came to more than a thousand pounds.

25.

In the autumn the whole family moved to Paris. It was a pleasant house at the far end of the Avenue Victor Hugo, near Boulogne-sur-Seine, but they soon found that it was too far out from the centre of Paris to be convenient. Elinor had had several objectives in taking the house. She wanted somewhere as dissimilar as possible from Essex, with its unhappy associations; she had always wanted to live in France; she wanted Margot to taste the delights of French society and Juliet to finish her education there. She wanted a home that was absolutely her own, decorated and furnished by herself for herself; and she wanted a home where she could receive and entertain Curzon in the style which he showed her at Hackwood and which she had not been able to reproduce adequately in Green Street. She wrote inviting him to come, but he responded, temporising.

One day, December 3, she saw in an illustrated paper photographs of Curzon and Milner, the two eminent statesmen who were her closest friends, and she was moved to contrast them in her diary.

> Today in an illustrated paper there is a picture of you, my King, as you sat when the speech was done, leaning your proud head against the wall. You look weary and rather sad as you gaze into distance and the picture pulls at my heartstrings. I long to draw you to rest and caress those lines of care away. Ah me!
>
> And side by side on the page there is my old friend addressing a vast multitude too. How strange that you should be so near together! How different are your personalities, both so great, both true and noble and splendid, and yet the sight of one picture moves every passionate emotion and the other stirs a gentle admiration. And you are both counted as cold and stern and indifferent. Women, they say, are things of naught in both of your lives!

Curzon finally came in the spring and was warmly welcomed by the whole family, including Juliet, who had been taken away from school at Eastbourne to attend classes in Paris. Elinor discovered to her astonishment that Curzon had not been to Versailles since he was a small boy and she took him there, leading him with closed eyes across the terrace, as she had led Innes-Ker nine years before.

"Now!" said Elinor, turning him round.

Curzon gazed at the great façade for a long time without speaking, while Elinor waited with bated breath.

Finally he gave his opinion. "Architecturally correct, but monotonous." Elinor, once again deflated, was left wondering whether anybody but she appreciated the most wonderful sight in the world.

During the winter she worked on a new novel, *The Man and the Moment,* which had been commissioned by her American publishers, and which they wished to appear in America before it appeared in England. The expenses of redecorating the house and living expenses generally had been heavy and Elinor worked fast and hard to meet the alarming bills which were now coming in. Juliet attended her classes and Margot experienced the fashionable merry-go-round of smart Paris society, which Elinor had enjoyed in her day.

Elinor herself entertained a certain amount at her big house. At one of these parties, reclining on a sofa in a purple alcove, she read aloud from her works, both in the original and in the French translation, to a resplendent assembly which included the Duchesse de Luynes, the Duchesse de Rohan, the Duchesse de Noailles, the Marquise de Mun and the Comtesse de Segur. Such readings were not unusual among established authors of the time and Elinor's books had a high reputation with French literary critics—higher than they had in England.

But France was changed and Elinor was troubled at the new atmosphere in Paris, the hectic, feverish pursuit after amusement, no matter how bizarre or distasteful. Even among the upper classes the reserve and dignity which Elinor had thought practically synonymous with French aristocracy seemed to have gone.

The onrush of the war took the French upper classes completely by surprise. Elinor had already arranged to return to England for the season, being dissatisfied with French society, and had fortunately made her travelling arrangements well in advance. On the Quatorze Juillet she took the girls to Versailles to see the fireworks, let off in front of a huge crowd assembled round the Bassin de Neptune. The holiday spirit seemed undisturbed and there was no suggestion of calamity in the air.

On July 23 they went to a château near Paris for the week end and both they and their hostess were surprised and offended at the sudden departure of the Austrian Ambassador, who was one of the guests. It was Fielder, Elinor's chauffeur, who mentioned that he thought there might be going to be a war, and everyone searched hurriedly in the newspapers to see what he could mean and with whom the war could be.

The family reached England on July 29 to find that English society was almost equally unaware of what was going on. Leaving Juliet staying with Lucy at her house in Lennox Gardens, Elinor and Margot went, as usual, to Cowes.

They found the place in commotion at a rumour that the regatta might be put off. Most people refused to take this seriously but Lord Ormonde, the Commodore of the Squadron, told Elinor that he thought there must be something in it, for Prince Henry of Prussia, who never failed to come, had cancelled his visit.

BOOK FIVE

The War Correspondent

1914–1919

I.

During the rest of 1914, Elinor and her family lived in London. Mrs. Kennedy took a flat on the ground floor of Shelley Court, Tite Street, Chelsea, while Elinor stayed at the Ritz. Margot enlisted as a V.A.D. and worked in the kitchen of a hospital in Park Lane. Juliet, not yet sixteen, refused to go back to school, and instead put her hair up, pretended to be older than she was, and became a V.A.D., too. Elinor herself hankered to be given some war work, and she was greatly attracted by a suggestion that she should return to France and write articles for the American press about the devastated areas in France. The necessary permits and authorities, however, were not immediately forthcoming, and she remained for the moment in London, writing articles for the English press.

In 1915, impatient of the delay in completing the arrangements for her to write her articles, she returned to Paris, leaving her daughters in the care of their grandmother at Shelley Court. She decided that her house in the Avenue Victor Hugo was too far out and she stayed now at the Ritz, where she would be nearer to the heart of things.

Paris had altered greatly from the hectic days before the war. Everything was very serious, sober, and quiet. But at the same time Elinor noticed none of the earnestness, the appreciation of the gravity of the situation, the desire to be doing something, too, which was so apparent in London, even though the war was being fought on French soil.

She was especially disappointed at the attitude of the aristocracy. Very few of them were fighting; most of them were living quietly on their country estates and the rest had obtained safe jobs. Etiquette did not allow any well-born French girl to be a nurse or to do any form of war work at all, and it was solemnly explained to Elinor that no girl who demeaned herself in such a way could possibly hope to make a good marriage. Elinor remembered her own daughters in the hospital kitchen in London and was amazed at the different attitude—an attitude which persisted to the end of the war.

Paris was a depressing place at this time and Elinor's diary makes gloomy reading. The war was not over by Christmas and no one had yet developed his second wind. A great number of Elinor's friends, many of whom had been regular officers or in the reserve of their yeomanry or county regiments, had been killed.

Her permits to visit the battle areas had still not come through and she used to pass the time by taking flowers and cigarettes to the British Hospital in the Trianon Palace Hotel at Versailles. She would spend much of the day there, talking to the men, listening to their accounts of the battles. On one occasion she arrived at the hospital, her arms full of red roses, just as a man was wheeled past on his way to the operating theatre. He looked ghastly, and the sister, when Elinor glanced enquiringly at her, shook her head sadly. On a sudden impulse Elinor pushed a rose into his hand and told him that if he held on to it he would be all right. The man's fingers closed on the rose and he smiled feebly. Later the surgeon told Elinor that the man had held on to the rose even under the anaesthetic and was now making an almost miraculous recovery.

The permits, however, still failed to appear, and Elinor began to feel that she was achieving nothing by remaining in Paris. She was becoming very depressed, both by the war news and by the lack of interest of all her French friends in the war. The news also came that Clayton was seriously ill, and in the summer of 1915, Elinor returned to London.

She took a flat on the top floor of Shelley Court while her mother and her daughters remained on the ground floor. As usual, Elinor redecorated the flat completely before she moved in, giving the living-room varnished purple walls.

In March, Duckworth published her new novel, *The Man and the Moment,* which had been brought out the previous year in America. It was a light romance, very slight and artificial, but it was written with a great deal of charm and skill. The opening chapters, indeed, have a gayety reminiscent of *The Vicissitudes of Evangeline.*

But perhaps the foremost claim that *The Man and the Moment* has to our attention is that in it appears the first mention of "it," that personal magnetic quality whose discovery and identification was later to bring Elinor fame and fortune almost as great as that brought her by *Three Weeks.*

> I know one particular case of it in a friend of mine. No matter what he does, one always forgives him. It does not depend upon looks either—although this actual person is abominably good-looking—it does not depend upon intelligence or character or—anything—as you say, it is just "it." Now you have "it" and the Princess, perfectly charming though she is, has not.

2.

For the summer of 1915, Curzon lent Elinor his villa, Naldera, at Broadstairs. Her personal feelings for him were, if anything, even stronger than they had been seven years earlier, though she could not help hoping that in due course their relationship might be established on a more serene and simple, though not less intense, basis.

But, if she could have seen it, the writing was already on the wall. On the twenty-seventh of May, Curzon joined the Coalition Government as Lord Privy Seal, and from that moment onwards his political ambition was once more in the ascendant.

Shortly afterwards she was present at a public speech which he made, and she wrote in her diary:

What magic in a personality! Oh! my heart! to see you there, master of those ten thousand people, calm, aloof, unmoved. To hear your noble voice and listen to your masterly argument. To sit there, one of a rough crowd, gazing up at your splendid face and to know that in other moments that proud head can lie upon my breast even as a little child. Ah me! these are moments in life worth living for. And what matters to me that sometimes you are cruel and aloof even to me? Have you not a right to be what you please since you are certainly king of my being? Did I write some while ago that my soul worship of you was dead! Poor fool! It is greater than ever. It slept, but not with the sleep of death. No other man and no other voice can move me ever. Only you, beloved one in all the world. I have been through many days of anguishing sorrow. You will never know, my heart, the agony. But now I am calm again and I have seen you playing your great part in the fierce light and I am satisfied.

Curzon had taken a long lease of Montacute House in Somerset, and he suggested now that Elinor might like to go down there in the autumn and winter and supervise its redecoration for him. This suggestion appealed strongly to her and she spent a large part of the rest of that year, and of the following year, 1916, at Montacute. Normally she could not endure room temperatures to be below seventy degrees and it is tribute to her devotion both to Curzon and to house decoration that she should have been willing to live in the wintry weather in the cold stone house, much of the time being spent on the top of stepladders in large, unheated rooms.

3.

In November 1915, Clayton Glyn died, his long years of illness and dependence at last over. Elinor had the painful task of going through all his papers and learning so much about him which he had never allowed her to know during his lifetime, and mourning again the decay of her once bright and happy marriage.

Soon afterwards she became ill herself and had to remain in bed for several weeks. On her recovery she determined that she must do something active to help in the war and she joined the canteen in Grosvenor Gardens, choosing the night shift, explaining that at her age it no longer mattered what happened to her.

> I was never a good waitress [she wrote], always stupid and muddling, but I could sweep and clean nicely and finally became one of the most expert of the washing-up staff.

In company with other voluntary workers she washed up thousands of greasy plates, knives, and forks, and scrubbed tables and floors with those immaculate, lily-white hands of which she was so proud. She was bullied by the professional canteen manager, who enjoyed humiliating the more aristocratic or celebrated members of her voluntary staff.

Elinor derived a considerable satisfaction from her work, feeling that at last she was doing something to help and liking the direct contact her work gave her with the troops. The worst part of the night shift was the trudge home at four in the morning to Tite Street, for there was no transport available and, petrol being unobtainable, no one kept a car.

In between her shifts she would go down to Montacute or sleep in her flat in Tite Street. She was also at this time writing articles for the British press, and in the intervals of everything else she was at work on her new novel, *The Career of Katherine Bush.*

4.

In the spring of 1916 the first suspicions came to Elinor that her friendship with Curzon was drawing towards its close. She wrote in her diary:

Oh, I realise no man matters but my Lord, and I must crush all that and be a cynic and when I see you, oh my heart, I must be gay and not feel, and there is some change, I know it, in me. It is the third stage, it is of a tender place that is growing a hard surface to protect itself. I am afraid of suffering but I must be gay, for of what good to be tortured? The moment might come when you would again think only of what was *best for you,* and then what would become of me? Should I die, or simply go to hell?

But how shall I feel when I see you, Oh my heart? That is what I do not know. I must of course be cold and friendly, since that is what you wished, but what will it be if, as ever, your much loved face moves me to the passionate tenderness of old. Surely I am strong and can meet you calmly. Surely my will has not been all in vain.

However, her will could not meet the demand she made of it.

Tonight I have seen you again and I know that, however

it goes for this world, I can never love you less. You are my darling, my beloved Lord. However you will, you can come back to me and I will love and soothe you and be tender and true, and some day, since I believe in God, I shall have peace and my heart's desire and no more pain.

Meanwhile let angels watch over you and keep you. I care not whether you are selfish, as everyone says, or no. I care not if you are famous, or no. Nothing can change my absolute love. Darling one, goodnight, and let my love bring you rest and peace.

Elinor had been trying for years to conquer either her love or her misgivings. She had not succeeded in doing either. When the blow finally fell, it fell with a suddenness that was overwhelming.

On December 10, 1916, Lloyd George formed his War Cabinet, with Curzon as a member; and on looking in *The Times* the following day to read about the appointment Elinor saw there the notice of Curzon's engagement to Mrs. Alfred Duggan.

There had been no letter beforehand warning her of what was to come; nor was there any letter afterwards. If only there had been some word of warning, some word of explanation, it might have hurt less. Their faithful, passionate friendship had lasted for eight and a half years, and now it was severed by one public blow of the axe. She never saw him or wrote to him again. His letters to her, nearly five hundred of them, she burnt herself—the funeral pyre of her last and greatest love.

5.

In April 1917, Elinor returned to Paris, since the arrangements for her to write for the American press and the permits to visit the battlefields had at last come through. She was astonished at the change that had come over France in the two years she had been back in England. The subdued, depressed note of Paris had completely gone. Now there were gay crowds everywhere. The Ritz swarmed with expensively dressed women in silver fox capes; both the *beau monde* and the *demi-monde* now congregated there and it was impossible to tell them apart. In the evenings, however, the Ritz would be empty, everyone having gone to the Café de Paris, where the best of the cocottes assembled, or to the Folies Bergère, at the bar of which a lower type of courtesan, usually only seen on the streets, was available. "They are the most appalling-looking creatures, painted, diseased, and half-drunk with absinthe or drugs," she wrote.

No one had any war work to do. Indeed, no one seemed to take any interest in the war. "The sight of the whole company of idlers at tea the first day struck me as dreadful, after seeing the hard work done in England and remembering the touching belief which still prevailed that everyone who had work in France must be a hero." Elinor was much chaffed at the appointment of a food controller in England; the thought of food regulations was to French society incredible, the sort of absurdity which only the English could think of. No one had any knowledge of or interest in the German submarine menace, then at its height.

A French Comtesse, hearing about Elinor's work in the canteen, commented, "I suppose it feels wonderful to work. I must try it—a new emotion."

Elinor loved France deeply. It was her second home and some of her happiest days had been spent there. She filled her books with French phrases, she spoke its language as easily as her own. She was a passionate admirer of French art, French architecture and furniture, French habits, French civilisation. She loved Paris. Above all, she loved the French nobility, whom she had been taught to admire from the moment she could understand human speech, and whom she had herself always thought to be the embodiment of the virtues that she most admired.

She was bitterly disappointed now. Apart from the Duchesse de Rohan, whose house was a hospital, and the Comtesse de la Beravdière who had turned her big *hôtel* in the Parc Monceau into a leave centre for British officers, none of the French nobility seemed to take the slightest interest in the war. She wrote in her diary:

> What has happened to the gallant French nation that I used to adore? So much of the aristocracy here in Paris seems to be just *fin de race*. They have no true outlook, only just some decadent remains of the *dixhuitième* and the Second Empire without the wit and dignified point of view of the former, and without the pinchback vigour of the latter. They seem to be wilted flowers revived by some chemical for a short time, but their roots no longer exist.
>
> The war only means something to those who have suffered by it; it means little in the abstract and less than nothing to the section it has not touched. The peasants are carrying on in the fields near the Front because it is their life. The little shop-keepers near the lines are carrying on their business with unruffled calm, but the real source of their contentment is not patriotism but merely greed. They charge exorbitant prices for every bundle of straw and every cup of water which they dispose of to the exhausted troops, filling their pockets out of the extremity of human need.

And later she wrote:

> The women have a sex urge but they are vicious with overcivilisation. They want men, they do not want children. Nature speaks, but sophistication diverts nature. Poor France!
>
> Among the lay population, to those who have lost no

loved ones and have suffered no decrease of wealth, the war is simply a *bore*—nothing further—"*Voyons!*—the thing has gone on too long—it is an *ennui*."

What has become of the proud old French race? The French of today are an astonishing people. Ungrateful, emotional, dramatic, crafty and self-seeking; witty, gay, brave and untrue; yet so fascinating and so brilliant that they will always be loved, not for their qualities but in spite of them.

6.

Soon after her arrival in Paris, Elinor made her first visit to the battlefields, nearly becoming a casualty on her first day, the American officer who was driving her misjudging the width of a tram. Fortunately she had had a premonition of disaster and had insisted on sitting in the back in lonely state instead of beside him, as he wished. He was much impressed by her premonition and she decided afterwards that she bore a charmed life.

She dined that night at the French G.H.Q. at Compiègne, and was considerably relieved to find that the French Generals took more interest in the war than the Parisians. She spent the night at Compiègne and set off next morning to see as much as she could of the front. The French authorities evidently attached a good deal of importance to her American articles and her permits gave her wide scope.

She had several narrow escapes. Once she was bombed on the road and several times caught in artillery bombardments; but the most frightening experience she had was in one specially heavy bombardment. She was made to take shelter in a deep dugout, where she suffered miseries of claustrophobia. "My tongue was dry and my forehead damp and only the memory of Grandmamma's teachings kept me from screaming aloud," she wrote.

She spent several nights sleeping in the car or in a ditch at the side of the road, in stern contrast to the high standard of living upon which she normally insisted. At one point she was arrested, the troops being suspicious of the beautiful red-haired lady—she was fifty-two, but she looked at least fifteen years younger—driving about just behind the lines. They were convinced of her innocence, not by her formidable permits, but, strangely enough, by the discovery of an elegant pink satin nightdress in her luggage, which they searched.

Her most moving experience of the war was a night she spent in a deserted house which had been sliced in half by a shell. The village, too, was deserted, and uncannily quiet, but to get away from any stray starving dogs she camped in the first-floor bedroom and there, lying on the hard skeleton bed, she watched through the space where the wall should have been the bombardment of St. Quentin a few miles away. The noise of the guns effectively prevented sleep and she lay there all night watching the scarlet flames sweeping through the town, the huge masses of earth and masonry hurled into the air and the gaunt old cathedral standing out black against the glow.

It was a solemn and terrible sight and it moved her later to write a piece called *Destruction,* a paean of lamentation against the horror of war.

Elinor's graphic pen stood her in good stead on these visits to the battlefields. She wrote in her diary after one visit:

As I returned to the car I passed once more the heaps of stones that marked the site of the shattered village and I noticed the pathetic evidences of family life protruding from the ruins—a poor old bedstead of iron, a sodden mattress, and in one place the head of a child's toy horse. A curious feeling of stupefaction came over me and I looked up into the blue sky for relief. Then suddenly the air was rent with the distant thunder of battle beginning again towards the south.

The country for miles around and beyond Bailly was one vast desolation rendered the more piteous to look at by the contrast of the tender spring green of any bush and sapling which had chanced to escape the blast of shells. And not merely of shells. One of the things which enraged me the most was the wanton destruction of all the young fruit trees by the Germans before their retreat. For miles and miles the smiling innocent trees, their early bloom still on them, lay prone, hacked down out of pure malice and brutality.

One of her tasks was to investigate the stories of German atrocities, and she spent a good deal of time interrogating the victims and witnesses of alleged cases of German torture and rape. Much as she had always disliked the Germans, she tried to be fair and impartial, but she came to the conclusion that there were few exaggerations in the stories told to her.

Elinor returned to Paris from her first trip to the battlefields deeply shocked and moved by all she had seen; but her diary entry of the day of her return ends with a description of a new Reboux hat which had arrived in her absence and which she was furious to find had got dented on one side.

7.

When Elinor was not touring the battlefields, she remained at the Ritz. She had a suite on the Cambon side of the hotel, which she retained for the next three years, and also, through the kind offices of Olivier, a corner table in the restaurant, where she and her friends could talk without being overheard.

Many interesting conversations took place there during the next three years, for Elinor was a good hostess and she was also exceedingly discreet. Colonel Le Roy Lewis, the military attaché, and his assistant, Colonel Spears (later Major-General Sir Edward Spears), often dined with her and discussed the war.

While she was in Paris, she undertook, besides the writing of her war articles, a subsidiary war job, becoming vice-president of a society called the Secours Franco-Americain. This had been formed to assist in resettling refugees as soon as possible in the recaptured battle areas and in starting them growing food again, wherever this was feasible. It was Elinor's first experience of a committee and she was most unimpressed. Many French noble ladies were also members, but they seemed unwilling to do any work and delighted in sidetracking the discussions on to subjects unconnected with the war. Everything was decided by sentiment, except when the question of subscriptions was raised, when the French members would sit for once absolutely silent.

Only the English and American members were willing to do any actual work, and Elinor, accordingly, found herself in charge of the building of the temporary huts for the resettled farm labourers and their families in the Noyon district. She spent a good deal of time at Noyon, doing a job which lay completely outside her normal experience, but from which she derived a good deal of solace and satisfaction.

This work involved a considerable amount of travelling to and fro between Noyon and Paris; and what with this and her journalistic work in the battle areas, there was little time left for that other essential activity, earning her living. However, her energy was very great and she somehow found time in between other duties to start a new novel, *The Price of Things.*

Her earlier novel, *The Career of Katherine Bush,* which she had been writing during 1915 and 1916, was published in April 1917.

8.

It was ten years since Elinor's discovery in the Nevada gold fields that gentle manners and aristocratic behaviour had no automatic connection with birth. She had been meditating upon this and upon its social implications ever since. The lesson had been repeated more recently in the Grosvenor Gardens canteen, where she had observed the admirable manners, without any suspicion of familiarity or awkwardness or affectation, of the British private soldiers towards the peeresses who were waiting on them.

She had also been watching the many American girls who had married into the British peerage and who, although they lacked what Elinor had once supposed to be the two prime requisites of aristocracy, birth and tradition, nevertheless succeeded in merging into their new social background as completely as if they had been born into it. Elinor had been gradually coming to the conclusion that there was no reason why anyone of any social stratum, given the intelligence and the will to learn, should be unable to become a personage of the highest social standing, accepted freely in all courts and houses, filled with *noblesse oblige,* and upholding proudly all the traditions of the aristocracy.

She accordingly took for the heroine of *The Career of Katherine Bush* not a young woman of ancient lineage, still less a Russian Imperial Highness, but a girl from the English lower-middle classes, the daughter of a Brixton auctioneer, the granddaughter of a pork butcher.*

* We may see how far Elinor had travelled if we compare a passage from *Beyond the Rocks.*

Lady Harrowfield tittered and whispered almost audibly to her neighbour:

"These are the creatures Florence insisted upon my giving an

Katherine Bush was the young, attractive secretary of a firm of moneylenders, and over the glass screen she heard the younger sons of the nobility begging loans against their future expectations. She thought how aristocratic and wonderful they were, herself imitating their voices and expressions against the time when she would be one of them. At home in Brixton she lived with her family, whom she despised heartily for their commonness, their lack of desire to raise themselves to aristocratic heights, and their petty snobberies. They in turn bore with Katherine despite her hardness, her refusal to marry the worthy Charlie Prodgers, and her *de haute en bas* manner, and they were glad of her ruthless efficiency.

Katherine had always refused all invitations from the aristocratic clients of her employers, feeling that these would only distract her from her principal objective. However, to increase her knowledge of high life, she agreed to go for a week end to Paris with Lord Algy FitzRufus, one of the more charming and impoverished of them. Here she learned which fork to use for oysters and that the nobility apparently had baths every day. She survived the week end without unfortunate consequences (due solely, we are given to understand, to her strength of personality, while her sister, a weaker character, was, under similar circumstances, less lucky), but to her astonishment she found herself passionately in love with Algy. She crushed this weakness ruthlessly, refused to marry him as he wanted, and insisted that they must never meet again, adding, for good measure, a pep talk about his idleness.

She resigned from the moneylenders and took a job as personal secretary to Lady Garribardine (a portrait of Teresa,

invitation to last night. Look at the man!" she added. "Has one ever seen such a person, except in a pork-butcher's shop!"

"I have never been in one," said Lord Bracondale agreeably; "but I hear things are too wonderfully managed at Harrowfield House—though I had no idea you did the shopping yourself, dear Lady Harrowfield."

She looked up at him, rage in her heart.

Lady Londonderry), helping her with her charitable work. Katherine's family despised her for being a paid employee and having to "live in," but Katherine was entirely content, living now in the houses of the great, learning all the time. She made mistakes, of course, but she only made them once. She used her physical charms to attract her employer's married nephew Gerard, so that he might teach her about Renaissance painting and lend her Chesterfield's letters and other good books. When he, not understanding, presumed to go further and start an affair with her, she sent him smartly about his business.

Usually she lived in her own room, eating her meals off a tray, but occasionally she was allowed into the drawing-room or dining-room, and here she would astonish everyone by the wisdom and sense of her remarks, by her discourses on the necessity for aristocratic government and especially for an aristocratic Foreign Secretary, by her strictures on the irresponsibility of some members of society, and by her emphasis on the general need for common sense.

Finally she went one day, by design as always, to the House of Lords to hear the Land Bill debated. One of the speakers was the Duke of Mordryn, a proconsular figure with a Curzonian style of oratory. She learned that he was a widower and she persuaded the unfortunate Gerard to introduce her to him without disclosing her subservient status.

The ending, of course, is inevitable, though there is one bad moment when Katherine, in her unswerving honesty of purpose, felt herself obliged to confess her affair with Algy to the Duke and at first to refuse his offer of marriage. However, we leave her a radiant Duchess, nursing the son and heir, and shedding a tear over the news of Algy's death in action at Mons—a strange touch of sentiment which Elinor later admitted to be out of character and artistically a mistake.

The Career of Katherine Bush is a product of Elinor's

cynical mood. Apart from a little perfunctory passion at the
end, there is no romance in it. One of Elinor's better known
aphorisms, which occurs in several of her books, was: "It is
wiser to marry the life you like, because, after a little, the
man doesn't matter." It was a sentiment which she alternately
resisted violently or accepted cynically, depending upon
whether she was in her romantic or her sceptical mood. In
The Career of Katherine Bush the man hardly matters, except
in so far as he provides the life that Katherine wants. The
Duke of Mordryn only enters the book three quarters of the
way through and it is not his character which entices Katherine. It is his title, his coronet, the greatness of his position
and—we must be fair—the greatness of his opportunities.

Ten years after publication, in 1927, Elinor wrote on the
flyleaf of her own copy:

At the time this book was written, to be an English
Duchess was the height of any young woman's ambition.
Now, of course, all that has passed away. But the great
lesson which the book still teaches is to make yourself the
round peg before you aspire to the round hole—never try
and force yourself into a position you are not fitted for.
Make yourself fitted for it; then in justice you can shout
and complain if you cannot obtain it. It is the shouting of
the square pegs for the round holes which makes all the
difficulty in life.

We may concede the sincerity of the author's purpose and
the effectiveness with which she makes her point, while at
the same time finding the book the social climber's vade
mecum. Katherine herself, snobbish, humourless, hard-
hearted, ruthless, selfish, and immoral, runs Ambrosine close
as the most dislikeable of all Elinor's heroines. As one reads
the book, ploughing onwards through the turgid sermons
about aristocracy and common sense, one cannot help longing

for some setback, some disaster, some form of suffering to overtake such a terrible girl. And one longs in vain.

The book is, of course, a Cinderella story, stripped of all its romantic atmosphere. But Cinderella, even such a hard, unloveable one, cannot fail, and the book was extremely popular, especially in Great Britain. Its ultimate British sale was surpassed only by *Three Weeks, The Visits of Elizabeth,* and *His Hour.*

9.

The Career of Katherine Bush was serialised before book publication in *Nash's Magazine,* like so many others of Elinor's novels. Elinor's literary agent, Hughes Massie, had in 1915, while Elinor was still planning the book, submitted the synopsis to the Hearst press for serialisation in America. Now, however, on receiving the finished manuscript, the editorial department had certain qualms about the story's acceptability in America. Mr. William Randolph Hearst himself read the manuscript and sent a message to Hughes Massie that he thought the character of Katherine was too hard for his readers; he would like her given some human faults and failings and made rather more lovable; he would like her to be less complacent about her early lapse from chastity; and he would like her to be less laudatory of English aristocracy in general —three criticisms which may be thought reasonable.

Hughes Massie passed these points on as tactfully as he could to Elinor, explaining that he thought it deplorable that she should be asked to alter her work by a newspaper proprietor or editor, but that perhaps in this case Elinor might be able to meet Hearst's points without compromising her objectives in writing the book. Elinor, however, refused to consider this, and cabled at once to Hearst—the first personal communication that ever passed between them:

WILLIAM RANDOLPH HEARST
  RIVERSIDE DRIVE
    NEW YORK CITY
YOUR EDITOR WANTS ME TO MAKE MY POWERFUL STORY
KATHERINE BUSH MORE SUGARY I KNOW BY EXPERIENCE
THAT MY OWN FLARE SUCCEEDS BEST WHEN NOT TAMPERED
WITH FEEL STRONGLY STORY WILL BE FAR MORE SUCCESS-
FUL IF LEFT RUGGED AND ARRESTING THOUGH WOULD NOT
OBJECT SHORTENING PSYCHOLOGY PROVIDED NOTHING NEW
INSERTED PLEASE CABLE YOUR PERSONAL FEELINGS

                      ELINOR GLYN
                        RITZOTEL
                        LONDON

The reply to this has not been preserved but it cannot have been favourable, for a few days later Elinor wrote Hearst a long letter defending and justifying the book. She was prepared to make Katherine less complacent about her early lapse, since this was, of course, a manifestation of the sex urge, which she was so soon to suppress. But Elinor would not give way on the other two points.

> I feel that if I have made myself clear I am sure you will see that I could not condemn any of her opinions which I respect for their honesty, but I could more strongly enforce the want of wisdom of her initial act. Her opinions are perfect sound common sense unbiased by emotion, and I should fancy would greatly appeal to the clever sensible American public who must be sick of mawkish sentimentality and unreal romantic sentiments.

> I feel it would be immoral if I, the author, showed that I condemn the heroine's opinions, because if I did that and still made her successful it would be preaching the most wicked doctrine, when on the contrary Katherine's conviction is that only perfect honesty must win, and this is also my preaching.

I could write a preface if you think fit explaining as I have in this letter. I have the highest opinion of the common sense of American readers and always feel I have their sympathy. They understood *Three Weeks* when the English did not. I know and feel this book will be of great interest and arouse controversy once we have made my point plain.

She also wrote to Mr. Edgar Sisson, the editor of *Cosmopolitan* magazine, which was considering the book.

My view of it is that I wished not to draw a lovable sweet heroine but a strong clever magnetic woman who wins out by sheer splendid courage and truth, even against the tremendous handicaps of her initial mistake. Every one of K.B.'s views are sane, logical, honest and full of common sense and show that she has deep psychological deduction. The whole explanation of what is true aristocracy I feel is the best thing I have ever done. K.B. was a true aristocrat and "the Duchess of Dashington" no better than a common barmaid. The pictures of English society before the war are photographic; so are all the portraits and will be recognised by everyone in England. Every single touch in the whole book is drawn from life.

K.B. is a proof of what strong will coupled with perfect honesty can do. Above all things, she *respects herself* and her act of renunciation when she tells the Duke her story shows sublime honour and courage. Readers will be deeply interested in her whether they like her or no. I believe there is no ridiculous snobby class in America like Katherine's family with their shams and pretences, but still it may interest Americans to hear about what such people are like in England.

But in her next letter Elinor wrote:

Dear Mr. Hearst,

On second thoughts I feel that if you would rather not risk Katherine Bush in your paper I shall quite understand, since you know your public best, and I could then make other arrangements. I have perfect confidence in your judgement of your public and think you are quite right to give them what you think best, only I write my books from inward conviction and make a study of my characters to get them exact to life, so I could not alter the principles in Katherine Bush which I have already explained. It would be like *Hamlet* without the Prince of Denmark.

I feel quite sure this will clear up all points and that even if Katherine Bush does not appear under your aegis we can have better luck next time. As you know your papers have all my sympathy.

Yours sincerely,
Elinor Glyn.

The Hearst press bought the serial rights of *The Career of Katherine Bush* for ten thousand dollars and it was serialised in *Cosmopolitan* with only the one agreed alteration. It was very well received by the American public and it was the beginning of Elinor's long association with the Hearst press. Most of her future novels were serialised in *Cosmopolitan*, which had an exclusive option on her work, and she was as well to contribute articles to other papers of the syndicate for the next twenty-five years. It was also the beginning of an oddly assorted but lasting friendship between Elinor and William Randolph Hearst.

In book form *The Career of Katherine Bush* did not sell well in America, its publication coinciding with the end of the war in Europe. Her American publisher wrote apologetically:

Just consider for a moment the last three weeks. I am replying to a letter of yours dated October 23rd. Since then terrific battles have been fought, the Austrian Empire, hundreds of years old, has gone to pieces, the great German Empire and its dreadful fighting machine have both entirely collapsed, 279 kings, princes and grand dukes and their families have abdicated and fled to neutral or unknown places, revolution started in all middle Europe and the war is done and finished. No other three weeks in all history can show anything approaching this. Can you expect people to buy novels at such a time with such events going on? And for two years this country has been going through this sort of thing in a milder form. The result is that fiction has suffered materially in this country.

This letter was shown to Hughes Massie, who commented drily:

I should say he is anxious not to offend you but is not very clear himself just how the small sales of *Katherine Bush* can be explained.

10.

Meanwhile, in 1917, Hughes Massie had astutely realised that with the changed conditions in Europe there would probably be now no objection to a stage presentation of *Three Weeks*. He considered, however, that it would be advisable to have a fresh dramatic version made, not only to ease its passage through the Lord Chamberlain's office, but also to bring the dialogue a little more into line with modern tastes.

Elinor agreed with this, and it was arranged that Roy Horniman, who had successfully adapted Locke's *Idols* for the stage, should write a new dramatic version. The play opened at the Strand Theatre on July 12, 1917, with Marga la Rubia as the Queen and Barry Baxter (succeeded later in the run by Basil Gill) as Paul.

One can fully appreciate Horniman's difficulties in casting

the book into a satisfying dramatic form, but at the same time his version must be open to some criticism. Most of the original dialogue, as might have been expected, has gone, the parts that remain standing out in startling and incongruous contrast. With the original dialogue has also gone the special atmosphere of exotic eroticism which was so essential to the story. The mysterious, passionate Slav Queen has been turned into a normal chain-smoking sex-starved woman called Sonia. Paul is a caricature of a stupid young Englishman; he whistles the "Eton Boating Song" just before each entry and after each exit as if it were a Wagnerian leitmotiv. The couch of roses, the feast of the full moon, the cupid fountain of Eastern perfume have all gone. The tiger skin just scrapes in; Paul twists his whiskers and calls him "Old Chap," a familiarity he would never have dared in the book. Paul's entire family, together with the English part of the story, has been cut out, thereby largely eliminating the point of the novel, Paul's awakening from intellectual and emotional sleep.

In place of these omissions Horniman put in a large number of Balkan courtiers and politicians, who, led by the King, continually interrupt the Swiss honeymoon to argue about politics or flirt with each other. There is even a distressing little romance between the Queen's maid, Anna, and a Swiss waiter. Elinor had carefully left the Balkan background vague, a suggested menace hanging over the pair; but in the dramatic version much of the time is taken up with arguments about the Constitution and the Legislative Council. The work became, not a passionate and original love story, but a Ruritanian romance played by stock characters in stock situations with stock dialogue and without the twists of plot and the pace which forms so necessary a part of Ruritanian adventure. Worst of all, the play was given a happy ending, which seemed to Elinor not only morally and dramatically indefensible, but also, by eliminating Paul's grief and subsequent regeneration, to remove the second point of her novel.

The Times dramatic critic gave the play a lighthearted review, concerned solely with the number of cushions on the stage and the fact that nobody ever sat on them. The *Daily Telegraph,* which had been so deeply shocked by the original novel, found now ten years later with surprise how mild and inoffensive the story seemed; oddly, because the adultery and the consequent baby were still there, made more flagrant by the happy ending, triumphant rather than tragic. But, in the critic's opinion, the play seemed unreal and melodramatic, though it was well acted apart from some moments of overplaying by Miss la Rubia.

Even the inadequate new version was sufficient to start again the arguments about the morality or otherwise of the Queen's behaviour, and it was on its opening night enthusiastically applauded by the audience. But it was taken off on October 20 after a run of a little over three months, and one cannot really feel that it deserved a longer run.

On tour it played to large houses. In Colchester the dramatic muse, presumably in outrage at the happy ending, gave the play a cataclysmic finale, which Elinor could not ever have bettered. The entire theatre burnt to the ground during the last act.

Elinor herself took little interest in the play, leaving the whole of the arrangements to Hughes Massie. She was not in England at any time during the West End run, and as far as is known, she never saw a performance of the play.

11.

Elinor's contacts in Paris in that autumn and winter of 1917 were sufficiently senior and well informed to let her have no illusions about the seriousness of the war situation. The conversations at her table with French Generals, with Le Roy Lewis and Spears, the letters she received from Milner, who was a member of the War Cabinet, while not disclosing any secrets, gave her a clear and anxious picture of future possibilities. She was all the more resentful at the uncaring attitude of French society to the war.

There was in Paris now a certain feeling that economy should be practised, but there was no suggestion among Elinor's French friends that they should go without food, petrol, or luxuries. It was, however, no longer good taste to wear sables and silver foxes in public—these were replaced by sheared rabbit, mounted on the most expensive materials and almost equally costly.

She wrote a bitter entry in her diary at this time:

Vice is rampant in Paris, Lesbians dine together openly, in groups of six sometimes, at Larue's. They are everywhere, and are freely spoken of without shame. Men are the same. Nothing is sacred, nothing is hidden, not even vice and avarice. The note is to be "natural" and "Nature" now appears to be a distorted thing. Oh! what is the matter with humanity?

Last night I dined with Princess ——, daughter of a very old noble family. We went on, all crammed into her motor (only the friends of Ministers or Generals can obtain petrol nowadays!) to the Lune Rousse and heard some very witty songs, and then on to Madame ——'s where we sat and watched the dancing.

The Young Comtesse ——, charming bacchante that she is, dances with perfect poetry of voluptuous motion, clasped close in the arms of an Argentine tango expert, their lips not two inches apart, eyes plunged in eyes, her unquiet body undulating against his, every movement of both in unison. The Argentine has been her partner—not her lover—for several months, though no one would believe it to see them dance. The real lover is an Italian, with whom she has been going about since she parted from a certain noble

Englishman, and rumour has it that she has been careless over this affair and is to have an operation. The old husband has been told it is appendicitis.

Imagine the mentality which could dance such dances night after night with a professional partner, when she was already aware of the existence of the lover's child! She does not know that there is a war and cares not a whit for the old and honoured name which she holds although she is highly born herself also.

Another entry reads:

One young widow was there tonight, her husband only killed four weeks ago, so bored, she said, with the funeral ceremonies and her mother-in-law's crocodile tears, that she had to come out and dance for a little! She was wrapped in a yard or so of black chiffon and apparently nothing else.

If God sent the war as a lesson to the world, it is not half learned yet I fear! Certainly not in Paris.

She was, however, encouraged by the arrival in Paris in December 1917 of Milner. He dined with her several times at her table and she later wrote, "I am proud to remember that he honoured me with his confidence and treated me as a reasonable and patriotic being, worthy of trust in matters of state."

Elinor's discretion was complete, and Milner had a great regard for her judgement of people, which, unlike her judgement of business affairs, was usually very close to the mark. On this occasion she was much cheered, not only by his company, but by his attitude to the war, so very different from that which she heard all around her. On his return to England he wrote to her:

Anything may happen. One lives in the presence of the most staggering possibilities of disaster. But so also does the enemy. If I am cheerful, it is because I am "all in" without any reservation whatsoever, or regrets for the past or thought of the future. *"On fait ce qu'on peut"* and the event is on the knees of the gods.

In December 1917 the first American troops began to arrive in Paris. Elinor was friendly with their provost marshal, General Allaire, but she was appalled by the indifference and ingratitude of her French friends towards the American Army. Even for Christmas the Americans were offered no private hospitality, no form of welcome; no effort was made to mitigate their loneliness. Only those officers who came with the correct social introductions were received in French houses.

Elinor felt very bad about it. Together with some English and American friends she persuaded the Comtesse de Sainte Aldegonde to lend her large house in the Avenue du Bois for a big New Year party to which every American officer in Paris was to be invited. To make it seem like a French party the invitations were sent out in the names of some grand French ladies, who had been persuaded to act as hostesses. Some two hundred American officers accepted and they were duly received by the official hostesses at the head of the great staircase. However, having shaken hands, the hostesses then turned their backs upon the company and spent the rest of the evening talking to each other and to a few American officers whom it was correct for them to know. The rest were cold-shouldered.

Elinor and her five friends did their best to make the remainder feel that they were being given a rousing welcome by the French, but they were only six among two hundred and there was a blank, depressed air over the whole party which nothing could shift. As midnight approached, Elinor noticed some of them slipping away quietly, unable to bear any more of it. She felt desperate; something drastic had to be done to retrieve this terrible evening. She seized a glass of punch, climbed up on to a table, and began to sing "Dixie."

The band joined in, and so, gradually, did everyone else. The action put Elinor socially beyond the pale, but at least the ice was broken and the party ended with some show of hilarity.

12.

In March 1918, shortly before the big German offensive, Elinor had a severe attack of influenza, followed by laryngitis; afterwards she was sent to the South of France to convalesce. She went as usual to St. Raphaël, and while she was there she read of the disquieting break-through on the British front. When she recovered, she went over for the day to Nice, a town she had always hated; now its gayety, its luxury, its shops full of jewellery and fashions and hats in the middle of the supreme crisis of the war seemed to her revolting. She returned to Paris as quickly as possible.

Paris was at the time being shelled by Big Bertha, and most of Elinor's French friends had fled from the city to their country estates. The remainder, to her astonishment, made a point of being personally rude to her about the British Army and British morale. One lady, whom Elinor had known intimately for thirty years, went so far as to write her an insulting letter about the British. Among those members of the resettlement committee who still remained in Paris there was special resentment that their work should have been wiped out so completely by the German advance.

Elinor refused to leave Paris. Someone, she felt, must remain in the city. Almost the whole of society had gone, and everybody else who could afford to—about a million altogether, it was said. Of Elinor's friends in Paris, virtually only the English and American war workers remained. On the evening of May 28 she and Lady Congreve were able to walk at half past eight in the evening round the Place Vendôme, down the Rue de la Paix and the Rue Castiglione without seeing a single human being or vehicle. There were rumours that the government was about to move to Bordeaux.

At the beginning of June, Sir Henry Thornton, the Assistant Director General of Movements, urged Elinor to leave Paris, pointing out that after her propaganda articles she might expect no very humane treatment if she were captured by the Germans. Milner was in Paris at the time and she appealed to him, asking if she need really go. Milner, however, was more optimistic about the situation at that moment, and it was arranged that Elinor could stay in Paris until or unless he sent a message to Sir Henry Thornton. The code word "Cherbourg" was to mean "Please arrange to move Mrs. Glyn to a place of safety."

On June 7 Milner wrote to her:

"I am very much struck indeed by what I see of your Americans—splendid men."

The use of the word "your" amused her, and she told him in reply of a proposal made by General Allaire that she should visit the American base camp at St. Nazaire. Milner urged her to accept and to try to make the Americans feel how much their help was appreciated by the Allies.

Elinor, however, was reluctant to leave Paris to visit any base camp at that moment, and on the twelfth of June, Milner wrote again:

I cannot say that I regard Paris as unsafe *yet* and it may never become so. But what makes me uneasy is that I think, if anything did go wrong, it might come suddenly, without previous warning, through some internal trouble which could not be foreseen here. I am not happy at the thought that you might be depending upon me for a signal which I should not have the knowledge to give in time. My advice is rather, that if your work with the Americans can begin now, you should not delay it. I know you would not like to leave Paris, unless you were doing something to help the cause. But as things stand, I really think that you might be rendering more service with the Americans and certainly your friends would feel easier in their minds!

The same day came news that the German advance had been checked and Elinor prepared to set out for St. Nazaire.

13.

She was deeply impressed by the American Army, which she now met in full scale for the first time. The grim, single-minded spirit, which she missed so badly among the French, reminded her of London in 1915. But she was also particularly impressed by the organisation of the American Army, by the care taken to draft every man to the branch where his own peacetime trade was likely to make him of most service. She went over the huge salvage depot near Blois and discovered that the gum-boot stores were in the charge of a leading rubber-boot manufacturer and the clothing-repair section supervised by the manager of a famous tailoring firm, both enlisted men. It had been very different in the British Army in 1914, with qualified engineers sweeping out stables and mathematicians working as navvies in labour battalions.

While she was at St. Nazaire, an American troopship arrived and she stood on the quay watching the men disembark. It was an imposing sight, and she was greatly struck by their fine physique, deep sunburn, and predominantly Anglo-Saxon appearance. This last surprised her, and she wondered whether the Anglo-Saxon strain was far more widespread in America than her travels had led her to believe, or whether it was in some way connected with their being volunteers. They were very different from the type of cosmopolitan American usually found in Paris; none of them had ever been to Europe before. In addition to seeing round the base camps she would also address the men in huge drill sheds or canteen huts, dwelling, as Milner had urged her, on how glad their allies were to see them on the soil of Europe. She would also sometimes declaim her piece *Destruction*. It was a dramatic and moving perform- ance, Elinor standing on the platform, a solitary figure in black in front of the American flag, one blinding white spotlight fall- ing on her red hair.

After her visit to St. Nazaire, Elinor came to London, where she visited her mother and daughters. She was back in Paris at the end of July and busied herself with the Secours Franco-Americain, her articles for both the British and Amer- ican press, with finishing her novel, *The Price of Things,* and starting a new one, *Elizabeth's Daughter*.

This last was a description of the American base camps at St. Nazaire by the seventeen-year-old Lady Ermyntrude, whose epistolary style was very reminiscent of her mother's. There were the usual gayety, the usual "Glynisms," and a slight romance with an American officer, whom she called Hiawatha because of his Red Indian appearance. But unlike its predecessor *Elizabeth Visits America, Elizabeth's Daughter* had a vigorous pro-American bias, so vigorous that it may have been less acceptable to English readers, particularly if they were members of the British Army. It was serialised in Great Britain in Newnes' *Novel Magazine* and by the Hearst press in America, but it was never published in book form, both her publishers feeling by then that it would be a mistake to bring out a war book soon after the armistice, and that by doing so they would divert attention from *The Price of Things*. With this view Elinor agreed.

Although *Elizabeth's Daughter** has many pleasant touches, we must feel that this decision was the right one, especially in view of the book's narrow scope and ephemeral setting. For us now, however, the chief interest in the story lies in the

---

* Serialised in America under the title *Elizabeth's Daughter Visits the S.O.S.*

acid comments which Elizabeth's uppish little daughter makes about the fading middle-aged beauty of her companion, a red-haired, green-eyed authoress who had written a shocking novel called *Nine Months*. Elinor's ability to laugh at herself was often buried deep in her moments of self-drama or self-pity, but it was never extinguished and it was always liable to reappear, most endearingly, at unexpected moments.

14.

With the final turning of the tide of war life in Paris became increasingly gay and cheerful. Society began to return, and the abuse of the British Army, which Elinor had endured so impatiently for the last three months, slowly died away, though even now her friends made a point of drawing her attention whenever possible to the fine achievements of the soldiers of other nations.

After the armistice Elinor decided that she had had enough of Paris. Her work in the devastated areas, both in journalism and resettlement, was over, though she continued to write for both the British and American press. She wrote a series of articles for Sir Frank Newnes on such subjects as "Are Women Changing?" "Is Chivalry Dead?" and "If I Were Queen," which were published in the *Grand Magazine* and for which she was paid her usual British price of sevenpence-halfpenny per word.

To write these articles Elinor wanted to get away by herself somewhere peaceful and quiet, which would at the same time not be too remote from the interesting events and people connected with the forthcoming peace conference. Accordingly she took a flat at No. 23 Rue du Peintre Lebrun at Versailles and spent some happy weeks redecorating it. She moved in in the early spring of 1919 and there, besides writing articles and reflecting on life, she began her new novel, which was later to be published under the title *Man and Maid.*

When she was not writing at Versailles, she would be at the Ritz in Paris, where she still kept a suite, watching the parade of personalities gathered in the city for the peace conference, meeting most of the principal participants, and learning something of what was going on behind the scenes. She had several old friends in Paris at that time; Lord Milner was there and also Lord Riddell, to whose newspapers she was contributing regularly. Both men often dined with her at her corner table.

In her diary she recorded her impressions and opinions of the statesmen gathered there. Lloyd George she met at dinner one night in the house in the Rue Nilot where he stayed.

He struck me as such a purely Celtic type that I felt that I was talking to some foreigner who spoke English well rather than to the British Prime Minister.

The conversation was nothing but chaff at first, but soon the P.M. began to tell us of his horror at the disgraceful way in which the French had thrown stones at the departing German delegates. He spoke strongly about the ungenerous vindictiveness of the French and I could see that his automatic sympathy for the underdog was turning him away from the French point of view about the terms of peace.

After dinner he talked to me for some time. He curled up his legs on the tiny hard French sofa and leaned across the little table towards my chair, gazing intently at me as he spoke. I noticed the pupils of his eyes kept expanding and contracting, producing a peculiar hypnotic effect. As far as I could tell, throughout our conversation he gave me his undivided attention, and this remarkable power of concentration struck me as the most wonderful of all his qualities. Most men are too vain to pay this compliment to a woman, but I feel sure that Lloyd George devotes the whole of his great capacities to everything which he undertakes and never misses a point by failing to attend to the evidence of a witness.

The next day, in the course of a rather more elaborate analysis of his character, she wrote:

The word which rises to my mind as I write of him is *Troubadour!* Perhaps it was his long hair and well-known love of music that gave me this odd impression, perhaps some momentary insight into an earlier incarnation. Whatever the cause, it was rather as a famous poet and minstrel, reciting his historic lays to the accompaniment of a strange musical instrument in the flickering fire-light of a castle hall, that I found myself picturing that peculiar Celtic visage, and never as the successor of Chatham and Peel, presiding over the British Cabinet at No. 10 Downing Street.

She was considerably less impressed by President Wilson.

Wilson's face is a mask. I feel that no one believes in him less than he does himself and that only a quarter of what he says and puts forward is real. The cultivated theorist in him has made him set out to accomplish a great task which he has now realised he is incapable of bringing to fruition, but he has not the courage to adapt his theories to fit the facts and continues to wear an air of supreme confidence which would be comic if it were not so tragic in its consequences. Despite his mask-like cheerfulness, I gained an impression of disappointment and of dreadful inward anxiety. There is a touch of Pan in him so carefully hidden and suppressed that it only shows clearly in his sudden automatic smile. The mistake which all the Allies have made has been treating him with too much respect, as if his views were really those of the American people.

At one time or another during those months she met most of the foreign delegates and described them in the locked pages of her diary: Venizelos, whom she regarded as the ablest man at the conference; Hughes, the Australian, whose deafness confined itself to inconvenient questions; Lord Riddell, with his curious trick of seeming not to hear or be interested in what was being said to him, and of suddenly referring to it again an hour or a week later; and, of course, Milner, the contrast and the complement to Lloyd George.

Several passages in her letters home at this time throw light on her relationship with Milner:

He is here—rushed out to see me as soon as he had signed Peace on Wednesday, and we spent the afternoon in the woods. He only signed the Peace to make the excuse to get over to see me. He told me he need not have done it, and yet he is one moment passionately loving, and the next, aloof and unapproachable. He is the most remarkable character of cunning, caution, sophistry and nobility one could imagine. We are just friends.

It was as the correspondent for Lord Riddell's papers that Elinor attended on June 28, 1919, the signing of the peace in the Hall of Mirrors at Versailles. She was one of the only two women present and she had to stand upon a precarious perch for a long time, waiting for the ceremony to begin.

She had expected the day to be a moment of triumph and thanksgiving, but instead she was overcome by a sense of foreboding. All she could think of was the empty meaning of the ceremony.

As I stood there upon the tottering bench, feeling that I must take care to be able to keep my balance, a sadness fell upon me. I did not want to see any more. It seemed as if the peace of the world must be as insecure as my own footing upon the bench had been.

BOOK SIX

Courts and Capitals

1920–1931

I.

In February 1920, Elinor paid another visit to Egypt, staying with Lady Congreve, whose husband was General Officer Commanding the Forces. Cairo at that time was full of friends. Lord Allenby was High Commissioner and Milner was also there on the abortive "Milner Mission," his recommendations being subsequently rejected by Lloyd George, despite the support of Curzon, the Foreign Secretary, and Allenby, the High Commissioner.

Before leaving for Egypt, Milner had written to Elinor:

I don't believe the Mission can do much good. First of all I was going in October, then I was firmly convinced I was not going out at all, now I am shot out at a moment's notice because the recalcitrant Nationalists have declared they won't have me— Send me a message to deliver to your friend the Sphinx and pray that the Egyptian malcontents may aim badly—they generally do!

But when she met him there, she found him thoroughly bored with the cloud of detectives who surrounded him all the time.

Elinor was always particularly sensitive to atmosphere and she found Egypt now very changed since her last visit eighteen years earlier. There was an uneasy, hostile atmosphere in the country, which had found expression in the serious riots ten months earlier. She could not help contrasting Egypt with what now seemed in retrospect to be the golden days of Lord Cromer's administration. The precincts of the Sphinx were now filled with unsightly shacks and boardings. The weather was cold and forbidding.

There was a change in Elinor, too. Since her last visit she had been through a great deal. Her health admittedly was much better now, but she was sadder, wiser, and older. Her prime of life was past. The easy, sunlit, civilised life of prewar days, which she had enjoyed so much, had disappeared, possibly for ever. At times the future seemed rather bleak and cheerless.

She stayed in Egypt only four weeks, and though she was received with every kindness by Lady Congreve and Lady Allenby, she was glad to leave when the time came.

The King of Egypt remembered her and the long hours she had spent in the Gezireh Gardens on her last visit, and he invited her to a magnificent banquet which he was giving for Milner. It was a splendid occasion, but very different in style from the banquets she had experienced in Russia. The hundred guests sat round a huge horseshoe table, and there was none of the ostentation and elaborate ceremonial which she had come to expect of state banquets. The food was simple and unexpectedly hot, while the general atmosphere was reminiscent of dinner in an English country house, except for the service, which was like something out of the *Arabian Nights*. There were a vast number of perfectly drilled menservants, dressed in scarlet and gold Turkish costumes, and they carried the dishes and plates high above their heads, moving always at a smart double. The whole dinner was over in forty minutes.

Elinor went also to a large number of balls and gay parties in Cairo that winter, given in honour of the Crown Prince (later King Carol) of Rumania. He invited Elinor, on behalf of his mother, Queen Marie, to come and stay with them in Bucharest on her way home to England. Elinor, to her deep regret, had to decline, as she was just off to stay with the Queen of Spain.

2.

Elinor arrived in Madrid for Holy Week and was accordingly able to be present at the magnificent Easter ceremonies of the Spanish court. Elinor loved court pomp and ceremony, especially when this contained traditional ritual whose origins went back far in history. She had been much interested in Russia by the ceremony of the Czar blessing the waters, but even more impressive now was the washing of the beggars' feet on Maundy Thursday. It was a moving sight, the Grandees in their glittering uniforms, the Duchesses in their high combs and mantillas, kneeling in stately dignity before the beggars, while the King and Queen passed down the line, washing and kissing the bare feet. She described the scene in enthusiastic detail in her book, *Letters from Spain.*

There were many other court ceremonies, and Elinor passed through Easter week and the two months following starry-eyed with delight. There is something a little pathetic about her longing for royal pageantry and her yearning to find in some modern capital the gorgeous court life of Versailles under Louis XV. She was fated ever to find such splendour only on the eve of its dissolution—a dissolution which she was, by conviction and temperament, never able to foresee.

King Alphonso XIII of Spain was a personal friend of hers; he himself on a visit to England climbed the four flights of stairs to her flat on the top floor of Shelley Court to see her. Now, in Spain, she specially approved of the dignified way in which he carried out his duties and upheld the cause of *noblesse oblige.* She likened him, curiously, to the Prince of Wales, especially in his zeal for social improvements and reforms, and she was unwise enough in her book to prophesy a long and glorious future for such a popular monarch.

She spent only two months in Spain, as compared with her six months in Russia and her year in America, and she was correspondingly less able to form a complete idea of the country. As in Russia, she moved almost exclusively in court circles and her contacts were confined almost exclusively to the upper classes. She conceived a great admiration for the Spanish male, despite his undoubted cruelty, jealousy, and his frequent fickleness as a husband. He was invariably completely masculine, without even a trace of the feminine in him.

There were, she found, two chief differences between the Spanish and Russian courts. In the Spanish court there was a strong atmosphere of piety and religion which found no counterpart in Russia. There was also, again in contrast to the rather hopeless cosmopolitanism of the Russian nobles, a feeling of intense personal pride which seemed to exist at all levels, and this showed itself in strange little ways. In Russia, for example, as in America, every servant's hand in hotel and private houses seemed to be held out continually for a tip; in Russia, Elinor had even had to tip the guards on the bends of the stairs in the royal palaces each time she passed. But in Madrid her attempt to tip the maid of the lady-in-waiting who had been assisting her caused only strong offence.

She attended two bullfights. One was a big *corrida* before the King and Queen, in which both Belmonte and Joselito fought. Elinor watched it from the box of the Duke de Tovar, who had bred the bulls. She was considerably revolted by the sight—the horses at that time were not padded—and even more by the cruelty of the crowd, which was extended not only towards the horses and the bulls but towards the matadors themselves. However, her training in the control of her emotions stood her in good stead.

Her second bullfight was a private one given for the Queen. This time they stood on a rickety plank gallery over the arena while young matadors fought young bulls. It was raining hard and, with the mud and the blood, it was a gruesome scene. On the slippery ground the matadors had several escapes, one having part of his face ripped open, and Elinor was considerably relieved when the Queen, who herself hated bullfighting, stopped the fight.

Even nastier to watch than a bullfight, Elinor found, was a cockfight, though there was the consolation here that the cocks were fighting to the death not at the instigation of a human master but for their own reasons. And she could not help being struck by the courage and the pride of the birds.

I was obliged to sit there and watch three *maines,* and really, horrible and even disgusting as it was, no one could fail to admire the courage and endurance of the birds: and what superlative belief in Self! For the fight is not caused by previous personal hatred for the adversary, but by resentment that *any* rival *could* exist! They do not hesitate a second to fly at each other once they are in the matting-covered ring, never having met before. Vanity and egotism are evidently the chief characteristics of cocks.*

Elinor was lavishly entertained as usual, going to a large number of private parties and balls: a concert and reception by the Duchess de Fernan Núñez; a tea with the celebrated Spanish dancers of the Countess de Casa Valencia; the Duke de Tovar's private entertainment at the opera; and the balls of the Countess Romanones and the Duchess de Parsent. Elinor had been warned beforehand that Spanish society was extremely exclusive and that she would probably not see the inside of any private houses, so she was especially pleased and gratified by the warmth of her reception. She was also sur-

* *Letters from Spain.*

prised to find that no one sat down to dinner till ten o'clock in the evening.

She was shown over the Prado and the Escorial—the last she found grim and depressing. She also stayed in country houses and visited Cordova, Seville, and Toledo.

You never enter a French village with its pollarded trees in the square in front of the Mairie, without some feeling that on fête days it will be gay; but you cannot think of any gayety in these grim towns of Spain. Romance may linger behind those barred windows, but of lightness there is no trace. Solemnity and resignation are in all faces.

What can the lives of the people be who live there? Their grave faces show no emotion whatsoever—and oh! what quantities of priests everywhere.

Again I say, why are priests generally so fat?

The countryside she thought gaunt and desolate, but she appreciated the architecture, especially where the Moorish influence was prevalent. The cathedral at Avila she admired greatly.

Best of all was Seville, with its wild *feria*. Her romantic spirit was completely overwhelmed by the Garden of the Alcazar, with its scents and sounds and lights.

Oh! such a garden! Fine tiled walks amid a riot of orange trees in full bloom, of roses, of jasmine and every voluptuous sweet-scented thing. What wonderful creatures those old Moors were! Even in the thirteenth century they knew how to construct the finest water works. You step on certain stones in the paths and set in motion little fountain sprays to cool each walk in front of you. Then there is the mysterious bath of the ladies of the harem, below the Palace. A cool place filled with glamour which Pedro the Cruel gave to the only creature he loved and was very good to, his adored mistress. The scent of the orange-blossom mingling with the roses and jasmine simply intoxicates you when you come out again into the garden.

How anyone can keep from desiring to be young again and walk there with a lover I cannot imagine! The whole of Seville is passionately romantic, but the Royal garden is the concentrated note of it.

BOOK SEVEN

The Film Producer

1920–1929

I.

In June 1920, soon after Elinor's return to Paris from Spain, she received a letter from Hughes Massie informing her that the representative of one of the principal Hollywood film companies, Famous Players-Lasky, was in Europe and wished to come to see her. There had been discussions going on for some time about the possibility of the sale of the film rights of *Three Weeks,* and Elinor assumed that the visit would be in connection with that.

The representative, however, a Miss Mayo, did not seem particularly interested in the film rights of *Three Weeks,* but sounded Elinor as to whether she would be willing to write original stories for films. Apart from one or two war films Elinor had seen no moving pictures at that time but, unlike many authors and literary people, she did not despise the new medium and saw at once its artistic and romantic possibilities.

The sequel to Miss Mayo's visit came shortly afterwards, when Hughes Massie transmitted an invitation from Mr. Lasky for Elinor to go to Hollywood and study the technical and other problems of moving pictures in the studios. She was then to write a scenario specially for filming and herself supervise its production as a moving picture. For this she was to receive ten thousand dollars plus travelling expenses plus the prospect of the renewal of the contract on better terms if the picture should prove a success.

Elinor accepted at once and she sailed for America that autumn on the *Mauretania*. At the bottom of the gangway, she recalled later, she paused for a moment, appalled at what she was doing. She was a lonely widow, almost fifty-six; she was uprooting herself from her familiar, well-loved background in London and Paris, and she was turning her back on her family and her friends; she was going, not to visit, but to live in a strange, utterly different world six thousand miles away, where she knew practically no one; she was going to try to master a completely new medium in severe, merciless competition with a crowd of talented people half her age.

She stood on the quayside staring up at the funnels of the liner, for almost the first time in her life scared and unsure of herself. Then she pulled herself together and went on up the gangway.

She had never been one to miss an opportunity for travel or adventure and this was just the sort of opportunity that appealed most to her. Not only was she going to a strange new challenging country but she had also been given the chance to open up a great new field for her stories and ideas, in particular for those romantic ideals which had seemed to her in the past so woefully missing in America. She had also the prospect of making a lot of money. Though she was by now accustomed to living from hand to mouth, she was uncomfortably aware that the moment must come when her skill, her energy, and her popularity must wane and she had no savings upon which to fall back.

At the moment, however, she had on hand as much work as she could manage and Hughes Massie had to send her a letter as she sailed reminding her of all her literary commitments. The Hearst press were taking advantage of her presence in America, not only to publicise her, but to sign her for a series of articles. There were a number of series of articles for English journals to which she was committed. There was her scenario for Lasky and there was also her yearly novel for Duckworth.

She was met in New York by a representative of Famous Players-Lasky and a full blare of publicity. It was suggested, on the strength of *Elizabeth Visits America,* that she was going to California because she preferred the Far West to the eastern seaboard. Elinor, however, tactfully but firmly, refused to make any such invidious distinctions. A few days later she arrived at the Hollywood Hotel, a homely place run by an old lady of over eighty. There she met the other authors whom Lasky had also invited to Hollywood: Maeterlinck, Edward Knoblock, Somerset Maugham, Gouverneur Morris, Gertrude Atherton, and an old friend, Sir Gilbert Parker.

2.

It is difficult now, more than thirty years later, to re-create the extraordinary topsy-turvy atmosphere of Hollywood in 1920. The lusty young film industry was finding its feet and was full of boisterous self-confidence. Everyone connected with the studios was firmly convinced that he or she knew all about everything, even ways of life far removed from his own, confirmed in this belief by the large box-office returns brought in even by the primitive silent films then being made.

They all believed they knew exactly what the public wanted and were perfectly capable of supplying it without any outside advice. Their efforts, however, were met with uncompromising hostility from almost all dramatic critics and a great number of distinguished people in the world of letters and art. The heads of the studios were pained by this criticism, to which they seem to have been particularly sensitive, and it was to combat this distrust and contempt for moving pictures in general that Lasky had invited his eminent authors to Hollywood.

It did not take the authors long to discover that their presence in Hollywood was only window-dressing. It was their names and not their literary abilities which were required by the studios. Elinor wrote in her memoirs:

> The blatantly crude or utterly false psychology of the stories as finally shown upon the screen was on a par with the absurdity of the sets and clothes, but we were powerless to prevent this. All authors, living or dead, famous or obscure, shared the same fate. Their stories were rewritten and completely altered either by the stenographers and continuity girls of the scenario department, or by the Assistant Director and his lady-love, or by the leading lady, or by anyone else who happened to pass through the studio; and even when at last, after infinite struggle, a scene was shot which bore some resemblance to the original story, it was certain to be left out in the cutting-room, or pared away to such an extent that all meaning which it might once have had was lost.

One by one all the imported authors departed in varying conditions of rage, disappointment, or sorrow. Maugham did not even stay to watch the shooting of his script but moved on quickly to his more familiar stamping-grounds across the Pacific. Elinor alone stayed on to fight it out.

There was, of course, another side to the story. Some of the authors whom Lasky had invited to Hollywood were no longer able or willing to learn their trade all over again. Their skill and their reputations were founded upon their mastery of words and they found it difficult now to adapt themselves to a wordless medium. Maeterlinck's first scenario was "a charming little tale about a small boy who discovered some fairies. I'm afraid," wrote Mr. Samuel Goldwyn, "my reactions to it were hardly fairy-like." Maeterlinck's second effort was a love story so daring that no censor could have passed it, and he returned to Europe in high dudgeon.

"A versatile woman, Elinor Glyn, [wrote Mr. Goldwyn] and one whose name will always figure in any history of the film colony—though she didn't think much of Hollywood."

It may well be thought that Elinor's success there, under the given conditions, was the most remarkable achievement of her whole career.

3.

Her first script, *The Great Moment,* was carefully devised for the silent screen and depended on plot, strong situations, vivid scenes, and clear-cut characters rather than the subtleties of human relationships. *The Kine Weekly* said of it:

> It is a highly-coloured, semi-sensational society drama but it has many good points to recommend it, including an original plot, definite characterisation, dramatic situations, a strong love interest and plenty of interest particularly suited to picturisation.

Sir Edward Pelham, a reserved, conventional English diplomat, has, in a moment of ecstatic passion, married a Russian gipsy girl, and in terror in case their daughter Nadine should grow up as wild as her mother, now dead, he keeps her virtually imprisoned in his English country house during her childhood. He also arranges for her to marry his distant cousin and heir, Eustace Pelham, a dull, pompous young man. Nadine, in her loneliness and yearning to escape, dreams continually of a Knight Bayard who will come and set her free. She sees from her bedroom window a handsome young man whom she imagines to be Eustace coming to propose but is in fact the manager of her father's American gold mine, Bayard Delaval.

Nadine is deeply disappointed by the real Eustace, who arrives later, but accepts him. She falls ill, and on the doctor's recommendation she, her fiancé, and her father go to Nevada to inspect the mine and to have a holiday. There, of course, she meets Bayard again and falls in love with him. Riding back with him from the mine across the desert, she is bitten by a rattlesnake, and Bayard in anguish saves her life by carrying her to a shack of his near by and pouring a bottle of whisky down her throat. Nadine becomes very drunk and, her gipsy blood coming out, she makes passionate love to him. At this strong and compromising situation, her father and fiancé arrive on the scene.

Sir Edward is outraged and tells Nadine he never wishes to see her again; he leaves her with the man whom he imagines to be her seducer. Nadine falls unconscious, and when she wakes she does not recognise Bayard. He, suddenly realising that her love the night before was only due to gipsy blood and the whisky, and not to love for him, sends her quickly away after her father, who forgives her a little bleakly. Poor Nadine, not understanding at all why her beloved Bayard should send her away so brusquely, is very unhappy. She goes to Washington to stay with friends and gets into the worst set. A millionaire called Hopper wishes to marry her and gives vast parties for her which turn into orgies and at which Nadine makes an exhibition of herself in her general misery and frustration.

However, through the influence of friends who understand the true story, Bayard arrives to claim her just before her marriage to Hopper. Nadine is radiantly happy, even at the thought of spending the rest of her life in a shack in the Nevada desert; and Bayard keeps as a surprise for her the knowledge that he is now retiring, a rich man, from gold mining and is taking Nadine to live at his ancestral home in Virginia.

As was later conceded, *The Great Moment* was admirable material for a Hollywood silent film of 1920. It was, however, at first treated with contempt, and the continuity writer proceeded to cut the story to ribbons. The director, Sam Wood, "in order to increase the suspense," decided to treat part of the film as a knockabout farce, and there were moments when Elinor herself was on the verge of packing her bags and returning to England.

One day, at a conference on the set, the director remarked, "Say, boys, I guess you all think you know just what ought to be done, but I certainly can't think how to end this story myself." In the moment of silence that followed, Elinor suggested tentatively that perhaps, as the author, she could suggest an ending. Cecil B. de Mille, one of the most powerful of Lasky's producers, was walking through the studio at that moment and he caught Elinor's eye and laughed out loud. That one laugh, Elinor later realised, did her film career more good than anything else. With de Mille's support and influence she was in a far stronger position to battle on for the ideals and objectives which had brought her to California.

The Great Moment was a considerable success at the box office, even in its mutilated, farcical form. This was due partly to the story itself, the hard core of which was still apparent, and partly to a vivid performance by Gloria Swanson as Nadine, wilful, passionate, bewildered, half child, half woman. Lasky was pleased and Elinor was signed on for a further picture on an improved contract.

4·

She had by now seen enough of Hollywood studios to know that, even with de Mille behind her, she was powerless to prevent her stories being altered almost beyond recognition. But at least she could do something to make the sets a little more realistic. Indeed, this aspect of film making seemed to her even more important than the story itself.

Few of the art directors, the scene designers, the costumiers or the hairdressers of Hollywood had been outside the States, but they would accept no advice or suggestions from Elinor. She was appalled to think that millions of Americans and Britons were going to see such travesties and presumably believe them to be accurate. In vain she protested that English Duchesses did not wear their hair like frizzy golliwoggs; that the drawing-rooms of English country houses did not contain bamboo tables, aspidistras, or the various knickknacks usually associated with seaside lodging-houses; that ducal castles did not have a line of spittoons, even gold ones, down the middle of the drawing-room.

Elinor had always a passionate love of truth, and she could not bear now to see the scenes she knew and loved so well misrepresented and held up to derision, even unintentionally. She was the sole representative of European high society in Hollywood and she felt her responsibility keenly.

It has often been said that Hollywood is a difficult place in which to retain a sense of proportion; Elinor found it as difficult as anyone else. One can sympathise with her indignation at seeing such travesties of English high life enacted on the sets, but at the same time one must feel that she often could not see the wood for the trees and that it would have been better had she conserved her combative efforts for broad principles and general atmosphere rather than for details of scenery or clothes. However, one has only to recall many of the Hollywood films of the thirties, with their greater desire for accuracy not only of sets and clothes but also of speech, atmosphere, and character, to realise how far the cinema progressed in those ten years, at any rate in authenticity. And for that progress Elinor must be given a good deal of the credit.

5.

"Elinor Glyn's name [wrote Mr. Goldwyn] is synonymous with the discovery of sex appeal for the cinema."

Elinor herself disliked the term "sex appeal," much preferring her own "it." But "it" was a quality which one either had or had not and which could never be acquired. Romance, that spiritual disguise so necessary to human happiness, was the teachable quality. In 1907 she had been shocked by the lack of romance in America, by the indifferent, mercenary attitude of American men and women to love, and although the pendulum was now swinging the other way, she felt that a great deal still could and should be done to bring romance into the lives of ordinary people and to teach all gold-digging girls that true love meant giving unconditionally and not receiving or bargaining.

But she was soon made to realise that American girls were not wholly to blame for this attitude.

I had not been long in Hollywood before I discovered that what I had always suspected was true; American men of those days simply could not make love! Not even the leading screen actors had any idea how to do it then. One after another screen tests of handsome young American film stars were shown me for approval, but in every case I considered that the performance was lamentable! I christened them all woolly lambs and besought the studio managers to find me someone who could treat differently, in front of the camera, the actress who was supposed to be his sweetheart from those who were supposed to be his aunts and sisters.

The best of them was Rudolph Valentino, not yet at his full fame, but even he had a lot to learn from Elinor in the art of making love convincingly before a camera. "Do you know," she would murmur in later years, "he had never even thought of kissing the palm, rather than the back, of a woman's hand until I made him do it!"

6.

It is not quite clear who suggested *Beyond the Rocks* for Elinor's second film. Lasky himself had considerable misgivings about it and, indeed, the book with its very slight plot would not seem to be good silent-film material. However, the story was approved and production started early in 1922.

Unlike *The Great Moment*, the whole action of *Beyond the Rocks* takes place in France and England, and this gave almost unlimited opportunities for those anachronisms and solecisms which Elinor so much abhorred. She and Sam Wood had disagreed many times in the first film; they were completely at loggerheads now and appalling rows went on between them on the set, each giving as good as received. Miss Ruby Miller, the Gaiety Girl, who was in Hollywood at the time, recalls that she went down to lunch with Elinor on the set, to find her in full battle over a shooting-party which was assembled in hunting pink before a cottage on which rambler roses were in full bloom. By the time Elinor had sorted this out to her satisfaction, the day was almost over and neither she, Miss Miller, nor anyone else had had any lunch.

> Like a lot of other women I know [wrote Mr. Goldwyn] she liked her own way, though it didn't always follow that she got it with me. She not only wrote the scenarios, but insisted on designing the dresses and arranging the drawing-room as a replica of her own room in London. When someone remonstrated with her about this, she retorted: "Do you think they would know how to arrange a gentlewoman's room but for me?"

The principal shortcomings in the completed picture of *Beyond the Rocks* were not in the settings, but in the acting and direction. The charm of the book, it will be remembered, lay in the effect of Theodora's innocence and purity upon Lord Bracondale's jaded man-of-the-world attitude. Both the principal actors seemed to misread their parts: Gloria Swanson played Theodora as a sophisticated minx and Rudolph Valentino, for all his charm and passion, portrayed Lord Bracondale as a young boy going through his first love affair. The continuity writers had taken every possible liberty with the story to introduce sensational effects. The scene at Versailles, in which Lord Bracondale tells Theodora the fairy story, was played in eighteenth-century clothes in and out of a sedan chair. Josiah, instead of dying quietly of a broken heart, was sent off big-game shooting in Africa to be brutally murdered by natives. There were also some rather surprising shots of Lord Bracondale galloping about a desert in a burnous, the studio having decided to put in some unused sequences from Valentino's previous film, *The Sheik.*

Altogether *Beyond the Rocks* was not, artistically, a great success. But with those stars and that author it could not fail at the box office. Exhibitors were advised to "Boom the Author!"

Conjure with the name of Elinor Glyn! The fact that the author has supervised this film may be mentioned but if it allows patrons to think that the book has been faithfully followed, they may be disappointed.

7.

Soon after her arrival in Hollywood, Elinor began to make a series of new friendships to replace those she had left behind in Europe. Douglas Fairbanks and Mary Pickford were, of course, the uncrowned king and queen of Hollywood at that time and Elinor, a connoisseur of queens, found in Mary Pickford the same gracious regal qualities she had found in the courts of Europe. The so evident love of this famous couple for each other was very moving, a thing utterly apart from anything else in the glossy, false-fronted life of Hollywood. There was an atmosphere of peace and happiness in their home, Pickfair, and some of the happiest hours of Elinor's years in Hollywood were spent there.

The parties there, always lively, were especially gay when Charles Chaplin was present. Elinor had met Chaplin a few days after her first arrival in Hollywood at Goldwyn's house. Chaplin had had a sudden fit of depression about his recently completed film, *The Kid,* and Goldwyn gave a small private party to show the film to a number of selected friends, including the authors so recently arrived from Europe. *The Kid* was the first Chaplin film that Elinor saw and she was deeply impressed. Her spontaneous words of admiration to him in that moment of misgiving began a warm personal friendship founded on mutual admiration.

Other close friends of Elinor's during those years were Gloria Swanson and Marion Davies, and she was a frequent guest at both their houses. She was also on pleasant if less intimate terms with a whole host of other Hollywood luminaries.

Hollywood parties at that time have come down to us with the reputation of being veritable orgies. There was certainly a great deal of drinking, particularly during Prohibition, but the notorious excesses did not take place at the parties given or attended by the more famous of the stars. But their parties were, all the same, unusual affairs. Married couples, or couples who were, in the slang of the time, "going with each other," sat determinedly side by side at meals, holding hands under the table. The conversation, especially when Chaplin was present, would range nimbly over a wide variety of subjects, controversial and intellectual.

After dinner everyone would do turns or play parlour games, charades, dumb crambo, act impromptu scenes, or make one-minute speeches on abstruse subjects. Elinor was amazed that people who had spent the whole day acting in the studio should want to continue doing it in private in the evening. It was part, she supposed, of the hectic, restless atmosphere of the place.

The speeches and scenes set were often very exacting and left no doubt in Elinor's mind that being a leading film star needed not only appearance, personality, and acting ability but also a more-than-average share of brains. She herself loved any form of amateur theatricals or charades and she threw herself into these entertainments with extreme enjoyment. She recalled one of these charades in her memoirs:

> Charlie [Chaplin] drew me as his partner and from the bowl I picked our subject which was "Hate." Our turn was last and as all the rest had treated their themes in a comic vein, Charlie decided that we would be serious. By some magic he got himself up into an alcove behind which the supports of the window appeared like a cross. He wore nothing but a cloth twisted round him and spread out his hands as if crucified. I knelt, draped in a white sheet, at the foot of the alcove, to represent the Mourning World, while Charlie's Japanese servant lit up the whole scene with a single candle, held low from the side where he could not be seen. The room was otherwise in darkness and the effect was extraordinarily moving. I remember the sudden reverent hush as the audience first saw his face, so wonderfully filled with agony and resignation.

Elinor was also a popular figure at the bigger and rather less intellectually strenuous parties. She had always been at her best in social company and now, even in that throng determined to outglitter each other, her great beauty, her regal presence, and her personality made her, effortlessly, one of the

outstanding figures. Her gift of quick and amusing conversation, practised and perfected at so many house parties in England, made her a welcome guest.

It was in Hollywood that she first actually met William
Randolph Hearst in person, and she went many times to his
amazing ranch, San Simeon, where each guest had his own
Spanish villa and everyone ate in a huge tapestried dining-hall
off one of the longest refectory tables ever seen. The table and
all the room were crowded with the relics of European culture.
Furniture, painted ceilings, Gothic choir stalls, complete Tudor
rooms lay about or remained in partly opened packing-cases.
It was all very bewildering to Elinor, who venerated English
stately homes strongly and could not reconcile herself now to
seeing so many of their treasures jumbled together as if in a
huge antique shop. The pick of the antique sales of the world
was here, higgledy-piggledy, uncatalogued, some pieces, it was
said, bought by mistake twice over. The noise, too, was terrific,
with a crowd of minor film stars shouting and laughing, and
gramophones blaring; and in the middle of all the hubbub was
Hearst himself, conducting his business with his secretaries.

Although they were so very different in character, Elinor
and Hearst took to each other. She had always admired strong
characters and she certainly found one in Hearst. She found
him, too, a generous and thoughtful host and a kind employer.
He, in his turn, liked Elinor, admiring her work and her personality, and finding her a social asset at his parties. He also
acted at times as her business advisor, cautioning her against
various deals and speculations to which she was being tempted.
Had his advice been more continually available, she might
well have ended a much richer woman than she did.

It was on her way to stay with Hearst in Mexico that Elinor
experienced another of her bedroom farces. A storm had
washed away the road and she, Chaplin, and his new wife,
Lita Grey, had to spend the night in a double-bedded shack.
It was filthy and very uncomfortable, but nothing else was

available at two o'clock in the morning. Chaplin and his wife bickered continually about the amount of bed the other was taking up. At last, just as Elinor, in a child's cot, with her feet on a packing-case, was dropping off to sleep, Chaplin suddenly sat up and said in a deep, sepulchral voice, "My God! Think of Charlie Chaplin and Elinor Glyn in bed together in the wilds of Mexico!"

Elinor burst out laughing and, thus stimulated, Chaplin delivered a long monologue, reciting imaginary press paragraphs describing the scandal, mimicking the voices and different reactions of all those who might read the news. Never had Elinor known him more brilliant and she felt quite weak from laughter. Finally, as dawn was breaking, they decided to get some sleep. Elinor was just dropping off when the sepulchral voice announced, "My God! There's a bug!" And he started all over again. This time the laughter and noise was so great that other members of the party who were sleeping in the saloon or in cars outside burst in to see what the trouble was and whether there had been a holdup.

It would, however, be a mistake to think of Elinor's time away from the studios being filled with continual parties. She had far too much work to do for that, and most evenings she would spend quietly in her room at the Hollywood Hotel, reading Plato in a dogged and rather touching effort to try to retain her sense of values in that crazy looking-glass world. She was only too well aware of the dangers to the human personality of what she called the "Californian Curse," and of which the most flagrant and tragic example was the breakup of that seemingly perfect love idyll between Douglas Fairbanks and Mary Pickford.

The Curse is nothing less than that of the Evil Fairy in the old stories, who was able to banish the real personality of those whom she bewitched, forcing them against their wills to carry out her commands, to forget the land of their birth, the purpose of their journey and many of the principles which they had hitherto held most dear.

The early symptoms of the disease, which break out almost on arrival in Hollywood, are a sense of exaggerated self-importance and self-centredness which naturally alienates all old friends. Next comes a great desire for and belief in the importance of money above all else, a loss of the normal sense of humour and proportion and finally, in extreme cases, the abandonment of all previous standards of moral value.

By her foreknowledge, by her determined concentration upon what she conceived to be the eternal verities, she was able for a while to ward off and delay the effects of the Californian Curse. As will be seen later, even she was not able to escape it altogether.

8.

During 1922, Elinor was approached by another film company, Metro-Goldwyn-Mayer, who proposed that, when *Beyond the Rocks* and her contract with Famous Players-Lasky were completed, she should join MGM to supervise the filming of *Three Weeks*. For years Elinor had been hoping that she would one day be given an opportunity to film her bestseller and she accepted the tempting new offer with alacrity—too great alacrity for the contract she might have won from them by harder bargaining.

The production was scheduled to begin in March 1923, and meanwhile Elinor decided to return to Europe to revisit her family and friends and familiar scenes. Her absence in America had prevented her, to her distress, from being present at either of her daughters' weddings, Margot's to Sir Edward Davson, and Juliet's to Sir Rhys Rhys-Williams, both of which had taken place in 1921. Now she was able to be present at a great family reunion and to meet her first two grandchildren (one of them myself), for whose schooling, with her newly acquired wealth and her instinctive generosity, she immediately started insurance policies. She installed her mother in a comfortable flat in Embankment Gardens and reopened her house in the Avenue Victor Hugo, Paris. She also went with Margot to Cannes, made another trip to Spain, and gave a series of lectures in Norway, Denmark, and Sweden. She was back again in Hollywood at the end of February 1923, living now in a suite on the sixth floor of the Ambassador Hotel, Los Angeles.

During her visit to Europe she had been working on the film version of *Three Weeks,* and we may with some justice regard the finished scenario as a considerable achievement, a yardstick of the degree to which in her first two years in Hollywood she had mastered the art of the silent film. Horniman had discovered how difficult it was to cast *Three Weeks* into a dramatic version. The greater part of the book, it will be remembered, is virtually one long love scene, and to get this across without any dialogue and without lapsing into either offensiveness or ribaldry made a considerable demand on Elinor's skill. To break up the love scene, and in the interests of clarity, she was obliged to insert some sequences of the Balkan background, to show briefly the King's depravity, his unpopularity, and the love and respect in which the Queen was held. She also put in, to increase the suspense, a fight on the edge of a Venetian canal between Vasili and one of the King's spies, but otherwise she stuck closely to the book, except that, at the demands of the studio, she was obliged to put in a brief reunion between Paul and the Queen in the villa before the final tragedy. The English part she left unaltered.

Her scenario, however, tested to the utmost the resources even of Metro-Goldwyn-Mayer's experienced continuity writer. For the scene in the Queen's boudoir in Lucerne where she lies on the tiger skin, quivering with emotion and passion, he wrote, a little helplessly:

SCENE 137 CLOSE-UP INTERIOR THE LADY'S SUITE

Better than describe this scene, I will simply mention that Mrs. Glyn will enact it for Mr. Crossland on the set. The lady makes her decision to accept Paul as her lover. She hears Paul outside and indicates for him to come in.

Elinor enjoyed working for MGM more than she had for the Lasky studios, finding the art department, under the direction of Cedric Gibbons, more amenable to her insistence on accuracy and beauty of setting. She cared terribly that *Three Weeks* should be worthily produced and several times she had scenes, which still dissatisfied her, reshot at her own expense.

There was also the shadow of the censor falling across this particular film. Elinor had cherished a faint hope that, in the interests of verisimilitude, Paul might be allowed to play the final love scene on the night of the full moon in pyjamas; but she was soon made to realise that this would never be permitted, and in the approved version the Queen tiptoed away, wracked with sobs, leaving Paul asleep on the couch of rose petals, still in full evening dress, his hair smooth and his white waistcoat uncrumpled. As a consolation for this MGM allowed Elinor real rose petals for the couch.

The part of the Queen was played by Aileen Pringle, looking astonishingly like Elinor, who had coached her assiduously. She gave a beautiful performance, dignified, regal yet passionate. Conrad Nagel's Paul was adequate, if a little weak, but the actor who played the King unfortunately burlesqued his part. As one critic remarked, the story as a whole could do with a little humour, but not in that particular character.

Three Weeks, however, fully deserved its enormous success at the box office. In England the censor made a large number of cuts, including, rather strangely, the title, which was not allowed to appear even on a by-line. But despite this handicap *The Romance of a Queen* did very well and provided a strong resurge of interest in the original novel.

Three Weeks has never been filmed as a talking picture, though a proposal from Metro-Goldwyn-Mayer to do so in 1933, with Gloria Swanson as the Queen and Irving Thalberg as director, reached an advanced stage before it was abandoned in deference to a "cleaner films" campaign then sweeping America.

It had occurred to several people that *Three Weeks* was well suited to musical treatment. In 1908 the book had been suggested to Puccini as a possible libretto, and we may well think that the intensity, the drama, and the passion of the story might have fired Puccini to write some of his most appealing music. He himself gave the book serious consideration but rejected it in the belief, erroneous as it turned out, that *The Girl of the Golden West* would have greater attraction in America. In any event, however, the projected operatic version must have encountered serious difficulties over the vexed question of the ownership of the American dramatic rights of *Three Weeks*.

In 1924 the Shubert brothers proposed to present the work as an operetta in New York. A musical score was commissioned and completed before the venture foundered on the unseen rocks that bar the way for so many Broadway productions.

9.

Elinor's views about American women, and perhaps the women themselves, had changed considerably since 1908. They were no longer the "fluffy little gold-diggers"; on the contrary, they were as capable of love as European women. Now they wrote to her in their hundreds, following the publication of her newspaper articles, asking for help and advice:

How were they to win the man they loved? How were they to hold his love? How could they rekindle his earlier love, now seemingly dead?

The popularity of Elinor's own novels, of Rudolph Valentino's films, showed only too clearly how desperately hungry the women of America were for love and romance; and Elinor thought it pitiful that they could find it only in print and in celluloid. Real life, she was convinced, was as full of potential romance as any book or film; but it was so easily smothered by dull, matter-of-fact routine, by sordidness, or by excessive familiarity. She had been puzzled, even in the days of *Three Weeks,* as has already been shown, by the way the marriage ties so often proved fatal to love itself; her own marriage had been a case in point. Her cynical, disillusioned spirit had, in *The Damsel and the Sage,* accepted this seemingly inevitable consequence of marriage with a shrug and a pout. It had always been so and would probably always remain so.

But her romantic heart rebelled. It should be possible, she argued—and the whole of her creed of life was based upon this premise—for men or women of any nationality to find all the romance they wanted in their own lives, not only before but even after marriage, without having to resort to novels and films—provided that they had the necessary skill and wisdom. And it was to provide this skill that she wrote for her American readers *The Philosophy of Love.*

The book contained many of the thoughts and conclusions of her own life, and much of it was taken from articles she had already written on the subject. It dealt with many aspects of love and marriage, and especially with the problem of how to make love last. She coined a new word, to "revulsh": less strong than to disgust, stronger than to put off, it covered all those little points of habit, speech, and hygiene, those minute pinpricks, all of them almost negligible, which cumulatively killed love far more completely than the greater matrimonial crimes of cruelty or infidelity. This point has since been made by many others in books and newspaper articles.

She also campaigned against the touching and "petting" which had become so prevalent since her first visit and which was partly a reaction from the chaperoned austerity of those days and partly, no doubt, the social consequence of the wider ownership of small, closed cars.

Don't cheapen all agreeable emotions by being so physically friendly with every girl—that is, touching her at every moment, taking arms and so on, when you are not the least interested in her, or she in you.

Touching ought to be reserved entirely for the loved one —that is, if you want to feel any thrills; and this advice applies to girls also. This continuous and promiscuous familiarity of pawing each other, is the first step towards destroying the capacity to love.

Quite apart from the practical results of disillusionment such pawing was, in Elinor's view, "servants' behaviour," and she fought against it unwearyingly for the rest of her life. We can imagine that she must have regretted the passages in *Elizabeth Visits America* in which she urged American girls to be less grudging and miserly with their kisses.

The Philosophy of Love also includes an extended analysis of the male and female characters and contains her division of the female sex into three parts, lover-women, mother-women and neuter-women; the characteristics of one or other group should, Elinor contended, be discernible even in early childhood.

The book is, on the whole, sensible and constructive, and is free of those wilder and more controversial theories about life which both enrich and mar Elinor's other works. It is full of earnest, practical advice, some of it dull and a little obvious, other parts strong and outspoken. It was written in a sincere attempt to bring romance into the lives of young Americans, particularly young American women, and for that reason it deserved the astonishing reception that America gave it.

When it was published in England, under the title *Love —What It Means to Me,* it caused no great stir. But the American nation has an almost inexhaustible thirst for books of practical advice upon human relationships. *The Philosophy of Love* sold a quarter of a million copies in its first six months of publication and its ultimate American sale was second only to that of *Three Weeks.*

The consequences of the book's widespread popularity were twofold. One was an enormous increase in Elinor's own mail —letters from girls, young husbands, young wives, asking her further advice upon some particular point, and to each of which Elinor replied fully and conscientiously, despite the demand which they made upon her severely limited time. She found herself, in effect, running singlehandedly a marriage-advice bureau and she continued this up to her departure from America in 1929. She liked the insight which it gave her into people's lives and problems, the feeling that she was bringing her romantic ideals into widespread practice, and especially the thought that she was repaying to the American people something of the kindness and hospitality they had always shown to her.

The other consequence of the success of *The Philosophy of Love* was more spectacular: an engagement to appear in vaudeville in New York, giving ten-minute talks on love, at a salary of five hundred pounds a week. This engagement she carried out during the winter of 1923; and one may wonder if, while she was waiting in the wings for her cue, she ever recalled the days when she would not have allowed anyone connected with the stage inside her house.

10.

Elinor's second film for Metro-Goldwyn-Mayer, *His Hour,* was produced early in 1924, and the making of this film was one of the happiest experiences Elinor had during her stay in Hollywood. She found her new director, King Vidor, a congenial person, and for once there was no difficulty about the authenticity of the sets. Hollywood swarmed with *émigré* Russians earning their living as film extras, and Elinor was both pained and amused to find several of them playing in her film very nearly the same parts they had played in St. Petersburg in real life.

The story was only altered very slightly, the duel between Gritzko and Boris in the darkened room playing a rather more important part, and the climax in the hunting-lodge being made a little less risqué. Aileen Pringle acted Tamara on rather a subdued note, as if she were determined to emphasise the difference between Tamara and the Queen in *Three Weeks.* John Gilbert as Gritzko showed very nearly as much "it" as the original Gritzko himself—a vivid, passionate performance in the Valentino manner which raised him at once to the heights of stardom.

11.

Elinor had always thrived on admiration. Any form of disparagement or deflation was fatal to her self-esteem and her creative impetus. During her visits to America she had always moved in a spotlight of admiration, the greater part of it genuine. But, like so many others who feed on admiration, she could never tell the real praise from the false; she could never detect the unscrupulous flatterer among the crowd of sincere admirers.

We cannot wonder now that, alone in Hollywood, six thousand miles from her family and friends and her familiar background, intoxicated by the success and fortune she was making in her new career, stimulated by her fame and popularity among hundreds of thousands of Americans, she should have been specially vulnerable to smooth dishonesty or glossy sharp practice. She had never had any kind of business sense, and now, with the thought of her large film earnings behind her, she launched into a variety of projects, speculations in land, gold mines, companies, and investments, from only some of which Hearst managed to dissuade her. "Everyone tells me," she wrote rather touchingly in one letter home, "what a wonderful business woman I have become." In blissful self-confidence over her deals she was robbed on all sides. She forgot her original intention to salt away a proportion of her earnings in gilt-edged investments against the time when she would retire.

Her personal expenses were also high, though perhaps not excessively so in view of the standard required to be maintained by successful people in Hollywood. She was also very generous to a large number of her compatriots who had been less fortunate than she. The full extent of these benefactions will never be known.

As always, she signed any contract laid before her, and became increasingly entangled with varying agents of conflicting interests, some of them of dubious integrity. One contract she signed entitled an agent to a 50 per cent commission on all her earnings from her books and films, past as well as future.

Something drastic had to be done, and in the summer of 1924, Juliet and her husband, Sir Rhys Rhys-Williams, a noted barrister, travelled out to Hollywood to disentangle Elinor's affairs. The first step was to free her from her commitments to these agents, in particular the one who was taking a 50 per cent commission. Rhys-Williams interviewed him and the man produced triumphantly the signed contract. Rhys-Williams explained that Mrs. Glyn always honoured her contracts and would no doubt do so in this case, but he must ask for the contract to be published. Rather than do this, the agent tore it up.

Rhys-Williams then turned to the tougher business of negotiating an improvement in Elinor's contract with Metro-Goldwyn-Mayer. This involved some hard bargaining with Mr. Louis B. Mayer, and in the end a satisfactory solution was achieved. Elinor was to make further films for MGM and to be paid not only lump sums for the purchase or lease of the film rights, and expenses, but also a royalty on the box-office takings, with a guaranteed minimum of ten thousand pounds per picture.

It was, however, not enough merely to get Elinor out of her mess. Steps had to be taken to prevent or at least to reduce the likelihood of such a position recurring. It was not easy to persuade her to agree to any safeguards, for her belief in her own judgement and abilities was unshaken. Finally it was decided that she should become a limited liability company, which would hold the copyrights of all her works and receive all royalties arising from them. Juliet was the secretary of this company and various members of the family its directors. Elinor herself was not on the board, and it was hoped by this means, if not to prevent altogether, at least to reduce the commitments into which she might rashly enter.

A more immediate result was that what remained of the fortune Elinor had made in America could now be invested for her in annuities.

12.

In 1924 the effects of Prohibition began to reach serious proportions due to the extensive indulgence in "hooch" or "moonshine" alcohol even by some of the lesser stars and film technicians. The whole level of character and intelligence of the rank and file of the film industry sagged badly, and on several occasions shooting at the studio had to be suspended for a whole day or more while some vital member of the cast or technical staff slept off the effects of his or her overintoxication. Elinor herself was furious at such behaviour. She was abstemious by nature and made it a point of honour to be punctual on the set every morning. The studio authorities would censure mildly the miscreant for the time and money wasted, but Elinor was deeply distressed to note that among the lesser people such behaviour was regarded with admiration.

Coinciding with the rise in drunkenness was an increase in lawlessness. Elinor heard continually of terrifying holdups, violent robberies, and strange, unexplained murders. The Chief Constable of Los Angeles told her that crime was far worse than anyone knew and that more murders took place in Los Angeles and Hollywood in a month than in the whole of France in a year. She had no means of confirming the statistical accuracy of this statement, but she was well aware of the prevalence and violence of the crime wave.

Practically every one of her friends had been held up and robbed at some time or other. All the leading stars were followed all the time by armed guards and their houses were patrolled by guards at night. Elinor grew accustomed to hiding her rings and her pearl necklace in her stockings before driving about at night. After an evening at Pickfair, Douglas Fairbanks would always send a car to follow her own car back to her hotel if there was no other guest going that way.

On one occasion Elinor, Chaplin, and Marion Davies emerged from Elinor's suite in the Ambassador Hotel to find, just outside her door, a murderer in the act of killing a man. Before anyone could realise what was happening, the lift arrived filled with police, who hurriedly removed both the murderer and the corpse. Elinor expected that the police would call and question her and that she would be subpoenaed as a witness. But nothing at all happened, nor was there any reference to the crime in the papers. She asked the manager about it, but he brusquely denied that any such event had taken place. Only an obstinate bloodstain on the carpet outside her door, which defied repeated scrubbings, reminded her that the whole thing was not a mere figment of her imagination.

On several other occasions she heard shots and screams from the garden under her balcony, and she became accustomed to finding that nobody knew anything about them the next day.

During the summer of 1924 she herself began to receive anonymous letters and mysterious telephone calls threatening her life. She felt disinclined to do battle with a murder gang, and on her son-in-law's advice she gave the letters to the hotel detective, promising a large reward if they could be stopped. The detective smilingly announced a few days later that the letters had been traced to a madman who had now been recaptured and that she would not receive any more of them. Elinor did not believe the story for a moment, but she paid up meekly and the letters duly stopped.

Looking back later, Elinor was horrified, not so much by the crime wave itself, which was in due course brought under control, but by her own placid acceptance of the normality of such events and the way in which they were hushed up. This stifling of her conscience, this blunting of her moral scruples she considered as yet another manifestation of the effects of the Californian Curse.

13.

In 1925, Elinor produced a film version of *Man and Maid* for Metro-Goldwyn-Mayer. This followed the story of her novel, but a silent film could not carry all the subtle overtones of character and relationships which had distinguished the book, and the film showed simply and rather sentimentally a poor typist marrying a rich hero. The settings included some glittering French interiors and the film was adequately acted by Lew Cody as Nicholas and Harriet Hammond as Alathea. There was also an excellent little performance by Renée Adorée as Suzette.

For her next film, *Love's Blindness*, which was made at the end of the same year, Elinor reverted to her English settings. Hubert, Earl of St. Austell, is involved in a spectacular money crash, and to save himself and, even more, his friends, he agrees to Benjamin Levy's conditional offer of help. Levy has social ambitions and his condition is that Hubert should marry his daughter Vanessa. Hubert, trapped and humiliated, loathes the thought of Vanessa; he does not notice her beauty, which is derived from her aristocratic Italian mother, and treats her with icy contempt. Vanessa, however, knows nothing of her father's machinations; she has adored Hubert from afar for some time and imagines that he is now marrying her for love. Hubert's treatment of her, the unconscious partner and witness of his degradation, breaks her heart and gives her a miscarriage. The final happy ending comes as something of a jolt.

The film's settings were costly and elaborate and evocative of an English country house, but it was acted by Pauline Stark and Antonio Moreno with almost excessive restraint, and it aroused little enthusiasm among either the critics or the public. The book version of the story was published by Duckworth in February 1926 and was called by *The Times Literary Supplement* a "capable romance."

For her next film, *The Only Thing*, which was the last that she made for MGM, Elinor turned again to a Balkan kingdom. She put in popular and well-tried ingredients: the heroine, the beautiful Queen; the old, unattractive King; the handsome English diplomat in love with the Queen;

the Queen's charming American girl friend, Sally; a handsome, upright Balkan politician in love with Sally; a sinister
blind beggar, the embodiment of evil, who stirs up the mob to
revolution, killing the King and throwing the Queen and the
diplomat into prison. Elinor had in the past five years learned
a great deal about negotiating with Hollywood film companies, and at this point her draft synopsis breaks off abruptly
with the words:

> The rescue from the prison and the final great situation
> which is very dangerous and exciting I do not propose to
> tell anyone, until the contract is made, as it is a unique and
> great situation.

Mr. Mayer accepted the bait thus held out to him, the contract was signed, and Elinor revealed the missing scene, a new
version of the *mariage de Nantes* in which the Queen finds
herself tied in the sinking barge to the diplomat, who is dis-
guised, to her unspeakable horror, as the blind beggar himself.
This scene was to be shot partly under water by a method
devised by Elinor herself. The closing sequences of the story
were to show the Queen and the diplomat married, living
quietly in his English country home, while the people of
the Balkan state acclaim their new republic and their new
President and his wife Sally—a startling denouement for such
a royalist author.

The film was made in the summer of 1926, with the
mariage de Nantes just as Elinor conceived it. But the
American continuity writers took out Sally and the republic,
and turned the diplomat, whom Elinor had made a commoner,
into a Duke.

14.

The Rhys-Williamses' efforts to minimise Elinor's general
expenditure and the possibility of further commitments were

only partially successful. She engaged a young man as secretary and personal agent, the intention being that he should obtain further lucrative contracts for her and in general manage her business interests. For this he was to be paid a salary of five thousand pounds a year.

The directors of Elinor Glyn, Ltd., appalled, cabled from England that this was an English Cabinet Minister's salary and surely there must be some mistake. Elinor replied superbly that she thought the figure entirely reasonable for the work he was doing, and the directors had no option but to pay this salary, to the considerable detriment of Elinor's bank balance.

Elinor had at this time virtually turned her back on the Old World, becoming more and more imbued with the technique and aspirations of the inhabitants of Hollywood, with the belief that wealth and notoriety were in themselves worthy ambitions. She was full of supreme confidence in her own judgement, abilities, and the rightness of all her actions, and she tended to treat with a certain amount of contempt any dissenting voice from the Old World, merely because it was the Old, and in her present view obsolescent, World.

A momentary check in this rising megalomania was provided by the arrival in Hollywood of Lady Ravensdale, on a tour round the world. Elinor was delighted to see her again; her mere presence brought back memories of Crag and Hackwood and Montacute, the gracious society world now so far away. Elinor showed her round Hollywood, introduced her to everyone she wished to meet, and gave a party for her. Together they attended Rudolph Valentino's amazing funeral. Later that night Elinor went to condole and discuss the Great Lover with Pola Negri, who, though never his wife, was wearing the blackest of widow's weeds.

15.

One of Elinor's principal literary activities at this time was a series of articles called *The Truth,* which she wrote for the Hearst press. There were more than two hundred and fifty of them, and they dealt not only with love and marriage, but with almost every other subject under the sun.

She adopted in these articles an uncompromising, forthright style, a ruthless didacticism, deliberately intended to strip away all self-deception and prevarication. She herself was both hurt and enfeebled when her own self-deceptions were stripped from her, but of these, her own self-deceptions, she was for the most part unaware. She had no compunction, when truth and honesty demanded it, in letting others see themselves and their actions in the cold light of realism.

But the most important and the most consequential piece of literary work which Elinor produced at this time was her famous *conte,* " 'It.' " In length " 'It' " is more a short novel than a short story. It was serialised in the *Cosmopolitan* and was published the following year by itself in America and by Duckworth in a volume containing four other short stories. " 'It' " was deservedly a great success and one must regard it not only as the cream of her American literary output, but as one of the most striking pieces she ever wrote.

" 'It,' " as the title suggests, is a study in personal magnetism. Since *The Man and the Moment* there had been in her novels and articles, letters, diaries, and even, it is understood, in her conversation, several mentions of "it." And now in her new story she defined it once again.

To have "it," the fortunate possessor must have that strange magnetism which attracts both sexes. He or she must be entirely unself-conscious and full of self-confidence,

indifferent to the effect he or she is producing, and unin-
fluenced by others. There must be physical attraction, but
beauty is unnecessary. Conceit or self-consciousness destroys
"it" immediately. In the animal world "it" demonstrates in
tigers and cats—both animals being fascinating and mysterious, and quite unbiddable.

Both the hero and the heroine of the story possess "it" to
a marked degree. The hero, John Gaunt, has raised himself
by his own exertions from the depths of the Bowery to the
head of a prosperous New York business, but despite this and
despite his attraction for women he realises that there is
something missing in his life. The girl, Ava Cleveland, is well
born, proud, impoverished, "a little sister of the rich," in continuous difficulties mainly through the financial irresponsbility
of her scapegrace but charming brother, Larry.

Gaunt, deeply attracted to her, has mentioned that he will
give her a job if ever she needs it, and finally in desperation
she takes it. She finds herself sitting at a desk immediately
outside his door, sorting press cuttings at a large salary, resented by the other girls in the office and the supervisor, and
acutely aware of her humiliating and invidious position. She
is as strongly attracted to Gaunt as he to her, but she holds
him firmly at arm's length.

Larry, also an employee of Gaunt's, continually runs up
bills, and Ava knows that her fate and Larry's are now completely in Gaunt's hands.

Gaunt names the price that he will require for forgiving
Larry. Ava puts on her loveliest evening dress and goes to
dine with Gaunt alone in his house, ready to pay the price.
The scene that follows is perhaps the strongest that Elinor
ever wrote. All through the dinner, behind their fencing and
sparring, lies their acute awareness of each other's "it," and
this gives a sharp tang to their words. After dinner Gaunt
suddenly offers Ava her brother's freedom and pardon with-

out demanding any price. Ava, almost overcome with longing for Gaunt, replies that her class does not accept favours from his, and that she prefers to pay.

He took her forward into the apricot-rose bedroom. It had evidently been prepared for someone to stay there for the night; for filmy, gossamer raiment lay ready on the bed.

Intoxication filled Ava's brain—a divine madness permeated her being—Her ears but dimly heard, but her heart registered that John Gaunt's deep voice was saying sternly —"Tell me the truth—Is it for your brother—or for a cat-like desire for the conquest of a man?—Is it for the pride of taking me from another woman, that you are here?— Or is it just for the love of me—Ava?"

Her eyes, wet with dewy tears, looked up at him, while her willowy body grew limp in his embrace. His passionate regard devoured her—His head drooped closer and closer to her—Then his lips met hers in utter abandon of desire, which filled them both.

"Ah, God!"—at last, she said divinely—"What do I care for a price—or tomorrow—or the afterwards—I came because I love you—John Gaunt!"

All the dreams of heaven which he had dreamed of as a child when once he had strayed from the Bowery, all dirty and ragged into St. Patrick's Cathedral and heard High Mass sung, now seemed to return to him—Here was his heart's desire, won and in his arms—His to have and to hold from now for henceforth till death them do part— Given of herself without reservations, without bargainings, without vows.

Then he gave her a number of presents, her creditors' bills, paid and receipted, her treasures redeemed from the pawn-broker, and last of all, a glorious necklace of virgin pearls.

"These"—he said as he fastened the diamond clasp—"are

for the lady I have *always* intended to marry"—Then when he saw that all the soul of love was gazing at him through Ava's tender eyes, suddenly he released her from his arms, and kneeling down, he kissed her ivory hands.

The Times Literary Supplement reviewer in the course of his notice wrote:

The first story gives us a situation much favoured by Mrs. Glyn in which a powerful and wealthy lover subdues the persistent coldness and reluctance of the girl he means to win. Ava, with her coolness and restraint, reminds one a little of the heroine of Mrs. Glyn's novel *The Career of Katherine Bush*. Despite the author's slipshod English and a curious feeling one sometimes has that she is burlesquing her own style, these stories certainly let themselves be read.

From this view there can be few dissenting opinions.

16.

In March 1927, Elinor paid a brief visit to England, during which Laszlo painted, in only three hours, the lovely sketch of her on the jacket of this book. In this sketch, hurried and unfinished though it is, the artist has captured not only Elinor's own appearance but also her personality far more successfully than in the formal and finished portrait which he had painted thirteen years earlier.

But as we look at the sketch, our chief feeling must surely be of astonishment that it should be a picture of a woman of sixty-two. There are, however, many photographs taken of her at this time to prove that Laszlo did not flatter her. Ever since her girlhood she had devoted much of her time and energy and thought to preserving her beauty, unlined and unwasted by the passing of time. She fought all her life a grim, implacable delaying action against old age, a battle which she came as near as anyone ever has to winning. She never disdained the use of artifice, employing everything from the secret treatment of El-Zair to the more commonplace face creams. In Hollywood in 1926 she had undergone a facial treatment so painful that her arms had had to be strapped to her sides for ten days. She would rise very early in the morning so as to have plenty of time to complete her elaborate toilet and beauty treatment, and, incidentally, to do some writing before going to the studio.

Whether the time and energy Elinor devoted to her appearance were worth while is a moot point. But worth while or not, we cannot, after looking at Laszlo's sketch, deny the effectiveness of her methods; and we may think that it was exactly because she was still, even in her middle sixties, so beautiful, and able to command such a quantity of spontaneous admiration, that she could carry out so successfully such a large and taxing programme of work.

Also in March 1927, Duckworth published *The Wrinkle Book,* a slim volume giving some extremely practical and up-to-date advice about face massage and exercises. It was in the preface to this book that Elinor produced two of her more startling aids to beauty. One was to scrub the face hard with a dry nailbrush till the skin glowed crimson. The other was always to sleep with one's head to the magnetic north. Both these treatments she faithfully carried out herself; the latter one, she explained, was "pure common sense."

17.

Elinor's last three films in Hollywood were made for her old company, Famous Players-Lasky, which was by now renamed Paramount. The films were all light comedies, a new genre in films for her. The first, *Ritzy,* was easily the worst of the three. It was founded very remotely upon a short story of Elinor's of the same name, about a bumptious American girl who tried to teach Paris society a lesson and got severely snubbed. In the film only the heroine's nickname and her dislikeable character remain. Ritzy Brown longs to marry a Duke, but to her annoyance falls in love with a commoner. The Duke and the commoner, however, turn out to have exchanged roles, to teach her a lesson, and so Ritzy gets it both ways. It says a good deal for the ingenuity and skill of all concerned that any laughs were got out of such a wretched little plot.

The second film was *"It."* Once again there was no obvious resemblance between the film and the original story except the title. But this time Elinor wrote the screen play herself. In the book the dominating character had been John Gaunt, but the Paramount studios wanted the chief part, the character who had "it," to be the girl. Further, it was to be a light comedy, and not, like the book, a tense study in human relationship.

For a while Elinor felt puzzled, but after she met Clara Bow, who was to play the heroine, she saw her way clear before her; and under the considerable stimulus and inspiration of Clara Bow's own personality Elinor produced the scenario of her most famous and successful film.

In synopsis form the story seems very slight. A New York store proprietor, Cyrus Waltham (played by Antonio Moreno) is strongly attracted by one of his shopgirls, the "pert and unabashed" Betty Lou Spence (Clara Bow). Going to call on her in her modest home, he finds her minding a friend's baby. He jumps to the conclusion that Betty Lou is an unmarried mother and offers her his protection. She is indignant at this supposed insult, but after some gay misunderstandings the story finally reaches a happy conclusion on Cyrus's yacht. The film was sparklingly directed by Clarence

Badger, and was in the words of one critic, "as entertaining as it is disarming."

> The screen's most piquant star [wrote the *Kine Weekly*] in an Elinor Glyn story, demonstrating the presence of an indefinable attraction. The comedy situations are excellently handled and the treatment is light, bright and vivacious.

"*It*" grossed more than a million dollars at the box office, at that time a prodigious figure for a film. It also boosted the reputations of all those concerned with the film, principally Elinor herself, who also reaped large financial rewards. The *Bioscope* wrote in a rather sardonic paragraph:

> Few authors have boomed themselves so successfully as Elinor Glyn. Her latest effort is as astute as it is likely to be effective. Having written a book called *It*, she proceeds to get a picture produced explaining what "it" is, and incidentally appears in the picture and tells the hero what "it" is. Then for the past year she has been lecturing on "it," and the new cult has spread across the continent to the east coast.

Elinor's fan mail had been large ever since the publication of *The Philosophy of Love*. Now it swelled to proportions reminiscent of the days of *Three Weeks*. All over the world girls wrote asking exactly what "it" was and how they could acquire it. To this last question, of course, there was only one answer—that "it" could never be acquired. Elinor also wrote numerous articles on the subject, listing some of the well-known figures who had "it,"* and trying to show the difference between those who had it and those who had not. The press could not leave the subject alone and were for ever interviewing her about "it"; and Elinor was deeply gratified, find-

---

* These included the Prince of Wales, Gary Cooper, and Lord Beaverbrook.

ing herself back on the peak of fame and fortune, as high if not higher than she had reached twenty years before.

The film also made the reputation of Clara Bow. She was later to play many other parts of very different character, but for the rest of her career she was always thought of primarily as the "It" Girl. She herself was keenly conscious of the debt she owed to Elinor. When she came on her honeymoon to see Elinor in England, she wrote on a photograph of herself, "To Elinor Glyn, whom I respect and admire more than any other woman in the world."

Elinor's last Hollywood film, *Red Hair,* was made by the same team, author-producer, director, and actress. The film, which was in colour, was designed as a vehicle for showing Clara Bow's versatility and for illustrating the passion inherent in redheads. The heroine was a little manicurist, who received presents from three male admirers, of whom one saw her as a demure young miss, one as a "vamp" and one as a temperamental young woman. She herself reformed when she met the right man, who was the nephew of two of her admirers and the ward of the third. They attempted to interfere with her new romance, but the handicap of their own pasts and the heroine's fiery temper frustrated them. The final and rather daring scene took place on a boat, in which she undressed and returned them their presents of clothes in each other's presence, to their great consternation, before going off with the right man.

Once again the story provided a series of nicely contrived comic scenes, expertly directed by Clarence Badger, and once again Clara Bow was in excellent form. *Red Hair* was almost as successful as *"It,"* grossing nine hundred thousand dollars at the box office, and Elinor decided wisely to relinquish her Hollywood career on this note of triumph.

She had successfully achieved her triple objective, for which she had first come to Hollywood seven years before. She had spread her romantic ideals, not only through her films but through her books and articles far wider through America than she had ever dared to hope. She had made her fortune. She had acquired a large number of new friends, and a considerable insight into the American way of life. And she had re-established her fame in a way she had never even dreamt. Now, at last, she could afford to retire and lead a more leisured existence.

18.

Elinor had never pulled her punches about America, either in the early days of *Elizabeth Visits America* or more recently. She had never been one to indulge the shortcomings of others, except, perhaps, her husband. Though she was not so ungracious as to stint her admiration for the good aspects of the American scene, she never hesitated to pass severe and sometimes scathing comment on the parts which pleased her less.

She had during her seven years in America consciously resisted all efforts to Americanise her. In her books, especially *The Flirt and the Flapper,* we may note that she had a considerable command of American slang, but she never used a single Americanism in her own conversation. There was no trace of an American accent in her voice.

We cannot be surprised at this. It would, indeed, have been surprising if she, her habits, manners, and speech trained in the style and tradition of the English and French aristocracy, should have moved so far from her rigid and proudly held standards as to adopt, even for protective colouring, a form of outward behaviour, habit, and speech which she had once thought uncouth. But underneath the purely outward, formal standards there had been a considerable change. In mind and in spirit she was now far closer to the American way of life, more nearly attuned to American ideals and geared to American tempo. She had also, not unnaturally, become very fond of a country and a people which had given her such splendid opportunities and which had rewarded her efforts so lavishly.

And so we find that when the moment came in 1927 when she was free to leave America and return to England, she found suddenly that she could not bear to go. She wanted, however, to leave California, even though she had so many friends there, and she went to live in New York, taking a flat on the top floor of the Ritz Tower, at that time the tallest inhabited building in the world.

Elinor loved the view from her flat, which had windows on all sides, the strange lights and shadows, the lightning and thunder and high winds around her and, especially on calm nights, the city lights twinkling far below her as if they were stars reflected in a lake. She lived there for nearly a year, writing articles for Hearst and magazine stories.

One of these stories, *Such Men Are Dangerous,* she sold for six thousand pounds, and it was the first of her stories to be produced as a talking picture. The story dealt with an immensely rich and rather unattractive man, married to a dull wife and longing for romance. In the middle of a flight across the Channel he jumped out of the aircraft and disappeared for ever. In fact, he parachuted down and was picked up by a midget, two-man submarine* which he had arranged to be at a certain spot. He then went to Vienna and placed himself in the hands of a plastic surgeon, who lifted his face, remoulded his nose, altered the shape of his hands, stretched him on a rack, carried out a difficult operation on his shoulder muscles to alter the set of his shoulders, and gave his vocal chords and hair drastic treatment. The millionaire was now unrecognisable in every way and he set out to find romance. His wife, in the meantime, had brightened herself up and in due course the millionaire met her, fell in love with her, and married her all over again, without ever telling her the true story.

* This was a remarkably prophetic invention of Elinor's for which some of the critics laughed at her.

The film followed the story in outline, if not in detail, and Warner Baxter gave a good performance as the millionaire. Elinor took no part in the production, but she was pleased by the finished picture, especially by the meticulous accuracy of the sets.

In the summer of 1928, Elinor returned to Hollywood, staying with Marion Davies at her beach house. She thoroughly enjoyed luxuriating in her new-found idleness in the warm California climate and seeing her friends again, and at Marion Davies' stern insistence she stayed there for six weeks before leaving for Washington.

Washington had always appealed greatly to Elinor, with its old houses, its cosmopolitan atmosphere, and its diplomatic society. Elinor had many friends in the city and she now decided to make her home there. She bought a pleasant house of the 1790 period in Georgetown and spent the whole of the autumn and winter of 1928 redecorating it.

Her ideas of house decoration, never austere, had been encouraged in Hollywood by the sumptuous sets she had designed for her films. It was many years since she had last decorated a home of her own, and in Washington now, secure in her newly acquired wealth, she gave her ruling passion and her lavish ideas full rein, denying herself nothing, however extravagant. The house in Georgetown was the costliest that she ever decorated for herself, and, ironically, it was the only one that she never lived in.

Shortly before she moved in, in the spring of 1929, she paid a visit to England, intending to spend a few weeks with her family and friends. In fact, she remained there for the rest of her life.

BOOK EIGHT

The Legend

1929–1943

I.

In considering Elinor Glyn's life and career one is struck by the way in which the pattern repeats itself. In 1908 she had returned from America flushed with her triumph, her pockets bulging with her earnings, her head turned by the adulation she had received, intransigent, indifferent to cautionary advice, her judgement unstable and unreliable. In 1908 her intransigence had been tempered, one might almost say her character redeemed, by the sudden shock of financial adversity. Twenty-one years later, the pattern repeated itself almost exactly, with the colours, if anything, a little heightened.

Elinor's American fortune was no longer as large as it had once been or as she herself still believed it to be. Much of it had disappeared in Hollywood without trace, melted like hoarfrost in the sun. She had been profligate with money, both in New York and in Washington, and there were, too, sudden large demands for income tax, for which she had made no provision and which she tended to ignore, vaguely thinking it unjust.

Her family rapidly appraised themselves of this true position of her finances and pressed her strongly not to return to America. There was no particular reason why she need live there now and she was quite capable of continuing her journalistic work there from England, where her family would be able to keep a closer watch upon her expenditure. Elinor herself was deeply affected by her return to familiar scenes and faces, and by a strong desire to live in closer contact with her growing family, and especially with her mother, who had had a stroke; she wanted, too, to pick up her old friendships and her own life.

A house, Wolsey's Spring, near Kingston, had been prepared for her return, and Elinor now settled in there. As a permanent residence it was not altogether ideal. It was too far from London to be convenient, although it was hardly remote by American standards. Elinor had been deprived, perhaps fortunately, of the opportunity of supervising the complete redecoration of the house and she felt a little aggrieved at this. It was large and there seemed to be too many servants about for her liking; apart from her personal maid in her own rooms Elinor always preferred the rest of the staff to be as little in evidence as possible. The house was also rather expensive to run. However, it provided, for the moment, a suitable milieu as well as the standard of living which she wished and still thought she was able to afford.

2.

In 1908, Elinor had brought back with her from America a number of new ideologies of dubious value, the chief of which was New Thought. In 1929 she returned home under the strong influence of spiritualism and the occult in general. She had always had an interest in occult and psychic matters. All her life she had been keenly attentive to, if not actually influenced by, the predictions of soothsayers and clairvoyants; she had worried over her children's horoscopes and tried hard to find a scientific basis for astrology.

She knew, too, that she was unusually imbued herself with psychic powers. Many times she had premonitions and forebodings which were so definite as almost to amount to second sight and which were usually fulfilled with uncanny accuracy.* Her first experience with ghosts took place when she was still very young. She had been staying in a country house in Hertfordshire, the owner of which lay seriously ill upstairs. At a quarter to one in the morning Elinor and several others, though by no means all, of the household, heard the passing bell toll from the neighbouring, deserted, and securely locked church. The owner of the house died twenty-four hours later, exactly to the minute.

Elinor had many other experiences of this sort both in England and France. In Kilkenny Castle she heard a disembodied voice sighing in the corner by the fireplace, a sigh which could be heard by those who were completely deaf. In one French château a weird white figure arose and wailed at the end of her bed. If there was a ghost about, Elinor usually saw or heard it, and these experiences cannot be attributed merely to her vigorous imagination, for in each case there was a strange story about the house or the room which she did not learn till the following day.

She was interested but not frightened by these experiences, regarding them as yet another example of her own susceptibility to waves and vibrations. The two ghost stories which she wrote herself* lack the eery, chilling quality of the great masters of the macabre.

Elinor's main interest in 1929, however, was not in ghosts but in spiritualism and all such efforts to make contact with departed spirits. She joined a circle of spiritualists and at-

* She warned the Mollisons in 1933 that their plane, the *Seafarer*, would crash on its forthcoming Atlantic flight unless it were painted some colour other than black. Mrs. Mollison explained why it was impossible to repaint the plane another colour, but she thanked Elinor for her warning. The plane duly crashed.
* "The Irtonwood Ghost" in *The Contrast and Other Stories* and "Why I?" in *It and Other Stories*.

tended several séances with a good medium, making contact with Clayton and many friends of hers who were now dead. At first Elinor was considerably impressed. The séances seemed to be perfectly genuine, and on one occasion she took a secretary with her to make sure that the words were actually spoken and were not merely imagined by her. Messages from Clayton and her friends contained references which could not be known possibly to any third person. There were also forecasts about the future which were sometimes correct.

Automatic writing was a variant which she also practised, and for which she found she had a gift. She would take up a pencil and block, make her mind as blank as possible, and after a little while she would find the pencil writing by itself in her hand. The handwriting was utterly different from her normal one, and once again messages came through from Clayton and others which were very difficult to explain if they were not genuine communications. The official explanation of automatic writing is, of course, that it is the expression of the subconscious. But Elinor refused to believe this. Not only were many of the messages extremely distasteful to her, but also, when she first experimented with automatic writing in Egypt in 1920, she wrote several pages of faultless Arabic, of which she knew not a word. She could not credit her subconscious with the power to write faultless Arabic when her conscious found it difficult enough to write faultless English.

After a while Elinor noticed that all the messages, whether addressed to her or to other members of her circle, no matter from whom they were supposed to come, were always in exactly the same style—pompous platitudes, minute instructions about ornaments or other trivia, detailed but quite useless remedies for her rheumatic knee, elaborate prophesies about the future which were usually quite misleading. Just as Elinor refused to think her own subconscious responsible for such utterances, so did she also decline to believe that Clayton, Wynne Finch, and her other friends could have lost their sense of humour and proportion so completely when they "passed over." In his lifetime Clayton had detested pompous, dramatic slogans and clichés; he had never been particularly interested in the ornaments in Elinor's bedroom or, for that matter, particularly concerned about her health. Nothing about the messages bore the hallmark of their senders' personalities and gradually Elinor came to believe that they were fakes, sent perhaps by some imp or sprite of the half-world in the intent of teasing and making mischief among gullible people like herself. She became sick of the whole business as her incredulity and her sense of humour reasserted themselves, and in due course she gave it up altogether.

At that time table-turning, planchette boards, and other minor manifestations of spiritualism were popular after-dinner entertainments at some house parties. Elinor participated in them with the utmost reluctance. Though her belief in the efficacy of such communications was fading, she still believed in the strength of her own pyschic powers and regarded them as too dangerous for use in casual parlour games. In one house party in Yorkshire, Elinor was at last persuaded to take part in a session at the planchette board. In her hand the trolley prophesied the death within a year of another member of the party, specifically named. This prophesy, which turned out to be correct, caused a good deal of consternation among the party and marked the end of Elinor's experiments in spiritualism.

Automatic writing, however, remained a considerable temptation, and it required a strong effort of will not to sit back and idly watch the pencil writing of its own accord when she should have been busy upon an article or a story.

3.

The British film industry at this time was at a particularly low ebb. With the end of the silent films many studios had closed down and actors and technicians were thrown out of work. Little finance was available for equipping either studios or cinemas for talking pictures, which themselves, by re-erecting the language barrier, had cut potential film producers from their lucrative foreign markets.

Elinor's re-entry into the world of films was largely prompted by a genuine desire to rehabilitate British films by placing her experience and her reputation as a film author at the industry's disposal. She also hankered again for the fame and fortune her Hollywood films had brought her. By making films herself in Britain, she told herself she would not only help to revitalise British films, now receiving some belated assistance from the recently passed Quota Act, but also create a new outlet for herself and her stories, and restore her fortune again to the pinnacle from which it had so sadly slipped in the past few years.

Accordingly she formed a small company, Elinor Glyn Productions, Ltd., and rented studio space at Elstree. She engaged a production manager who had been well recommended and placed the lighting and photography in the hands of the man who had been Mary Pickford's cameraman for eleven years. She asked Edward Knoblock, who had been one of her fellow authors in the early days in Hollywood, to collaborate with her on the script. United Artists guaranteed a release and promised a large advance payment on delivery of the negative. The prospect for the moment seemed fair and the production, which was financed entirely by Elinor herself, began in the autumn of 1929.

The film, *Knowing Men,* was based on a story Elinor had

written for Clara Bow but which had been rejected in favour
of *Red Hair*. It was a very slight and improbable comedy
about an heiress who pretended to be a poor companion to
her aunt so as to discover the real characters and intentions of
her male admirers. Several of the scenes were rather risqué
and the critics found them shocking. Elissa Landi played the
Clara Bow part with great charm and Carl Brisson did his
best for the stupid but athletic hero; the cast also included
Helen Haye and Jeanne de Casalis. H. Fraser-Simson wrote
a catchy theme song and Elinor herself directed her first talking picture.

The production went smoothly and was finished in only
two days over the scheduled time, to the amazement of the
Elstree studio manager. The first night took place at the Regal
Cinema (now the Odeon), Marble Arch, in February 1930.
For years Elinor had been protected and insulated from the
blasts of criticism by the organised publicity campaigns of the
big film studios and she had not realised what it was like to
be entirely on her own. She was aware that the film was not
as good as her Hollywood productions, but she hoped that the
reviewers would be indulgent, as it was her money that she
was spending. In this she was sadly disappointed.

She had been unwise enough to appear in a prologue to the
film delivering a scathing speech about the failings of the male
sex, and this alienated the audience from the start. The notices that *Knowing Men* received were so bad as to be news
in themselves. One of the kinder of the critics wrote:

> Neither plot nor direction display originality and the pic-
> ture suffers from the writer's deep and apparently incurable
> mistrust of men, first displayed thirty years ago when she
> introduced Elizabeth, the child of her fancy, to a sniggering
> public.

We may note with some surprise that the critic's hostility was
so widespread as to envelop in retrospect Elinor's first novel,

which had been so highly praised by the critics of the time and which was not at the moment under review.

The morning after the disastrous first night Edward Knoblock obtained a temporary injunction preventing the picture being shown again, and the film had to be taken off after one performance, pending the hearing of the case. Knoblock lost the case and a permanent injunction was refused, but the damage was done and the release missed. Except for the guaranteed advance, the film was a dead loss.

In London at the time was the head of United Artists, Mr. Schenk, and he thought sufficiently well of *Knowing Men* to urge Elinor to make further films, which he would distribute for her. He even spoke hopefully of an American release. Elinor was riled by the treatment that *Knowing Men* had received and allowed herself to be persuaded by his suggestions.

The Price of Things was chosen for her second film in the hope that a more dramatic story would appeal to those critics who had taken exception to her comedy, but despite Mr. Schenk's promises no release of any kind was forthcoming and it too was a complete loss to the little company.

4.

Elinor was now back where she had been twenty years before, reduced to writing novels in haste to pay off her debts, and in the next four years she published four novels and a book of short stories. To live on, she had only the annuity which the Rhys-Williamses had bought for her out of the savings from her first four American films and it was obvious that a policy of severe retrenchment was necessary. Wolsey's Spring was sold and Elinor moved into a small flat in Hertford Street, near Shepherd's Market, Mayfair.

She could also no longer support her mother. The flat in

Embankment Gardens was given up and Mrs. Kennedy went to live at Miskin Manor, the Rhys-Williamses' country home in Glamorgan. Here she remained for the last seven years of her life.

They were in some ways the happiest years since Douglas Sutherland's death. Mrs. Kennedy had her own suite of rooms where she lived with her devoted maid, Frances, and from which she could see across the fields to the bluebell wood. She would come down ceremonially to lunch and dinner each day, a manner of life which reminded her nostalgically of the better days at Lamberts. Especially pleasant were the moments in the summer and at Christmas when there was a large family gathering in the house.

Following her stroke her memory was strangely elliptical. She remembered only the happy days of her life and a few of the minor unpleasantnesses—the journey in the schooner to South America, the smell of the slave ships in Rio. The major horrors, the winter journey home from Turin to England with her dying husband, his death, the whole of her marriage to Mr. Kennedy, were effaced altogether.

She died on April 20, 1937, at the age of ninety-six.

5.

Elinor lived in her Hertford Street flat till 1934, when she moved to a larger one in Connaught Place, Bayswater, with a lovely blue and gold drawing-room overlooking Hyde Park. Both these flats she filled with her own taste and personality. Her fine collection of French furniture and pictures, her beautiful silks and brocades, her tiger skins gave her drawing-room a unique and piquant atmosphere. One American visitor complained later that "There wasn't a darned chair in the room you could relax in," but Elinor herself, except when she was curled up on a sofa, always sat upright in a chair.

There were five of her tigers on view: "Paul" (the original one from Lucerne), "Curzon," "Milner," and two anonymous ones. She loved them for their own sakes, but their presence invariably stimulated reporters, who came frequently to interview her about love, marriage or "it," into keeping the tiger-skin legend alive.

Elinor also acquired about this time a pair of marmalade-coloured cats whom she named Candide and Zadig, as a tribute to Voltaire. They were beautiful, proud, independent creatures of enormous character and "it," in many ways very like their mistress. Elinor was devoted to them and they became as much a feature of her life as her tigers.

She was at this time continually in the public eye, an almost lengendary person, a red-haired, green-eyed Queen of Passion, who spent her day, so it was supposed, reclining on her tiger skins. The "it" vogue showed no signs of abating, and hardly a day passed without some reference to this personal quality in some paper or magazine. Her opinion was sought on all sorts of current controversial problems, and she contributed a large number of articles both to the British and American press on topics of the day, principally, of course, love and marriage. Her own name was another factor, a fortuitous one, in keeping her name before the public, and jokes about Nell Glyn pattered regularly from variety comedians.

Although it was now thirty years since she had published her first novels, her books, in particular the earlier ones, showed no signs of waning popularity. In 1933 Ray Smith's Twopenny Library reported, with a certain amount of surprise, that the three women authors most in demand were still Ethel M. Dell, Elinor Glyn, and Marie Corelli, in that order. The overseas demand for Elinor's novels was also well maintained. In the same year a Lisbon statistician stated that the seven novelists of any nationality most widely read in Portugal were Edgar Wallace, Rafael Sabatini, Conan Doyle,

A. E. W. Mason, E. M. Hull, P. C. Wren, and Elinor Glyn.

Elinor's own taste in books had altered little in the last sixty years. She read no modern or recent fiction other than her own novels. Her favourite books, to which she turned again and again, and which she now possessed in sumptuous calf-bound copies, given to her by Curzon, were the ones which she had come to love during her childhood in Jersey: the Greek classics, Sterne, Chesterfield, La Rochefoucauld, Voltaire, and, pre-eminently, Kingsley's *The Heroes*. To these she had later added Symonds' *Renaissance in Italy*, Pater's *Marius the Epicurean*, Landor's *Pericles and Aspasia*, and James Bain's *A Digit of the Moon*, the latter's thoughts on reincarnation coinciding strongly with her own beliefs.

6.

Elinor had little difficulty in re-establishing herself in her old background, and during these last years she went out and about a good deal, staying with friends in the country, going to lunch, dinner, and cocktail parties in London, attending first nights, lunching, as so often before, with friends at the Ritz. She loved dancing, but her enjoyment of this favourite pastime was reduced by her rheumatic left knee, which was often very painful. A heavy fall from a bus which moved on while she was still climbing on board damaged this knee severely, and she was obliged to spend most of 1932 on her sofa.

She went several times to stay with Hearst at St. Donat's in Glamorgan, where he had bought the old castle. Into the thick castle walls he had built dozens of new bathrooms and decorated them lavishly with genuine mediaeval tapestries and suits of armour. Downstairs gramophones blared and minor film stars shrieked; and presiding over everything was the genial but autocratic figure of Hearst himself, resplendent in bright pink tie and Tyrolean hat.

Elinor was a popular figure at these gatherings. The starlets called her Grandmamma and liked to think they were shocking someone who had herself shocked an earlier generation. Elinor was by this time practically unshockable, but she dutifully pretended to be shocked by their clothes and behaviour, and everyone was pleased.

She was, however, considerably surprised at the way the members of the house party chose to amuse themselves. They played ceaselessly a game called Monopoly, and Elinor, who was bored by most games, was very puzzled.

"They play all night as well," she commented on her return to London after one of these visits. "The boredom of it! And not even for money!"

It had not been thus in the great days at Easton.

Elinor also did a certain amount of entertaining herself. These parties were pleasant occasions, for she was a good hostess, able to listen to two or three separate conversations simultaneously and careful to see that no one was left out in the cold. One might expect to find there a cross section of the different worlds in which she had lived: peers and peeresses, politicians, diplomats, soldiers, university professors, foreign royalty, American film stars—a wide and varied circle of friends. There were always as well a large number of young people, partly because Elinor liked to have their company and partly because she remembered how much she had owed to the kindness of Lady Fitzharding in her youth. She would take special trouble over debutantes in their first season, advising them on hair styles, clothes, and make-up, introducing them to eligible young men or to any others of her friends whom they might specially wish to meet.

It was a pleasant pattern of existence, a serene and golden sunset after the tempestuous, crowded life she had lived earlier. The only dark cloud was the eternal problem of finance. The income from her annuity was adequate for simple living, but Elinor found it difficult to cut her cloth accordingly. Over her chief mania, house decorating, she was as incorrigible as ever, and her family were for ever persuading her out of her yearly plan to make a fresh home for herself somewhere else.

"Money!" she exclaimed at one family inquest into her expenses. "Don't let's any of us ever mention the subject again. We get on much better when we don't."

It was finally decided that she must no longer have control of her own bank account. For the last eight years of her life she never signed a cheque. The bank paid all standing expenses, such as the rent of her flat, and doled out the rest to her in cash. With this she paid for everything, and by this means she was constrained to live within her income. It was typical of her financial scrupulousness that she should have accepted this ignominious and inconvenient arrangement so completely. Not once did she attempt to evade it, although she could have obtained credit anywhere with ease. One must feel that Clayton Glyn's reaction to such a plan would have been very different.

7.

"Vanity," Elinor wrote in her commonplace book, "is one of the hideous burdens the gods imposed upon mankind, knowing that it would for ever keep human beings out of Olympus."

All her life Elinor inveighed against vanity. It was, she considered, responsible for those shortcomings of human behaviour that she despised so much—shyness, bumptiousness, self-consciousness, affectation. These were all forms of bad manners, she considered, owing their origin to vanity. It was because the person was vain and preoccupied with the impression he was making on the other person rather than with the person himself that he became tongue-tied or loud-mouthed, clumsy or precious, whichever way his self-consciousness took him. The characters, both in real life and in her books, whom she admired most she called *sans gêne*—at ease. It was the mark of a gentleman to be always poised and without affectation, completely unaware of the excellent impression he was making.

Yet it would take a brave man to declare Elinor herself free from vanity. She was always deeply conscious of the effect she was creating. She longed for admiration and thrived on it, and one may well feel that she herself ought to have been the very last person to despise vanity.

But it would be harsh to regard this as simply an example of practising herself what she condemned in others. We may think it more just to look on it as yet another contradiction of the two sides of her character, her dramatic instincts at war once again with her eighteenth-century training in self-restraint.

Elinor herself would have had no difficulty in explaining the inconsistency. It was merely the difference between vanity and pride. She wrote in her commonplace book:

Vanity is the desire for the esteem of others, which, subconsciously, we know that we do not deserve.

False pride is the result of sub-conscious knowledge of inferiority which makes the individual experience a profound urge to receive all the outward and standardised proofs of honour.

Real pride is the consciousness that there is God's image within us, which must not be degraded.

"It is vanity which makes you cry," she would observe to a child sobbing after a rebuke. "Pride would prevent it."

When R. J. Minney, the playwright, was going to Hollywood, Elinor gave him a number of letters of introduction to her friends there, including one to Irving Thalberg, the producer.

"And tell him," went on Elinor, producing a copy of Lytton Strachey's *Elizabeth and Essex,* "that this is to be the subject of his next film. And I wish to play Queen Elizabeth." She went on to illustrate the various gestures and expressions she would use to portray Queen Elizabeth's various moods.

When Minney got to Hollywood, he duly passed on Elinor's lighthearted message to Thalberg. Thalberg commented:

"Well, it's quite an idea. She could certainly manage the part. Why, she's always acting."

This remark was not passed back to Elinor and her reaction to it cannot be judged. She might have taken it in the same frivolous spirit in which she had sent her own message, or she might have been hurt. To be "always acting" was hardly consistent with being natural or *sans gêne.*

Thalberg's comment, though at first sight true enough, is too simple and sweeping. Elinor, undoubtedly, was usually playing a part, adopting a pose; but she did it for reasons very different from the usual reasons. People who are "always acting" normally borrow their poses from others they admire in order to hide some inadequacy, some interior hollowness. Elinor borrowed her poses from no one. She drew them up out of the rich storehouse of her own personality.

There were four principal poses and we have met them all already. The one which fortunately predominated was her Elizabeth pose—gay, witty, sophisticated, and affectionate. There was also a pose of queenly passion reminiscent of *Three Weeks.* There was the Halcyone pose, fey, simple, naïve, openhearted. And, fourthly, there was the Ambrosine pose, a particularly tiresome one, full of misunderstood self-pity. She adopted one or other of these poses as the mood or the occasion suited her, changing it as easily as a dress, sometimes to the bewilderment of her friends.

But her poses were not artificial; they were the products of the many-sidedness of her own personality. They were, if the contradiction in terms may be allowed, genuine poses. And in so far as she was "always acting," she was acting—and we may think sometimes burlesquing—the part of Elinor Glyn.

Nor was there any interior hollowness to conceal. A great number of people have testified that even a single meeting with her was an unforgettable experience. A few minutes' conversation with her was enough to reveal a highly charged, full-blooded personality, with a richness and a vitality rarely encountered in any walk of life.

8.

In 1931, Elinor went to Hungary at the invitation of Baron and Baroness Rubido-Zichy, staying for about two months, and getting background for a new novel which she was planning.

Hungary had been a republic ever since the breakup of the Austrian Empire in 1918, but Elinor found, to her great pleasure, that many of the aristocracy hoped that the monarchy might be restored at a not too distant date. Hungarian society was the most exclusive that she had yet met. Despite the general impoverishment of the landed classes after the Treaty of Versailles, it was not yet possible for any upstart, however rich, to buy himself into the aristocratic set, an exclusiveness of which she approved.

There were, she discovered, two separate aristocratic circles in Hungary. One was rich and cosmopolitan, at home in Budapest or Cannes or Paris. The other comprised members of the old and famous families who had not had the means to travel abroad. Their behaviour towards Elinor was equally courteous and well bred, but because of the narrowness of their experience and interests it was difficult, even when they spoke English well, to keep up a long conversation with them.

The Hungarian people as a whole she found surprisingly different from all their neighbours; practical, unlike the Austrians; casual about financial gain; proud, independent, and still, at that time, completely feudal. No Hungarian lord would dare treat his servants or his peasants in the curt, peremptory manner Elinor had observed in Russia and Austria; and no Hungarian peasant, no matter how poor, would dream of letting his wife work for hire.

The Hungarian people, Elinor decided, were, if anything, nearer to the British people than to anyone else in their attitude toward life, in their mutual respect between the various classes, in their love of sport, and above all, in their love of horses. Hungary was, she discovered, the land of horses. Everyone seemed to be a born rider and the advent of the motorcar had apparently made no difference. There were statues of horses in the streets of Budapest; everyone took a keen interest in racing, hunting, polo, and driving. On the country estates the horse was supreme.

Elinor's Hungarian novel, *Love's Hour,* which was published in March 1932, was, as the title shows, intended to echo her best-selling Russian novel of twenty-two years before. There are, indeed, many points of similarity, in the delineation of minor characters, in the construction, and especially in the evocation of a country, a people, and a society, which was the chief feature of *His Hour.* If the picture of Hungary seems less striking, that is perhaps due to the fact that life in a Hungarian château was not so very different from life in an English country house.

But Elinor's gift of description never failed her and we take away from *Love's Hour* an impression of a civilised, aristocratic, if once again, rather idle society; Budapest at night; gipsy music and Tokay; plains and castles; stags roaring in the deer forests; above all, horses—those well-groomed, high-mettled thoroughbreds handled by their masters with such complete *expertise* and sympathy. It is difficult, as one reads

the descriptions of horses in *Love's Hour,* to remember that
Elinor was, even in Hungary, a confirmed and unswerving
horse hater.

Had *Love's Hour* remained a love story told against this
colourful background, it might have deserved the same fame
and success as its predecessor. But unfortunately it misses the
simplicity and bold sweep of *His Hour.* It is cluttered up with
a motley collection of Elinor's other ideas and interests, which
were now so deeply imbedded in her personality. She tossed
them in casually, hardly noticing that she did so, not realising
how inappropriate some of them were to a Hungarian love
story—reincarnation, Greek philosophy, French furniture,
noblesse oblige, the need for aristocracy, the law of the boomerang, the hunting instinct. The book gives one a comprehensive picture of Elinor's mind, but the story and the
background are in consequence often a little blurred. The romantic pair, both of them rather unreal characters, are paying
off their "karmic debts" incurred in a former life, and the
strange, occult atmosphere, which Elinor tried with some success to establish in several scenes, does not mix well with the
detailed factual descriptions elsewhere.

There are, however, some magnificent moments of passion.
The English heroine is, as so often, haughty and disagreeable,
a Circe enslaving all men's hearts and despising them, and in
desiring her the hero gives a remarkable example of the vigour
of the Hungarian hunting instinct.

9.

The visit to Hungary was the last of Elinor's journeys, for
we cannot count the several visits to Paris she made in the
remaining years of peace. She had in her life travelled far
and wide, from California in the West to Russia in the East,
usually in the cause of her art, always with relish. She be-

lieved strongly in the educative influence of travel, in its
broadening effect upon the mind, illustrated so completely by
the two Hungarian societies. It was vital, she thought, to meet
people of other races, other ideas, other customs, even though
in her case she so often saw foreign countries from the same
queen's-eye view.

But, wherever she went, her chief interest was in the pursuit of the romantic ideals which were, to her, an essential
to true living. She herself admitted that the search for romance, her felicitous definition of which is printed in the
first pages of this book, was the guiding principle of her life
and she was prepared to travel far and wide in her quest.

She summarised her conclusions about one aspect of romance in a characteristic passage in her commonplace book,
though one must think that it was derived more from general
observation and deduction than from firsthand experience.

As Lovers—

American	Fatherly and uncouth
French	Passionate and *petit-maître*
Austrian	Sentimental and feckless
Hungarian	Passionate and exacting
Scandinavian	Psychological and scientific
Russian	Passionate and unstable
Spanish	Jealous and matter-of-fact
Italian	Romantic and fickle
English	Casual and adorable
German	Sentimental and vulgar
All the Near East	Passionate and untrustworthy.

10.

Elinor's appearance during these years was as astonishingly
youthful as ever. Miss Christina Foyle recalls that at a literary

luncheon in 1939, a young man asked to be introduced to "the beautiful young girl." Even when one was close to her, there were no visible telltale signs to show that she was in her middle seventies.

The number of her admirers, too, showed no signs of falling off, and she was carrying on at this time an amorous correspondence with a Polish Prince in America, an Austrian Prince in Vienna and, of all people, Field-Marshal Mannerheim of Finland, whom she had known both in St. Petersburg and in Paris. These affairs, if they may be so called, never progressed beyond the correspondence stage, and Elinor treated them with lightheartedness, although she answered the letters gravely and carefully (observing of the Austrian Prince, "One has to be so careful with Austrians, they commit suicide so easily"). She was, however, considerably gratified to think that even in her seventies Princes and Field-Marshals still wished her to fly with them.

Her heart was never engaged. After the Curzon episode she was never again capable of supreme self-denying love. The most she could achieve was fondness and affection, notably for Milner. She had been badly hurt once and she was thankful to find that she was never so vulnerable again.

The effect upon her of her relationship with Curzon is more evident at this stage than immediately after its end. Then there had been no outward or visible effect. We may recall a phrase from her diary quoted earlier in this book about a friend of hers similarly forsaken: "But she is a person of the old school and she gives no sign." It was the same with Elinor. It would have been unthinkable to give any sign. Private emotion, private suffering must be held in an iron self-control and must be concealed from the world. That had been the teaching of Mrs. Saunders; it was Elinor's own teaching, too.

She bore no resentment against Curzon. Rancour was an emotion of which she was always wholly incapable. His qual-

ities never seemed to her less than admirable, and during these
last years she spoke of him frequently, not as the great love
of her life, but as the most interesting of her many friends;
and it is in this guise that he appears briefly in her autobiography.

Curzon's influence upon her may be seen in the fact that
she now took it for granted that all young men should wish
to be exactly like him. He was the *beau ideal.* She assumed,
as a matter of course, that her grandsons would wish to follow
in his footsteps, would enter politics, and would be inspired
by the Curzonian triple crown of ambition—Captain of the
Oppidans at Eton, Viceroy of India, and Prime Minister—
the last tier of which had eluded even him. (Three of her
grandsons did achieve this position at Eton. But none of them
have gone into politics, and the viceroyalty of India is no
more.)

II.

Elinor's autobiography, *Romantic Adventure,* was published in June 1936. She had had a serious illness and operation the previous year and it was a considerable effort and
achievement to deliver the manuscript on time. There were
many aspects of her life and career with which, of course, she
could not herself deal and she could not be expected to examine, except by implication, her character or her work with
the objectivity that has been possible here. But at the same
time she was able to give a spirited account of her vivid and
varied life, and it would be ungracious for me not to acknowl-
edge here the great help I have received in writing this book
from *Romantic Adventure,* especially in the early chapters,
where few other sources of information are available.

The book was well received by the critics. *The Times
Literary Supplement* atoned for many early blows with a

charming review, appreciating the solace she had given to innumerable readers and wishing her many adventures and much more romance. The side of herself which she revealed in her autobiography came as a considerable surprise to her public, who, in default of any other information about her private life, had vaguely identified her with the heroine of *Three Weeks*. For the first time they learned something of the true background of her life; of the aristocratic circles in which she moved and the eighteenth-century standards and manners which she maintained so inflexibly; of her hours of adversity and the courage with which she always met them; of the various adventures of her life which she entered upon so gayly; above all, of the sheer, slogging hard work that lay behind her success.

It was very far from being the popular picture of Elinor Glyn. Mr. Beverley Nichols wrote at this time in an article in the *Sunday Chronicle*:

I looked again at the beautiful woman who was still beautiful because of her strict and almost Spartan respect for her body and her looks. It was Elinor Glyn.

Reputations are curious things. I suppose if you asked the average young man in the street what sort of woman Elinor Glyn was, he would tell you that she spent most of her time on a tiger skin, smoking scented cigarettes, writing passionate passages with a purple pen and occasionally sipping a liqueur.

This is so exactly the opposite from her normal mode of life that it is worth noting.

Elinor Glyn does not loll about on tiger skins, nor on anything else. She sits bolt upright on a hard chair. Hence she has the shoulders of a young girl, although she is a grandmother. She does not drink liqueurs. She drinks water —lots of it.

*Discipline—discipline—discipline—*that is the rhythm of

Elinor Glyn's life. Mental discipline as well as physical—
because she is one of the few women I know who goes
daily to the fresh stream of the classics for her inspiration.

And yet in the popular imagination, she is a whirlwind
of eroticism.

12.

During the summer of 1936, Elinor rented a cottage near
Taplow and the following year, still temporarily bored with
London, she took a flat at Saltdean, near Brighton. This she
redecorated in her own individual style, impervious to the contrast between the square block of flats, with its low rooms and
modern doors, and her Louis XV furniture. The ceilings she
painted the same bright colours as the walls, a technique of
decoration which in such small rooms caused an almost painful intensity of colour.

Both at Taplow and at Saltdean she would wander about
the village, talking to the people, learning about their lives
and families in a way she had never done in Essex. She was
much mellower now. The haughtiness, the arrogance, the
class-consciousness were almost all gone. She was more toler-
ant, too, of shortcomings, even in the things that mattered
most to her, though from time to time her old self would still
flash out. To her thirteen-year-old granddaughter, who came
to see her without wearing gloves, she observed icily, "Are
you especially proud of your hands?"

Elinor's health had been weakened by the operation and
she no longer had the same buoyant energy, the same creative
urge. She still wrote her diary and long, amusing letters to
friends, but her literary career, as far as the public was concerned, was almost over. Her knee, too, continued to pain her
and restricted her activities. She liked, however, to walk along
the front at Saltdean, getting as near as possible to the great

waves which crashed against the cliffs during the equinoctial
storms.

13.

In February 1939, Elinor returned to Jersey for the first
time since Mr. Kennedy's death in 1888. It was something
of a triumph; parties and receptions were given for her, both
at Government House and elsewhere. The Bailiff of Jersey
presented her with the Great Seal of the Island. The shops
where she had dealt in her youth sent presents; autograph
books arrived by the hundred. The Rotary Club gave a lunch
for her and she wrote in her diary:

> They were delighted with my speech apparently. Not
> one person made me any compliments or expressed surprise
> that I looked so young, or said anything personally ap-
> preciative—although what I must have looked like among
> them I can't think! All hats too big in the head and rammed
> down, like ten years ago. Just too comic and behind the
> times. I wore my brown suit and my sables as it was too
> warm for the mink coat, and the fur hat that Margot likes.
> They, however, clapped to the echo. They are awfully proud
> of me *as their own!*

Elinor also met some relatives of her last governess who
had died shortly before, aged ninety-five. The governess apparently had prided herself on having taught Elinor Glyn,
who was such a brilliant child, a verdict at variance with her
expressed views at the time.

When Elinor was not attending functions or receptions, she
would travel about the island, reliving the memories and re-
visiting the haunts of her youth.

We passed all the old landmarks. The college high on

the hill, up on top of it along the parapet was where I received the first kiss from my "Eton boy!!" I remember I felt obliged to be very insulted and angry and not to speak to him for some days, but I really enjoyed the excitement very much!!

No. 55 Colomberie had been pulled down, but Richelieu was still there, strangely naked with all the ivy pulled off. She searched for, but did not find, the house where she had been born. But there were many other things for her to show Margaret, her maid. "That house where an actress once stayed—we were not allowed to look up when passing." She could not help mourning the spoliation of the green island in the last fifty years, the shacks and bungalows spreading like a blight along the shore.

Elinor stayed at Government House and noted sadly the decline from the earlier standards of elegance. The atmosphere of the place was changed.

The *nil admirari* note strong! The whole atmosphere with no deference to the Governor or the hostess was just too astonishing in contrast to the etiquette of our day. We just walked anyhow into dinner and the Governor indicated that I was to sit on his right hand. No ceremony at all, or names by plates. I am not saying whether this change is for the better or worse, nor do I mean any snobbish criticism. I am merely putting down the astonishing change. To us the Governor meant the representative of Queen Victoria and as such was reverenced and we paid him homage. Now everyone is "hail fellow well met!"

The exclusive Government House set, of which the Kennedys had been such jealous members and to which entry was only to be obtained by having the correct introductions, was gone. Elinor saw, with mixed feelings, that both the Lieutenant-Governor and his wife were now, in Mrs. Saunders' phrase, "familiar with the wrong people." Guests were now invited to Government House who would not have been permitted inside the grounds fifty years earlier. All the splendour, all the sacrosanct etiquette seemed to have gone, though Elinor noted thankfully that the loyal toast, "The Duke," (of Normandy) was still drunk at dinner.

Most shocking of all to Elinor was the realisation of the petty rivalries and spiteful gossip which went on and from which the Kennedys, in their aloof and exclusive society, had been to some extent insulated.

The impression grew and grew upon me that the whole island is now full of bad, petty and envious vibrations. I found it almost impossible to concentrate upon my prayers and golden light, as if some dirty mist were between.

We must have been really strong characters under Gran's [Mrs. Kennedy's] aloof influence, always to have struggled away from the small petty gossips and never to have become as the others were. "I want to get out, I want to get out" like Sterne's starling, I always used to cry! Lucy married really for no other reason but—to get away. I remember now feeling on the boat in 1888 when we finally left, that prison doors were opening at last. It cannot be good for human beings to be on so small an island with no outside interests. I never wish to go back again.

But I only found kindness and welcome and honour in my short time there now. For good or ill I was born there and spent the years there, on and off, from 1873 to 1888.

This was my last night in Jersey. We left for St. Malo early next day with bouquets of violets and homage, and France seemed free and wonderful on landing.

14.

The outbreak of the Second World War found Elinor at Saltdean. Her reaction to the news was characteristic. The passing of time and the buffets of life had left her idealism undimmed and her view was simple and unshakeable. Part of her diary entry for the fifth of September, 1939, reads:

17A Curzon House, Saltdean.

War was declared on Sunday last with Germany—that pagan doomed country ruled by a mad upstart, evidently under the strong influence of very evil forces. So that it is not like an ordinary war waged between greedy human beings. This seems to be the first war since the inspired Crusades, which on our side is for purely altruistic reasons. So that we shall certainly win it presently, if we learn the lesson of it in time.

It may be the means of removing for ever oppression and class-hatred and selfishness and injustice. The last war gave great liberty from custom and convention. It broadened people's outlook, but the misery had been so great that many of orthodox religion lost faith and seemed afterwards to drift. Immediately after, the younger generation seemed to become putrid. Vices never spoken of openly before were chaffed about and thought quite ordinary. To say a young man was a "pansy" was no longer a crushing disgrace. But while all that generation grew more and more disgusting, education was advancing and gradually a keener under-standing of everything began to appear and now the very young seem to be splendid people. The Forces of Good are fighting upon our side against the forces of evil. So the end is sure to be glorious. We have only to bear the terrible intermediate period. Thus, at nearly 75, I look on with, I hope, wise, experienced eyes.

Equally typical was an incident which she recorded later in the same extract.

> On Sunday, just as I was going to Rottingdean to have lunch with Margot and the boys, an air raid warning sounded. A foolish woman was creating a mild panic in the hall. I am afraid I snubbed her, but immediately calm was restored.

One can imagine the withering scorn with which she must have castigated the woman. Her lack of self-control, her outburst of "servant's behaviour" would have been deplorable at any time. Now, with a war on, it was not to be passed over in silence.

In due course Elinor returned to London, to her new flat in Carrington House, Shepherd's Market, the part of London which she loved most. In this flat, smaller than her ones in Connaught Place or Hertford Street, she established her own characteristic milieu, and it remained her home for the rest of her life. Her move was fortunate and well timed, for both the Connaught Place and the Saltdean flats were severely damaged in later air raids.

October 17, 1939, was Elinor's seventy-fifth birthday, and she attended a large celebration lunch at the Berkeley. Although she fought the appearance, mind, and habits of old age as resolutely as ever, it was not part of her attitude to conceal her real age. She was rather proud of the advancing years and of the little mark they left upon her. One of the few signs of the passing time may be detected in the increasing terseness of the daily entries in her diary. The entry for the seventeenth of October concludes:

"Dozens of roses. People so kind. Lose gas-mask." The gas mask had had a short and inglorious career; she had never been much interested in it.

The blackout, however, intimidated her a good deal. Two days later she wrote:

"Have fall in black-out by stupidity of Sir A. ——."

And the following day:

"Not well enough to go to wedding. Sir A. —— brings flowers because of having been so stupid."

The fall damaged her knee again, and for the rest of that winter she went out as little as possible at night. Instead she wrote a new novel, her last. *The Third Eye* was her only attempt at a thriller and was inspired by the stories of secret service which had been related to her by Sir Paul Dukes, a close friend at this time.

Elinor's other literary work were her occasional articles in the British press and, more notably, her regular contributions to the Hearst press in America. She was the only British writer admitted now to the columns of the Hearst newspapers and she liked to think that her articles about wartime England were doing something to help the war cause.

15.

When invasion was feared in May 1940, her family sent Elinor, protesting, to the Rhys-Williamses' country house, Miskin Manor, in South Wales. There she remained for several months. She recognised that her presence in London was a liability and an anxiety to her family but this did not prevent her feeling bored and out of things, suddenly cut off from the social intercourse which had always formed such a part of her life.

When other members of the family were there on leave from the Army, or on holiday from school, the atmosphere of the house was, even under the war conditions, almost as agreeable and gay as it had been in the old days. But for much of the time she was alone there with her adolescent granddaughter, to whom she gave continual advice about poise and deportment. Out of sheer boredom she came to adopt far more

frequently than usual her Ambrosine pose, till it almost
ousted her normal Elizabeth mood.

Sometimes, however, other moods would show themselves.
The house was being requisitioned by the Army for a field
ambulance unit and an R.A.M.C. major came to inspect it.
Partly to amuse herself and partly as a demonstration to her
granddaughter of feminine attraction, Elinor set herself out to
bewitch the unsuspecting major. Assuming her *Three Weeks*
pose and dressing with elaborate care, she sat under a magnolia tree and greeted the major on his arrival with that special
mixture of imperiousness and hidden passion which she had
captured so successfully in her best seller. She commanded
the major to sit down beside her and in her most dramatic
manner she read *Three Weeks* aloud to him. She had lost
none of her own charm and the major left a few hours later,
having made only the most perfunctory inspection of the
building, but deeply impressed by Elinor Glyn.

It was not, however, boredom or loneliness which finally
drove Elinor away from Miskin, but horror of old age. Her
mother had lived the last seven years of her life in the rooms
at the end of the big passage and her aura still hung about
them. Mrs. Kennedy had never resisted old age as her daughter did. Indeed, she had almost seemed to welcome it. She was
a gracious, serene old lady, lace-capped and ebony-sticked, and
she had been like that for the last forty years of her life,
hardly changing in outward appearance. In that house, in
that passage, Elinor, her daughter, could see the shape of
things to come only too clearly. The image was already materi-
alising for her, ghost-like, photographed upon the air, herself
with lace cap and ebony stick, white-haired, fumbling.

It was to her the ultimate horror and she shrank from it.
Better anything, better bombs than that. She must get away
from Miskin now, quickly, before old age got too firm a grip
upon her.

16.

The air raids were now at their full violence, but Elinor, back in London, was not daunted by them and was happy at her return to her well-loved setting. She was even able to pick up something of her old life. On the twelfth of September, 1940, she wrote to Margot:

> The raids are truly too interesting! One has to keep saying "I am not dreaming, this is *really* England and not a wild west show of incessant shooting." Irene's [Lady Ravensdale's] house was hit on Monday night.
>
> The Foyle luncheon was very interesting yesterday. Duff Cooper made an excellently *worded* speech but he has no magnetism or good voice or delivery. Now we must get ready for invasion I suppose! The curious thing is that everyone is speaking of it just as if it were a new oyster season opening or some quite natural ordinary thing!
>
> I am enjoying it all! Fondest love to you all, darling.

Her general health, however, was weaker. In her diary there are an increasing number of mentions of feeling ill: "Did not feel well" or "Too tired to go out."

This physical ill-health and weariness brought with it a certain amount of mental and emotional depression. But, as ever, she kept this concealed, as far as possible, from her family and friends. In the company of visitors she was stimulated into being her normal, buoyant Elizabeth self, ready to discuss the war news, or Greek philosophy, or eighteenth-century furniture, or love with all comers. I remember visiting her on her birthday, bringing her some oysters. She was in rather low spirits when I arrived and was staying in bed—that big bed with the silk canopy which was the most striking feature of her bedroom. As we talked, she blossomed out into her old self, ending by measuring my Sam Browne belt to compare it with her own waistline at the same age.

During the summer of 1942 she fell ill again, this time more seriously. On September 20 she wrote to Marion Davies in Hollywood, in a handwriting so weak and shaky that it is hardly decipherable:

Marion darling—

How good you are sending all these lovely things. W.R. [Hearst] so kind too with the two packets. I know you will forgive me writing so badly. I have been very ill. I had a kind of sudden turn (not the usual old age stroke or high blood pressure). Just a turn of faintness. However, I am much better now, so I thank you as soon as I can hold the pencil.

This ugly war! It is getting a turn for the better so perhaps the end may come soon. I shall always carry on and say Cheerio! till the end anyway. I know we shall win all right.

Fondest love and oh do thank W.R. I'll write when I can. I *am* grateful.

Elinor

The flesh was now very frail but the spirit was still as vital as ever.

She recovered from this illness, but old age, so triumphantly held at bay for so long, was now coming in on the flood tide. Neither her memory nor her concentration was as it had been. When one talked to her, one had often the impression that her mind was a long way away, that her spirit was already beginning to move out of her failing body.

In the summer of 1943 she fell ill again, and on September 15 she was removed to a nursing home. On the evening of the twenty-second of September she lost consciousness and she died in the early hours of the following morning, the twenty-third of September, 1943, a few weeks before her

seventy-ninth birthday. Her funeral took place at Golders
Green Crematorium.

17.

Despite the severe restriction on the size of newspapers
and the demands of their space, *The Times* wrote a full,
thoughtful, and appreciative obituary notice, surveying Elinor's life and works and ending:

> At first she dealt in scarlet passions and risqué innocence;
> but beneath her pretensions to sophistication and dalliance
> with "naughtiness" she was an incurable romantic. She de-
> fined romance as "spiritual disguise created by the imag-
> ination with which to envelop material happenings and
> desires and thus bring them into greater harmony with the
> soul." In accordance with that conception she regulated
> both her life and her work. She was by nature intense and
> lived every moment of a long and adventurous life. Despite
> some foibles and petty vanities she was a vital and coura-
> geous woman.

It is by her own standards that she should be judged. In
My Religion she wrote, "I believe Deception, Lying and
Cruelty are the three deadly sins. And Love, Understanding
and Courage the three greatest virtues." She sometimes deceived herself but she never consciously deceived other people;
nor can one imagine her, under any circumstances, lying or
cruel.

Of the three virtues that she prized so highly, she sometimes failed in understanding. But her courage and her love
never faltered—that love which embraced not only those who
were nearest and dearest to her, but also her uncountable
readers, whom she had tried so hard to help and to whom she
had given so great happiness.

SOURCES AND ACKNOWLEDGEMENTS

This book is derived from the following sources:

Elinor Glyn's published books and articles; the synopses, scenarios, and continuities of her films; certain preliminary drafts and unpublished manuscripts.

The diary which she kept intermittently from 1879 to 1942 and which she used to record thoughts and impressions rather than the events of her life; the journals which she kept on special journeys; the notebooks which she used for miscellaneous records and descriptions; the commonplace books in which she wrote aphorisms and definitions.

The recollections of her own family and friends; information supplied by those who had business dealings with her; my own memories of her during the twenty-one years that our lives overlapped.

The letters which she wrote to the members of her family when she was away from home, and the bulk of which have been preserved; such of her business and personal correspondence with her friends as has survived; certain other relevant family papers.

The contemporary press notices of her books and films; various newspaper and magazine articles about her.

I am deeply grateful to all those who sent me information and reminiscences, or who allowed me to come and ask questions, and in this connection I would particularly like to thank the Baroness Ravensdale, Lady Moore-Guggisberg, Miss Mary Dixon, Miss Alice Head, Miss Christina Foyle, Miss Ruby Miller, Miss Evadne Price, Mr. Alan Arnold, Mr. Jonathan Cape, the Honourable Mervyn Horder, Mr. George Milsted, and Mr. R. J. Minney. My thanks are also due to Miss Joyce Weiner for valuable suggestions

347

and advice, and to the librarians and staff of the British Museum Newspaper Library and the National Film Library for kind and patient assistance. But my principal debt is to the members of my family for much encouragement, for a wealth of reminiscence and factual material, for entrusting me with a mass of family papers, and for reading and checking this book in typescript. It is a debt that cannot be adequately acknowledged in one sentence.

I must, however, make it clear that this book is not intended as a family tribute to Elinor Glyn. I have tried to see her as objectively as possible, consistent with the demands of filial piety, and I am solely responsible for the selection and the arrangement of all material and, except where otherwise indicated, for all opinions expressed.

My thanks are also due to Elinor Glyn, Ltd., Gerald Duckworth & Co., Ltd., Ivor Nicholson & Watson, Ltd., and The Amalgamated Press, Ltd., for permission to quote from Elinor Glyn's published books and articles; to Harper & Brothers for Mark Twain's letter to Elinor Glyn, previously published in *Mark Twain's Letters*, edited by Albert Bigelow Paine; to *The Times* for an extract from Elinor Glyn's obituary notice; to Mr. Beverley Nichols and the *Sunday Chronicle* for part of an article by Mr. Nichols; and to the *News of the World* for some sentences from an article by Mr. Samuel Goldwyn.

For permission to quote from private correspondence I must record my gratitude to the Viscountess Milner; Mrs. Gerald Duckworth; Elinor Glyn, Ltd.; Hughes Massie & Co., Ltd.; and Appleton-Century-Crofts, Inc.

The drawing-room at Connaught Place, 1936. Elinor, aged 72, two Persian cats and three tiger skins.

Elinor with the Nevada miners, 1908.

Drawing of Elinor in *Three Weeks* pose, 1907.